H. M. Hozier

The Invasions of England

A History of the Past, with Lessons for the Future: Vol. II.

H. M. Hozier

The Invasions of England
A History of the Past, with Lessons for the Future: Vol. II.

ISBN/EAN: 9783337203764

Printed in Europe, USA, Canada, Australia, Japan

Cover: Foto ©ninafisch / pixelio.de

More available books at **www.hansebooks.com**

THE INVASIONS OF ENGLAND.

THE
INVASIONS OF ENGLAND

A

HISTORY OF THE PAST

WITH

LESSONS FOR THE FUTURE.

BY

CAPTAIN H. M. HOZIER,
AUTHOR OF "THE SEVEN WEEKS' WAR."

IN TWO VOLUMES.
VOL. II.

"Happy England!—happy with a special reference to the present subject, in this, that the wise dispensation of Providence has cut her off by that streak of silver sea."—*Edinburgh Review.*

London:
MACMILLAN AND CO.
1876.

[*The Right of Translation and Reproduction is Reserved.*]

LONDON:
R. CLAY, SONS, AND TAYLOR, PRINTERS,
BREAD STREET HILL,
QUEEN VICTORIA STREET.

CONTENTS.

CHAPTER XVI.

(Continued.)

	PAGE
INVASIONS TO RESTORE THE STUART DYNASTY	1
Invasion of 1745	1

CHAPTER XVII.

INVASIONS IN CONNECTION WITH THE AMERICAN COLONIES	172
Invasion in Connection with the Independence of America	199

CHAPTER XVIII.

INVASIONS OF THE WARS OF THE FRENCH REVOLUTION	214
Invasion of the Irish Rebellion	293

CHAPTER XIX.

ATTEMPTED INVASION BY NAPOLEON 309

CHAPTER XX.

PROSPECTS OF INVASION 370

THE

INVASIONS AND ATTEMPTED INVASIONS OF ENGLAND.

CHAPTER XVI.
(*Continued.*)

INVASION OF 1745.

WE now come to the romantic enterprise of the Young Pretender, which for a brief space raised so high the hopes of the Jacobites, and spread alarm and dismay amidst the supporters of the established government. The former were crushed down and stamped out in the torrents of blood that flowed on the heath of Culloden.

The state of Scotland was considerably changed during the thirty years which elapsed between the descent of the Pretender at Peterhead and that of his son at Moidart. The sequestrations and attainders that followed the rebellion of 1715 had made the Highland noblemen cautious, and unwilling to embark in civil war, which, unless successful, was certain to entail severe penalties. The measures taken by the government after the defeat of the insurrection of Mar had also tended to render the success of a rising much less probable than formerly. Soon after the suppression of the rising of 1715 the clans were disarmed by Act of Parliament, and detachments of regular troops were employed to receive the weapons of the Highlanders. The loyal clans gave up their arms, but among those dangerous to the ruling dynasty the Act was as far as possible evaded. Still, as arms could only now be kept by stealth and in secret, they were obtained with much difficulty, and as the population increased a far larger proportion of the clansmen were unprovided with weapons. On the other hand, good roads had been made through the Highlands by the military labour which allowed of the passage of troops and guns into the wilds that were formerly inaccessible. Permanent garrisons of regular troops were stationed at the military posts of Fort William, Fort Augustus, Ruthven, and Inverness. These were also supported by independent companies of Highlanders, who were taken into the pay of the government to suppress the thefts and depredations of the lawless spirits of the North. These were in 1739 regimented and formed into the distinguished corps then known as the Black Watch, and which bears now, concurrently with its former appellation, the title of the 42nd Highlanders.

In the Lowlands, as the effect of the Union was more and more perceived to be beneficial, as trade became more and more developed, the party of order gained strength, and the Jacobites, who could only look to a restoration of

the Stuarts through disorder and civil strife, lost ground.
Had a more enlightened policy been pursued it is
probable that by the middle of the eighteenth century
not a single adherent of the Stuart cause would have
remained in the Lowlands. But through a fear of
admitting opponents to the dynasty into any position
of trust, oaths of office were rigidly maintained and
a bitter political feeling on the part of those who could
not take the pledge was fostered and nourished. The
conscientious men whom oaths would have bound were
averse to stigmatise as treasonable the opinions of their
fathers and relatives, though perhaps they themselves
were gradually sliding away from their views. Those
who had no consciences had little scruple in taking or in
breaking an oath as opportunity might require. Thus
many of the best men in Scotland were unable to obtain
employment in their native land, and were driven into
foreign service, where, surrounded by a Catholic atmo-
sphere and in communication with the agents of the
Stuart line, they nursed a morbid hatred to the government which exiled them from home, and hoped for the
restoration of a dynasty which would alone permit their
return to useful employment in their native country.

Both in the Highlands and the Lowlands the capacity
of the people for war was reduced. In the north the
feudal power of the chieftains had been considerably
sapped by the Clan Act and the sequestrations made
after the last rebellion. The improvements in firearms
made the military profession a more special employment, and among the Highlanders there were few but

the gentlemen who possessed muskets or understood their use. The private clansmen still trusted to the broadsword and dirk, and many did not even have them, but were contented to take the field with scythes lashed to long poles. In the Lowlands, the greater technicality of military training, the presence of regular troops, and the consequent preservation of order by public means, had for nearly half a century relieved individuals of the care of their personal safety and of the security of their goods and families. Armour had been entirely discarded and the use of arms forgotten except by the militia, which was generally contented with one annual parade as a mere preliminary to a dinner on the King's birthday. The only clan in Scotland which was at all fitted by training to cope with regular troopers was that of Fraser. The notorious Lovat, the chief of this tribe, had the command of one of the independent companies, and passed all his retainers in rotation through a course of drill in the ranks which gave him the command, in case of outbreak, of a battalion of about one thousand strong. This Highland chieftain, who thus anticipated on a small scale the system by which Scharnhorst raised the army that freed Germany from Napoleon, professedly held his soldiers for the service of the government. But the policy of this wily chieftain was regarded as so suspicious that his commission in the Black Watch was withdrawn in 1737, and he failed to obtain the arms from the government to equip his force, that would have been thrown into either scale according to his own interests.

In England the Jacobites, thirty years after the disaster of Preston, still remembered with dread the insurrection of 1715, and although among the High Church party, and especially at the University of Oxford, there were yet many who looked with favour upon the restoration of a sovereign endowed with hereditary right, the mercantile community had gained strength. This important bulwark of peace and order was a serious impediment to the organisation or execution of any plans of insurrection.

After the failure of the attempted invasion from Dunkirk in 1744, Prince Charles Edward returned to Paris, and there sought to incite the French government to aid him in a further attempt against England. But the ministers were cold and heartless in the extreme. They were engaged in Continental war, and recked little of the Stuart cause, except so far as it might be of avail to cause difficulties to England at convenient moments.

Murray, who had been sent as an emissary to Scotland to find out what chances of rising there were among the Highland chieftains, returned to Paris and reported that the Highlanders would rise if the French government would aid them with one thousand auxiliary troops, ten thousand stand of arms, and ninety thousand louisd'or. Without this assistance the Scottish chiefs declared that a rising would not only be useless, but would bring ruin and disaster on all concerned.

To obtain such assistance from the French Court was found to be impossible, and at length Charles, wearied out and disgusted with the perpetual procrastination of the French ministry, resolved to start with only such force as he himself could command. From such a rash undertaking all his Scottish friends, except the Duke of Perth, strongly disadvised him, but the Young Chevalier was not to be swayed by either their arguments or entreaties. He calculated that the defeat of the allies at Fontenoy, which had taken place in April of the same year, would tie the British regular army to the continent, and that during its absence he might with the Highlanders and the Jacobite partisans alone sweep away the militia, the recruits, and the trainbands, and secure the crown.

When he had formed this resolve he preserved it a close secret, and did not even communicate it to his father. The only member of the French ministry that was made aware of the design was Cardinal Tencin, who rather acquiesced in than approved of the undertaking. A considerable sum of money was borrowed from a firm of merchants, Rutledge and Walsh, who made a business of fitting out privateers against the English trade, and from the same source Charles obtained a ship of war named the *Elizabeth*, on board of which were stowed twenty guns and a considerable number of stands of arms. A frigate named the *Doutelle* was also chartered. She carried eighteen guns, and received a cargo of two thousand muskets, about five hundred swords, and nearly four thousand louisd'or.

The rendezvous was appointed at Nantes, and on the 2nd July, the Prince, accompanied by some half dozen Scottish partisans exiled on account of the rising of 1715, embarked in the *Doutelle*, and, in company with the *Elizabeth*, set sail from St. Nazaire, at the mouth of the Loire. Till the 13th the two vessels were detained off Belleisle by contrary winds, but on that day, with a favouring breeze, they stood out to sea and bore away northwards.

On the fourth day out from Belleisle a man-of-war carrying English colours hove in sight. She was the *Lion*, of fifty-one guns, and bore down upon and engaged the *Elizabeth*. The Prince was extremely anxious to take part in the action with the *Doutelle*, but the master exerted his authority, kept out of gunshot, and declared that if the Prince attempted to interfere in the command he would order him down to his cabin. After a contest of several hours the *Elizabeth* and *Lion* were both so severely injured that they were mutually forced to put into friendly harbours to refit. The latter made away to Plymouth, while the former with difficulty gained a shelter in Brest.

The *Doutelle*, which had held aloof from the encounter, now stood away alone for Scotland. Avoiding another man-of-war which appeared on the horizon, she arrived in safety off South Uist, one of the western isles, which owned the feudal seignoralty of Macdonald of Clanranald. Clanranald himself was away upon the mainland, but was represented by Macdonald of Boisdale, who was summoned on board the *Doutelle* as soon as she dropped anchor. He came on board, but on being urged by the Prince to take up arms and to engage in the cause his powerful neighbours Sir Alexander Macdonald and the chief of the Macleods, he sturdily refused to do so, and declaring the adventure to be so rash as to verge on insanity, avowed his intention of using all his influence with his nephew Clanranald to prevent his entering into it. He stated that the Macdonalds and Macleods were only willing to rise if the assistance were brought from abroad on which they had stipulated, and that they would certainly abide by this determination. During the conversation the anchor was weighed, and while it continued the *Doutelle* steered towards the mainland. In vain Charles argued, remonstrated, and endeavoured to persuade, Boisdale remained firm, and was at length permitted to take his boat and return to his island. On his departure the Chevalier called his friends together and asked their advice. He himself seemed for a moment prepared to relinquish the enterprise, and of those present only one voice was raised in favour of its further prosecution. Sir Thomas Sheridan, an Irish gentleman, who had been the Prince's tutor, and had considerable influence over him, argued that to return without at least further testing the feelings of the Highland chieftains, would expose them all to ridicule and contempt, and imply on the part of the Prince an eternal renunciation of his birthright. These views determined Charles to consult at least the chieftains on the mainland, which now lay close under the bows of the *Doutelle*.

The course of the frigate was laid in the bay that lies between Arasaig and Moidart, and entering Loch-na-Nuagh, she there cast anchor. The Prince at once informed Clanranald of his arrival, and the chieftain attended by his kinsman Macdonald of Kinloch Moidart, came on board. The same arguments which had been in vain exhausted on Boisdale were now applied to Clanranald as he and Charles paced up and down the deck, while the rest of the adventurers rested and refreshed themselves under an awning which had been raised near the poop. Clanranald was as firmly of opinion as his uncle that a rising could without foreign assistance prove only ruinous, and the interview was near being closed without result, when one of those little accidents occurred on which so often mighty issues hang. A young Highlander who was brother of Moidart, and accompanied his chieftain as an armed escort, beginning to perceive in whose presence he was, became feverishly impatient at the reluctance of his chief to join the long-expected Prince, and with nervous excitement began to dally with the handle of his claymore. This notion was noticed by Charles, who, turning to the dhunie-wassal, with a happy readiness exclaimed, "You at least will not forsake me." "I will follow you to death," cried the henchman warmly, "though there were never another to draw a claymore for you."

Shamed by the eager enthusiasm of their youthful kinsman, the chieftains could not be surpassed in loyalty. Argument, foresight, and prudence were cast aside, enthusiasm and excitement carried them away. They avowed themselves ready to support their Prince to the utmost of their military power and to the last drop of their blood. Charles, secure of the clan that marched under Clanranald, landed on the twenty-fifth of July and occupied the house of Borrodale as a temporary residence. The place was well suited for concealment, and afforded easy communication both with the clans of the Hebrides, who it was now hoped would join, and who could bring fifteen hundred warriors into the field, as well as with the chieftains of the mainland, who were most devoted to the House of Stuart. Seven persons only came ashore with the Pretender to the crown of Great Britain and Ireland and the claimant to the title of King of France. These were the Marquis of Tullibardine, who had been attainted for the rebellion of 1715, and was known by the Jacobites as the Duke of Athole, though the government had conferred the title on his younger brother; Sir Thomas Sheridan, the Prince's tutor; Sir John Macdonald, an officer in the Spanish service; Francis Strickland, an English Catholic gentleman; Kelly, who had been implicated in the affair of Bishop Atterbury; Æneas Macdonald, a banker in Paris, brother of Moidart, and Buchanan, the envoy who had summoned Charles to France to undertake the expedition from Dunkirk. One who either came with him or immediately joined him was a Macdonald, who was father of the celebrated Marshal Macdonald, Duke of Tarento, whose brilliant military genius was torn from our country and placed at the disposal of an enemy through political discord and civil strife.

Cameron of Lochiel was one of the first chieftains summoned to an interview with the Prince at Borrodale. He arrived fully prepared to combat the intention of a rising, and in hopes of convincing the Chevalier of the madness of the attempt. He was cautioned by a relative, Cameron of Fassiefern to write his views, and not to trust himself within the sphere of the Chevalier's fascination; but, confident in his own firmness, he attended the meeting. The result proved the justice of Fassiefern's forebodings. As long as Charles argued Lochiel was firm, and replied with reason to reason and with argument to argument. But the sting of being suspected of failing his sovereign in the hour of danger told more powerfully on the feelings of the high-minded chieftain. Charles, as if in conclusion, said, "I have come determined to claim my rights or to perish in the attempt. I am determined to take the field with those who will join my standard. Lochiel, whom my father considered his best friend, may stay at home and learn from the newspapers the fate of his Prince." Cameron's sagacity gave way, his good sense was overborne by his devotion, and, much affected, he vowed his own assistance and that of every man over whom he had influence. His decision was the real commencement of the rebellion, for it is generally understood that not a clan would have risen had the head of the Camerons persisted in remaining quiet.

As soon as the adherence of the Camerons was secured the fiery cross was sent out far and wide in every direction to summon the friendly clans to join with all their power the royal standard, which was to be raised at Glenfinnan on the 19th of August.

Clanranald was despatched on a mission to the Hebrides, where it was hoped that he might persuade

Sir Alexander Macdonald of Sleat, and Macleod of Macleod, each of whom could bring several hundred men into the field, to join. But both alleged that their engagement was to rise only if the foreign auxiliary force stipulated for was brought to Scotland, and both stood aloof from the enterprise. Their absence was but indifferently compensated for by the zeal of the lesser chieftains, who came in with less numerous followers.

The departure of Prince Charles from France was skilfully kept secret for some time. It was not till the 30th of July that Lord Tweeddale, the Secretary of State for Scotland in London, was aware of his sailing from Nantes, and it was not known in Edinburgh by the 8th of August. How this delay occurred has not been sufficiently accounted for, as the *Lion* must have brought back to Plymouth the news of her encounter with the *Elizabeth* by the 20th of July. But the suspicions of the government had already been aroused by a stir and activity that was noticed among the Jacobites, and measures were taken for the arrest of several suspected persons. Among these was the titular Duke of Perth, who was living at his seat of Castle Drummond, when Captain Campbell of Mocraw, who commanded an independent company lying in the neighbourhood, received orders to secure him. Campbell, in a manner little customary with a British officer, obtained an invitation to dine at Castle Drummond, and was received as a guest. When the ladies withdrew he informed the duke that he was his prisoner. The latter affected to treat the matter with indifference, and said that as it was so there was no help for it. But on leaving the dining-room he made Campbell pass before him, as if by an ordinary action of courtesy, and as soon as the officer was across the threshold quickly closed and locked the door upon him, then fled by a side door into the woods, where he found a pony, on which, although barebacked and with only a halter as a bridle, he made his escape into the Highlands. There he lay hidden till he heard of the landing at Moidart, when he immediately joined the Chevalier.

John Murray of Broughton in the meanwhile had performed the dangerous duty of having the manifestoes printed in the Lowlands, and joined Charles at Kinloch Moidart, whither he moved after a short stay at Borrodale. He was at once appointed Secretary of State to the Prince, and intrusted with the internal administration of the undertaking. Murray formed a plan for seizing Fort Augustus and Fort William by sending false information to the governors, which it was hoped would cause the garrisons from those posts to be sent out to disperse alleged meetings of Jacobites in the vicinity. But the commandants were not to be deceived, and held their men within their parapets.

Yet in the vicinity of these forts civil war broke out before the standard of the invader was raised. The commandant of Fort Augustus, anxious for the safety of Fort William, which lay near to the disaffected clans, sent two companies to reinforce its garrison under the command of Captain Scott. Scott left Fort Augustus early in the morning of the 16th of August with the object of reaching Fort William before nightfall. His route lay along the military road which passes by the lakes now joined by the Caledonian Canal, and is on both sides flanked by high and intricate mountains. He seems to have marched without the ordinary precaution of an advanced guard, but as he afterwards rose to be a general this can hardly have been the case. Still, after the detachment had passed the lakes, and was within eight miles of Fort William, it approached a narrow defile, named High Bridge, where the road crossed the river Spean on a steep and narrow bridge sunk among the rocks and woods that overhung the ravine cut by the river. As the troops were marching down to the bridge the silence and solitude were suddenly broken by the shrill notes of a bagpipe and the shouts of Highlanders, who appeared in arms among the stones and bushes on the further bank of the Spean. These were a party of Macdonalds of Keppoch, and consisted only of a dozen or fifteen men; but as they rushed from rock to rock and from bush to bush, constantly disappearing and as constantly appearing at different points, it was impossible for the captain of the regulars to make out their strength. A sergeant and private, sent forward to ask their meaning, as the country was then at peace, were taken prisoners and not allowed to come back.

There was no doubt now of the hostile intentions of the clansmen, and Scott wished to push forward and force the defile. But the other officers were averse to a rash advance through a difficult pass against an enemy who had the advantage of position, and whose strength could not be guessed at. The privates who were newly raised showed some symptoms of hesitation. Under these circumstances Scott attempted to retreat along the road by which he had advanced under cover of a rearguard that was quickly engaged by the Highlanders. The firing alarmed the country, and more mountaineers quickly appeared on the scene, and were increased by fresh arrivals. With superior activity, they could run along the mountains faster than the regulars could march on the road, and were able to line the rocks and thickets overhanging the path, from which they overwhelmed the regulars with a destructive fire. These could only return random shots at invisible enemies, and, rapidly losing all confidence, and demoralised by the yells of the pibroch and constant appearance of fresh adversaries, ran in confusion for five or six miles. Then they were stopped in their flight by the presence of another party in their front. Their ammunition was exhausted, and being closely pressed in flank and rear, and cut off in front, they lay down their arms and surrendered. Captain Scott and five or six of his men were wounded without having been able to maim a single mountaineer in return. This success gave great confidence to the Highlanders, and showed their power in difficult country against the more heavily-equipped and more tightly-clad regular soldiers. The prisoners were treated with great humanity, and taken to Lochiel house, where the wounded were carefully tended. As the governor of Fort Augustus would not allow a surgeon to go out to attend Captain Scott, Lochiel sent him on parole to the fort, so that he might not be deprived of medical assistance.

War was then openly commenced, and on the 19th Charles arrived in the narrow vale where the Finnan cuts a way through high and craggy mountains to the sea. He was attended by two companies of the Macdonalds, whose chief, Clanranald, was absent raising men in every quarter where he had influence. Charles expected to find the narrow valley filled with tartans and studded with bonnets; but on entering the glen his eye rested on a solitude as complete as if no summons to arms had been issued, and no fiery cross had sped forth. Two hours passed, and no waving tartans came in sight, no distant bagpipe nor clank of weapons of marching men fell upon the ear. The prospect was gloomy, and the Prince retired into a hut, and seemed uncertain and anxious for his fate. Then the strains of the bagpipe were heard, and the columns of the Cameron clan wound into the glen. They marched in two long lines, escorting as prisoners in the centre the two companies which had been taken at High Bridge. Three hundred Macdonalds arrived shortly afterwards under Keppoch, who, but for a dispute with his clan on account of not allowing their Catholic chaplains to come out with them, would have brought more men into the field.

The standard was then unfurled by the Marquis of Tullibardine. The manifesto of the Chevalier was read, as well as the commission of regency granted to his son, and Prince Charles made a short speech, saying that he came for the happiness of the people, and was willing to shed the last drop of his blood at the head of his adherents.

For a few days the Prince remained at Auchincarrie, the house of Cameron of Lochiel. Here he was joined by the men of Glencoe, the Stuarts of Appin and Glengarry, and his force was swelled to about two thousand combatants. News came that the regular troops were advancing to quell the rising, and the intelligence was received with joy, for Charles was determined not to imitate the policy of procrastination which had proved so fatal to Mar, but to avail himself speedily of the fierce activity and ardent energy of his Highland followers. He determined at once to advance; but as the Highlanders were most loath to carry baggage, and no horses could be obtained, and the roads were miserable, he was forced to leave behind a quantity of swivel guns and pioneers' tools, for which he could not obtain conveyance.

Only when the insurrection had already gained some strength were the representatives of the government in Edinburgh made aware of its existence, and though the adventure was rash, the time of its occurrence made it extremely formidable. George II. was absent in Hanover, and the government was entrusted to a Council of Regency, termed the Lords Justices, whose actions, as those of most conglomerate bodies, showed neither vigour nor sagacity. Early in summer they had received intelligence that the young Chevalier was preparing to sail from Nantes with a single vessel, and on the 30th July it was known in London that he had actually started. It was not till the middle of August that the landing at Moidart was known certainly in Edinburgh to the officials who there presided over the direction of affairs in Scotland. These were the Commander-in-Chief, Sir John Cope, the Justice Clerk, Andrew Fletcher, Lord Milton, and the Lord President Duncan Forbes. The last was a devoted and unwearied asserter of the Protestant succession. On the first rumour of the rising he hurried down to his seat, Culloden House, which lay near Inverness, and inspirited the Sutherlands and Mackays to support the government.

When the news of the landing of Charles was indubitably known in Edinburgh, there was considerable alarm, for the regular troops were chiefly on service on the continent. There were not in Scotland, exclusive of garrisons, three thousand men, and of these only one battalion was an old corps, while one battalion and a half were quite newly raised. Two regiments of dragoons, Hamilton's and Gardiner's, now the Thirteenth and Fourteenth Hussars, were the youngest in the service. There were some independent companies hired for the purpose of completing regiments in Flanders, and there were also several companies of the Highland regiment of Lord Loudoun, but these, being Highlanders, were not to be implicitly trusted in the present emergency. Out of this small force two of the newly-raised companies had been captured at High Bridge. Nevertheless Sir John Cope considered the strength at his command not only sufficient to defend the passes into the Lowlands, but to justify offensive action, and he proposed to the Lords Justices in England that he should at once advance, bring the rebels to action, and crush the revolt. His proposal was warmly approved, and he was ordered by the Lords Justices to carry it out. At the same time they provided him with a proclamation which had been issued in the *London Gazette*, and which proffered a reward of £30,000 to any person who should seize and secure the son of the Pretender, so that he might be brought to justice.

Sir John Cope, in obedience to his instructions, issued orders on the 13th August for the several parties of his troops to draw together at Stirling, whither arms and ammunition were sent from Edinburgh; and on the 19th, the day on which Prince Charles was unfurling his standard at Glenfinnan, he himself set out to place himself there at the head of his army, which consisted of Murray's regiment of foot, eight companies of Lascelles' regiment, two of Guise's, five of Lee's, one hundred and eighty-three men of the Highland regiment, and Hamilton's and Gardiner's dragoons. On the 21st the General advanced from Stirling with his infantry, six field-pieces, and two culverins; but he left the dragoons behind in the south, as they could not be of much service among the hills, and it would have been extremely difficult to find forage for them in the mountainous country. He took with him, however, a large quantity of baggage, a drove of black cattle to kill for food in case supplies from the country failed, and about a thousand stand of arms for the use of such loyal clans as might be willing to rise in his favour. As none such could be found, he sent back about seven hundred stand of arms from Crieff to Stirling. His march was directed on Fort Augustus, as a central point from which he hoped to strike a decisive blow. His road was the same by which the Highlanders were advancing in an opposite direction, and on his arrival at Dalnacardoch he heard that the Chevalier was advancing with the purpose of meeting him and giving him battle at the wild and precipitous pass of Corryarrack.

While the Prince lay at Invergary, behind Corryarrack, a messenger arrived from the false and fickle Fraser of Lovat, who was most anxious to obtain the patent of Duke of Fraser and the Lord Lieutenancy of Inverness-shire, which had been promised to him, without compromising himself by giving in exchange for these ideal advantages any solid aid that might imperil him with the government in case of the failure of the rebellion. It was easily seen that Fraser was anxious to obtain his reward without fulfilling his engagements; but as his influence in Inverness-shire over the Macphersons, Mackintoshes, and Farquharsons was very great, it was highly desirable to conciliate him, and the patent and commission were sent to him. At the same time Fraser was in daily communication with the Lord President; but his conduct in its result only proved the truth of the old adage, that honesty is the best policy; for notwithstanding his playing fast and loose with both sides, he was ultimately detected and brought to the scaffold.

While these negotiations were in progress, the

Chevalier was kept constantly informed of the proceedings of Sir John Cope by deserters from the Highland regiment, who constantly stole away from the regular troops to join the rising. As the forces of the government marched along the military road which led through Dalnacardoch on Fort Augustus, the Prince determined to secure the pass of Corryarrack, and there bar the way, hoping in the rugged ground, eminently favourable to the Highlanders, to inflict upon the enemy a defeat which would allow him to sweep them away before him in hopeless rout even beyond the passages of the Forth.

On the twenty-sixth of August, the Highland army, after burning and destroying its baggage and all encumbrances that could impede its march, occupied Aberchallader, within three miles of Fort Augustus, and early on the 27th was on the mountain slopes of Corryarrack.

This high and steep mountain is ascended on the southern side, whence Cope was expected by Wade's military road, which painfully gains the summit of the pass by seventeen zig-zags or traverses, that gave to this portion of the way, in the language of the country people, the name of the Devil's staircase. The mountain side, except where cut by the road, is almost inaccessible, and the line of road itself is repeatedly intersected by gullies formed by mountain torrents, crossed by bridges that could be rapidly broken down. Everywhere rocks and thickets, where an ambush might lurk, or unseen sharpshooters gain an inaccessible cover, overhang the way. It offered a splendid battle-field for agile irregular troops, such as the Highlanders, against the heavily accoutred and stifly clad soldiery; for inconvenient accoutrements and uncomfortable dress were then considered as indispensable necessities to a well-drilled army. Charles discerned the advantages which the steep mountain offered to him, and at early dawn moved forward to seize the crest.

While the clansmen were stepping cheerily up the northern face, two officers were hurried up to the summit to reconnoitre. In haste and breathless, they gained the highest point of the road, and ran forward to peer down the further side of the mountain, expecting to view the long line of Cope's bayonets, artillery, and baggage slowly toiling up the Devil's staircase.

But to their astonishment, the road was perfectly solitary and still. No clank of arms, no buzz of men, no beat of drum, no loud word of command was wafted up to them. The cry of the curlew and blackcock alone broke the silence of the hill side, and not a movement caught the eye but the waving of the heather, or the quivering of aspen in the morning breeze. For a time not a single man was to be seen, then a few Highlanders came in sight. These were at first taken to be scouts of the enemy, who it was only natural would be furnished by the Highlanders of Lord Loudoun's regiment. But though they came steadily forward, no advanced guard and no columns followed in their wake. They proved to be deserters from the scouts of Cope's army, and they brought the astonishing intelligence that their general had turned aside to avoid the expected action, and was now in full march for Inverness. The fact proved to be that Sir John Cope, on approaching the Highland army, found much greater difficulties in attacking it than he had previously anticipated. He was met in the way by an officer who had been taken prisoner by the rebels, and had been present at the raising of the standard at Glenfinnan, and who had been released by Charles. This officer reported the numbers of the rebels to be far greater than had been expected, and Cope now saw all the difficulty and danger of attacking Corryarrack, though it seems that it would not have required very much prescience to have foreseen that the Highlanders would rise in considerable numbers, and that an irregular army in a mountainous country would probably take post in a difficult defile. But this does not seem to have been considered beforehand, and the chief, devoid of confidence in his own abilities, and overwhelmed with a sense of responsibility, had recourse to the favourite refuge of an incompetent leader, and summoned a council of war. It was now too late to decide whether it would not have been better to remain at Stirling, and hold the Forth, while troops were sent to the north to raise the loyal clans near Inverness and act against the rear of the Highland army. To attack Corryarrack seemed impossible; to remain before the pass might check the Highlanders, but expose Cope himself, to be attacked in rear by other clans whose want of loyalty had been proved by the fact that they refused to take up arms on his forward march, and then even if they could make no serious impression against disciplined troops, could certainly prevent him from drawing supplies from the country, and could eventually starve him out. There seemed no course open but either to return to Stirling or to move on Inverness and gain there an accession of strength from the well-affected clans. To retreat before a dispersed and undisciplined enemy would be ignominious; it was decided to move on Inverness, and it was hoped that this movement would draw the army of the Pretender in the same direction, for it was but natural to suppose that the Highlanders would scruple to move forward into the Lowlands, and leave their countries, their families, and their cattle uncovered and unprotected from the British force at Inverness. In this view Cope was misled. He did not understand the wild enthusiasm with which the mountaineers had thrown themselves into the cause of the Young Chevalier, an enthusiasm which urged them to spare neither land, nor property, nor child, nor life to secure his accession to the throne. He also made a false calculation as to time, for before he could press on in the Highland glens, so as to call back the clansmen to protect their homes, the Highland army was already threatening his own base of communication and the capital of Scotland, and he was forced to hurry back to protect the seat of the government.

Fortified by the opinion of the council of war on the 27th of August, the same day that Prince Charles occupied Corryarrack, the British troops turned off by the other branch of the military road from Dalwinny and moved for Inverness.

Great was the exultation in the Highland army when

the flight of Sir John Cope—for such his retreat was considered—became known. There was a general call to follow him, and some of the chieftains proposed to march five hundred picked men over the mountains, who should throw themselves across the Inverness road ahead of the regular troops, and detain them till the whole force of the Highlanders could come up in their rear and destroy them. But the Prince perceived that the Lowlands were the decisive point where the campaign must be decided, and in deference to his views the proposed attack on Cope was abandoned, and the Highlanders pushed down from Corryarrack towards the south.

A detachment was sent to attack the barracks of Ruthveld, but was beaten off by the bravery of the little garrison of regular troops that was posted there. But it did not rejoin the army entirely empty-handed, for it brought back the chief of the Macpherson clan, who was son-in-law of Lord Lovat, and was made prisoner either accidentally or on purpose.

After passing through the mountains of Badenoch on the 30th of August, the Prince entered the vale of Athole, and occupied Blair Castle. Here he remained two days, and was joined by several new adherents, and on the 4th September made his public entry into the city of Perth amidst the acclamations of the people.

The possession of Perth opened the way to the towns of Dundee and Montrose, whither parties were despatched to search for horses and to levy the public money. The halt that was necessary to carry out these measures was employed in drilling and organising the troops. This work was not one of such long duration as would be requisite with wholly untrained levies, for the Highlanders were already familiar with a species of manœuvre well suited to their own irregular tactics. As Sir Walter Scott says, "They marched in a column of three abreast, and could wheel up with prompt regularity in order to form the line, or rather succession of clan columns, in which it was their fashion to charge. They were accustomed also to carry their arms with habitual ease, and handle them with ready promptitude; to fire with a precise aim, and to charge with ready vigour, trusting to their national weapons, the broadsword and target, with which the first rank of every clan, being generally gentlemen, were armed." The clans were from their native training ready to act as battalions, and it was only necessary to model them into brigades.

While this was being done two most valuable personages joined the standard of the Chevalier. These were the Duke of Perth and Lord George Murray. The former brought with him about two hundred of his tenantry: the latter was most useful in inducing the men of his brother, the Duke of Athole, to enlist, and both were made Lieutenant-Generals of the Prince's army. Lord George Murray was in other respects an important acquisition; he had served in the Sardinian army, had studied deeply the military art, and, what is far more important, had meditated upon it much. Indeed he was the only person in the Highland force, beyond the Prince himself, who seems to have strategically considered the campaign, for the chieftains considered their duty confined to leading their clansmen gallantly in action, and the French and Irish officers had been so carelessly selected, that their knowledge was little more than what is necessary for inspecting a company or relieving a guard. Over such men Lord George Murray had a great superiority; but this was damped by a failing of temper and manners. Proud of his superior attainments, he was unconciliatory to the feelings of others, impatient of any opinion that differed from his own, and blunt and dogmatic in putting forward his own views.

During the halt at Perth news was received that Sir John Cope was directing his march from Inverness to Aberdeen, and had ordered transports to be sent to that seaport with a view to embarking his army and carrying it by sea to aid in the protection of Edinburgh. Charles was determined not to imitate the inaction of Mar, but to anticipate the movement, and himself seize Edinburgh before Cope's arrival. On the eleventh of September he broke up from Perth, and although it was not easy to draw the Highlanders away from the comforts of a town, that night occupied Dunblane. On the thirteenth the passage of the Forth was made at the fords of Frew, where Mar had failed although at the head of a more numerous army. The passage was effected without difficulty, on account of the drought of the weather, and thus the bridge of Stirling, which was commanded by the guns of the Castle, supported by some vessels of war, was turned. As the heads of the Highland columns filed down to the Forth, the outposts of Gardiner's dragoons fell back before them and retreated to Linlithgow, although they could have much impeded the passage of the river had they boldly charged the head of each column as it emerged from the stream. The sight of the Highland clans filing past, and of their royal standard, drew a few shots from Stirling Castle, one of which is said to have fallen within twenty yards of Charles himself; but the cannonade was ineffectual, and the town of Stirling opened its gates and furnished provisions. Everything was paid for, and discipline so strictly maintained, that Lochiel, finding one of his men plundering in spite of his orders, shot him dead with his own hand.

The army marched across the plain of Bannockburn, and on the fourteenth was billeted in the town of Falkirk or bivouacked among some broom-fields round Callender House. At that mansion the Prince was entertained by Lord Kilmarnock, its owner, who informed him that Gardiner's dragoons had occupied Linlithgow bridge with the intention of disputing the passage there next day. A thousand Highlanders were sent forward under Lord George Murray before day-break in the hopes of surprising them, but found that the dragoons had decamped the previous evening. Without any opposition Lord George took possession of the town and of the ancient palace. A few hours later they were joined by the Prince in person, and the advanced guard was pushed on, and occupied Kirkliston, only eight miles from the West Port of Edinburgh.

Edinburgh had long been a peaceful town, little accustomed to the din of arms. No one in the middle of the eighteenth century, in that capital, seemed to imagine that the wild Highlanders could cross the Forth, and, even after the intelligence arrived that the Young Chevalier had landed at Moidart, appeared to give credit to serious danger. But a sudden awe seemed to burst upon the city when the unexpected news arrived that General Cope had passed from the front of the rebel army to Inverness, and left the road to Dunedin uncovered. The capital was abandoned in great measure to its own resources, and the inhabitants were swayed either by fear or by joy, according to their hatred or their love for the Stuart cause.

In a military point of view, Edinburgh was almost an open town. The squares, streets, and monuments of the new town, which have now gained for the capital of Scotland the not unfit appellation of the Modern Athens, had in the middle of the eighteenth century, and for a long time afterwards, no existence. The city was strictly limited to its original boundaries, which had been established as early as the fourteenth or fifteenth century. The defences were of a character merely calculated to exclude wayfarers, vagrants, and tramps, but of no nature to resist the slightest attack of troops, accompanied even with a weak field-train of artillery. A high wall enclosed the city from the West Port on the west, to the Canongate, and then, turning northward, ascended the ridge on which the town is built, formed one side of the suburb called St. Mary's Wynd; and extended to the Netherbow Port; hence the wall ran down Leith Wynd, and terminated at a hospital close on the banks of the

North Loch. Above the town towered indeed the Castle, armed with artillery, and occupied by an English garrison under the command of a veteran general; but the views of that officer appear to have been entirely confined to the maintenance of his own fortified post, and not to have embraced any defence of the city.

The population were little fit to supply the want of that artillery which the town wall was too narrow to carry. Such as were able to bear arms were indeed embodied under the name of trained bands, and had muskets, which were kept in the town magazines. Their numbers amounted nominally to a force of sixteen companies of about eighty or one hundred men each; but there was little discipline, and not much military ardour among the inhabitants of Edinburgh. It was not doubtful that if these trained bands were to be called out, nearly as many of them would probably declare for Prince Charles as for King George. There was a small body of infantry, called the City Guard, that consisted of perhaps 120 men, who acted as the police of the city, but were hardly calculated to defend their town against the inroads of Highlanders. The only regular troops, except the small garrisons of English in the castles of Edinburgh and Stirling, in the Lowlands, were the two regiments of Dragoons which General Cope had left behind him when he passed into the mountains to engage the rebels. Yet the citizens of Edinburgh, especially among the upper classes, were generally friendly to the Government and the House of Hanover; and a certain necessity of demonstration of military courage urged them not to yield up the metropolis without a blow to a few wild insurgents from the hills and valleys of the north.

As soon as, on the 27th of August, it was known in Edinburgh that General Cope had, with the regular troops, marched to Inverness, and uncovered the road to the Lowlands, a meeting of the friends of Government was held, at which it was resolved that the city should be put in a state of defence. Some fortifications were indeed commenced under the direction of a professor of mathematics, but the great hope of the burghers lay upon the arrival of General Cope.

An aide-de-camp to that officer came in from Inverness by sea, with directions that a number of transports then lying at Leith should be despatched without loss of time for Aberdeen. Captain Rogers—this aide-de-camp—stated that General Cope intended to move with his troops from Inverness to Aberdeen; embark them at the latter seaport, by means of the transports from Edinburgh. It was hoped he would thus be able to return to the Lowlands by sea in time to interpose between the city and the advance of the Pretender. The probable approach of the regular infantry increased the military ardour of the citizens, and as a regiment which had been voted by the town could not be levied without the warrant of the Government, several of the burghers petitioned to be allowed to enroll themselves as volunteers for the defence of the city. The numbers of these volunteers soon increased. On the night of the 31st August the news of the rebels having entered Athole came to Edinburgh. The drums beat to arms, and Hamilton's (now the 13th

Hussars) Dragoons, encamped close to the town. Gardiner's Dragoons, which had been left at Stirling, were intended to cover the road towards Edinburgh in the direction of Linlithgow.

By the time that, on the evening of the 11th September, the Highland army had reached Dunblane, the confusion in the capital was greatly increased. The volunteers had at no time amounted to more than four hundred men, and of those who had taken arms, several had done so merely out of an enthusiasm which threatened to evaporate the more closely it was brought to a serious test before the wild courage of the Highlanders.

As the advanced guard of the mountaineers, formed of detachments of the best men of every clan, pushed forward, the Dragoons of Colonel Gardiner fell back before them, and retired as far as Corstorphine, within three miles of Edinburgh. There Gardiner decided to make a stand; and sent for the second regiment of Dragoons from its quarters at Leith. At this time the van of the rebels was at Kirkliston. General Guest, the Lieutenant-Governor of the Castle of Edinburgh, then proposed to the Lord Provost, Archibald Stewart, who commanded all the forces of the city, that the volunteers, instead of waiting to be attacked, within the town, since they were numerically too weak even to man the wall, should aid in an offensive movement, which he intended to make, in order to protect the city, by engaging the vanguard of the enemy at once. With this view Guest proposed that Hamilton's Dragoons should march from Leith and join with Gardiner's at Corstorphine; in accordance with the request of the latter officers; and that the mounted men should be supported by the infantry volunteer corps, numbering about four hundred combatants. The Provost, having agreed to this proposal, also consented that ninety of the city guard should march out along with the armed citizens to engage the Highlanders. Not the whole of the volunteers were willing to pledge themselves to instant conflict, but about two hundred and fifty, it was understood, were prepared to expose themselves to the dangers of the claymore. Orders were sent to Hamilton's dragoons to march through Edinburgh, and take their way to Corstorphine.

The following day, Sunday, the 15th of September, Hamilton's dragoons broke up from their quarters at Leith and marched into the city, on their way to join Gardiner. As they passed through the town it was considered necessary that the volunteers should parade at once, in order to march directly in their rear, and to support their movement. Accordingly, although divine service was in progress at the time, the fire-bell (an ominous and ill-chosen signal) began to toll, and the volunteers slowly commenced to fall in upon their parade ground. As the dragoons passed, the volunteers cheered the horsemen, who clashed their swords and responded also with loud huzzahs. The sound and sight of the swords filled many of the volunteers with consternation; and those who did not perhaps at first feel much dread for themselves were considerably moved by the terror of their relatives and friends. A general decrease of martial ardour was apparent among the civic soldiery. As the author of the *Tales of a Grandfather* so truly remarks, there is nothing of which men in general are more easily persuaded, than of the extreme value of their own lives ; nor are they apt to estimate these more lightly, when they see that they are highly prized by others. A Calvinistic divine, who was brought from his pulpit by the sound of the fire-bell, stated as his opinion that such valiant men as the city volunteers ought not to sally forth, but reserve themselves for the defence of the city and the peaceful inhabitants, of which he (the clergyman) was no doubt one. This exhortation of the reverend gentleman fell upon ears probably more willing to obey his injunctions on this than on other occasions, and a great part of the volunteers themselves were speedily convinced that their lives were too precious to their city to be risked three miles away from it. As the regiment was ordered to move towards the West Port, the route by which the field of battle could be gained, the files grew gradually thinner and thinner on the way down the Bow ; and by the time the Grassmarket was passed, not above forty-five volunteers remained to reach the West Port. After some difficulty a hundred more were collected, but only on condition that the advance to Corstorphine should be abandoned ; and out of Edinburgh not one of the volunteers ever issued. They had to be led back to their parade ground and dismissed for the evening. So hazardous is it to trust to the native valour of undisciplined troops in the hour of danger. No men, unless accustomed to military discipline, and to act together in time of peace, can ever be relied upon to suddenly become heroes in the moment of peril. The citizen soldiers of Edinburgh on this occasion were probably men of not less courage and nerve than any other men, either in the regular army, or perhaps in the Highland clans that might have been opposed to them; the want of discipline allowed the nervousness of each individual to be communicated from himself to others, and so to permeate through the whole body.

But on this occasion the prudence of the volunteers was not destined to be entirely eclipsed by the valour of the regulars. The two regiments commanded by Gardiner and Hamilton were the youngest in the service, and were composed almost entirely of recruits. It was still hoped that the town might be protected by these two regiments of dragoons which Colonel Gardiner, who has become so justly celebrated for his private worth, his bravery, and his devotional character, now commanded. On the night of the 15th September, General Fowkes, however, who had been sent from London by sea, arrived at Leith and superseded Gardiner.

Early the next morning, the new General drew up the two regiments of dragoons near the north end of the Colt Bridge, which spans the water of Leith about two miles nearer Edinburgh than Corstorphine. The Highlanders were already advancing from the latter village. In front of the vanguard of the kilted clansmen rode a very few mounted gentlemen as scouts, to reconnoitre the enemy. As these came near the dragoons they fired their pistols, after the usual manner of skirmishers. The young recruits, who formed the pickets of the dragoons, were immediately seized with an unaccountable panic; and wheeling their horses, they fled towards the main body, without returning a shot. The panic communicated itself immediately to the squadrons, who also turned and galloped as fast as possible to the rear. The officers, unable to rally the ranks, were compelled to join in the flight. At full gallop, the flying dragoons tore along the fields on which now the new town of Edinburgh is built. General Guest from the castle ramparts, and the inhabitants of the city from the walls, could see this scandalous flight, which is now so well known in Scotland as the canter of Colt Brigg. Even at Leith, whither, as the regiments had lately encamped there, the men turned by a sort of instinct, it was possible to halt them only for a few moments. Before their nerves had recovered from their trepidation a cry was raised that the Highlanders were approaching, and the retreat was renewed as rapidly as before. A second time, near Preston, the officers succeeded in rallying their men; but one of them falling into a waste coal-pit, his cry for aid was supposed to be a Highland slogan, and the retreat again was resumed in the darkness of the night, and was only stopped on the sea coast near Dunbar and North Berwick.

The retreat of the dragoons deprived the town of Edinburgh of all hope of defence from without. At the same time a message was received from the camp of the invaders, informing the citizens that if they opened their gates their town should be favourably treated; but if they attempted resistance the inhabitants must not expect to be considered as prisoners of war. This uncomfortable message, which was speedily followed by sight of the flying dragoons passing into the horizon on the other side of the city from the enemy, caused a general aversion amongst the inhabitants to any idea of defensive measures. The Provost called a meeting of the magistracy, and also solicited the advice of the Crown officers : but the latter, with a prudence even superior to that shown by the dragoons, but more quiet than the volunteers, had already quitted the city and taken refuge some distance from it.

During the meeting of the magistracy, a letter was received from the Chevalier, signed, "Charles Prince Regent," informing the city that if any opposition were made the rebel leaders could not answer for the consequences, being firmly resolved to enter the town. This letter was read against the protest of the Provost. Its contents drove the citizens to almost a desperation of terror. Crowds gathered in the streets, and surrounded the Provost, entreating him to give up all thoughts of defending the walls. The volunteers, on a false report that the Highlanders were immediately approaching, resolved as a measure of personal precaution rather than of general protection, to disembody themselves, and return their arms to the magazine in the Castle. Thus by the flight of the dragoons, and the disbandment of the volunteers, the armed force of Edinburgh was reduced to the city guard and the few recruits of the newly-raised Edinburgh regiment, who were in the Castle. It was agreed to send a deputation of the Town Council to wait on the Prince at Gray's Mill, within two miles of the city. These were instructed to beg for a suspension of hostilities until the magistracy should have had time to deliberate on the letter which had been forwarded from the rebel camp.

Not long had this deputation passed out of the West Port, when intelligence arrived informing the Provost that Sir John Cope's army had arrived in the transports from Aberdeen; that the vessels had been sighted off Dunbar, where the General was about to land his troops, and move instantly to the relief of Edinburgh. A message was sent to recall the deputation to the Pretender; but it had already passed within the rebel lines. The news of the advance of Cope stirred up again martial ardour in the breast of the citizens. General Guest, the Governor of the Castle, was bombarded with various proposals. He was begged to recall the the dragoons; but wisely replied, that he considered it better for the service that they should unite with General Cope. Some of the more fiery volunteers requested a new issue of arms; but Guest seems to have been unwilling to place weapons again in hands which had certainly hardly proved staunch in danger, and contented himself with an intimation that the magistracy might arm those whom they could trust from the city magazines. About ten o'clock on the same night, of the 16th September, the deputation which had been sent to the Pretender returned with an answer of much the same purport as was contained in the first summons to surrender the city. At the same time a demand was made that a positive reply should be made before two o'clock in the morning. This made the magistrates sensible that the leaders of the assailants were as alive as they could be to the value of hours and minutes under such critical circumstances. It was determined to send out a second deputation to Gray's Mill with instructions to entreat for further time to parley; and this deputation was carried to the Highland head-quarters in a hackney-coach which has since not become undistinguished in history. When the deputation reached Gray's Mill the Prince refused to admit its members into his presence, and they were obliged to return without an answer.

During the anxious night of the 16th September the Heir of the Stuarts, within a few paces of the early capital of the founders of his race, slept only two hours, without taking off his clothes. In his council several plans were agitated for carrying the city by a sudden surprise; and there were various points at which it would have been easy that an attack by coup-de-main could be made. Conscious of the value of time, and with a determination to seize any advantage that might suddenly present itself, Lochiel and Murray of Broughton, with five hundred Camerons, were sent forward during the night to watch any favourable opportunity; and they were already beneath the walls of the city before the second deputation had left Gray's Mill. Without being perceived, this force crept close to the Netherbow Port, and there lay in ambush, provided with a barrel of gunpowder, to blow up one of the gates if necessary. But the hackney-coach, which had carried the second deputation to the rebel camp, prevented the necessity of the Camerons having recourse to this petard. After the coachman had deposited the members of the deputation, on his return from the camp, he wished to return from the main part of the city through the Netherbow Port to his stables in the suburb of the Canongate. The sentries of the city guard, knowing that the man had been engaged that night in the service of the magistrates, readily opened the gate to let him go home. Close behind the portals lay hidden, in the shadow of the wall, an advanced guard of twenty Camerons, clustered against either side of the gate. In deep silence, a few paces further down St. Mary's Wynd, was huddled a support of sixty mountaineers; and the remainder of the five hundred of the Cameron clan were in reserve at a further distance, near the foot of the lane. An attempt to have the gate opened for one of the Highlanders, disguised in a riding coat and hunting cap, had already failed, and the Camerons were about to quit the foot of the wall, when the portals were thrown open for the passage into the Canongate of this famous hackney coach. No sooner had the leaves of the gate been unfolded than the leading Camerons rushed in and secured and disarmed the few watchmen of the city guard. With the same ease they rushed into the guardhouse and disarmed such soldiers as there were found. Once inside the walls, it was a work of small time to occupy the other military posts and the gates without a drop of blood being spilt. As day dawned the Camerons were found in possession of the city; and with no more noise and tumult had they gained the place, than if one guard peacefully had relieved another. Shortly after daybreak the clan was marched up to the Cross; when the Castle, angered by the news of what had happened, fired a shot or two to annoy the Highland occupants of the town. The most part of the citizens of Edinburgh were roused by the shots, and awoke to find the city in the hands of the partisans of the Stuart cause.

Strict seems to have been the discipline maintained by Lochiel, for from six to eleven the Camerons remained drawn up in perfect order at the City Cross; and the Highlanders, refused the whisky which was offered to them by the citizens, and refrained from all plunder, though even a continental army might have claimed booty in a town thus taken as it were by storm. At noon of the same day, 17th September, another striking ceremony was enacted at the Old Cross of Edinburgh, already so famous in the annals of Scottish history. The heralds and pursuivants, arrayed in their antique and glittering dresses of office, were forced by the clansmen to proclaim King James VIII., and read the royal declaration and commission of regency, while the bagpipes played triumphal strains; and, as is usual, from the populace, which ever sides with success, acclamations were not wanting.

At nearly the same hour as King James VIII. was being proclaimed at the Cross, Prince Charles Edward, who till then had remained at the head of his vanguard, prepared to take possession of Holyrood House, the palace of his ancestors. To avoid the fire of the English garrison in Edinburgh Castle, he made a considerable circuit to the south, and coming round by the village of Duddingston, halted in the hollow between Arthur's Seat and Salisbury Crags. He entered the King's Park by a breach which had been made in the wall, and approached Holyrood House by the Duke's Walk, so called as it had been a favourite place of exercise of his grandfather the Duke of York during his residence in Scotland. So surrounded was the Prince by the populace, that although he had commenced to walk on foot, he was forced to mount on horseback, so as not to be thrown down by the people who crowded round him in enormous numbers, and with loud shouts of welcome. Thus mounted, he rode on to the palace, having on his right hand the Duke of Perth, on his left Lord Elcho, the eldest son of the Earl of Wemys, who had joined him a few days before, and followed by a crowd of Highland chiefs and Lowland gentlemen. The personal appearance of the Chevalier was prepossessing; his figure was tall and well formed, his limbs athletic and active; he excelled in all manly exercises, and was inured to every kind of toil, especially long marches on foot, having applied himself to field sports in Italy, and become an excellent walker. His face was striking and handsome, of a perfect oval, with a fair complexion; his eyes light blue; his features high and noble. Contrary to the fashion of the times, which prescribed perukes, his own fair hair usually fell in long ringlets on his neck. His manners were graceful, and most courteous. Such was Prince Charles Edward Stuart at the time of his entry into

Edinburgh; how different from him in his later years, when his constitution was ruined by intemperance, and his temper soured by the ill-health which resulted from indulgence in that vice! The dress that the Prince wore was national. A short tartan coat, a blue bonnet with a white rose, and the order and star of St. Andrew, seemed all chosen to identify him with the ancient nation that he called to arms. So far as the acclamations of the mob, and smiles of the most fickle part of the populace, the women, could be taken as a test, the Prince was so favourably received on his entry into Edinburgh that few who judged from appearances could doubt that he might have levied a thousand men from the town in half an hour, if he could have had the arms with which to equip them.

Even those who are most convinced of the blessings which have fallen upon this country through the accession of the House of Hanover, and who are most certain of the miseries that would have crushed our people and our land had the Stuart dynasty seized the crown, which it lost through the assertion of dogmas intolerable to free subjects, can hardly fail to feel a sympathy for the brave young Prince who, in defence of the rights which he considered inalienable, had the courage to land on a lone portion of the western coast, with less than a handful of supporters, and to throw himself, his fortunes and his life, on the generosity and valour of followers bound to him little by interest, though greatly by affection. Nor is it possible not to admire the sturdy fidelity of the clansmen, who clung with unfailing hope to the Stuart cause. The chiefs indeed may have followed the dictates of prudence, and have trusted that by playing a high stake for the return of the Stuarts they might, if successful, have secured for themselves position, emoluments, and rewards; but the lowly herdsmen and hunters of the glens and the hills had little thought of appointments under government in London, or of lucrative positions in the south. Yet out of pure devotion to a cause which they could but little comprehend, they were ready to penetrate at the call of their chieftains into what to them was a mysterious, a dangerous, and a far-off land.

Those who were able to see beneath the clamour or the crowd, discerned internal symptoms of weakness in the means by which Prince Charles Edward hoped to carry through his daring enterprise of driving a popular and beloved dynasty from the throne of these islands, and of tearing from the hearts of the great bulk of the people of England and Scotland the affection that they already felt for the House of Guelph. This affection was the more sure and constant, as it had already been evoked by the kindly hearts which so consistently beat within the breast of the House of Hanover. Even one hundred years ago the loyalty towards the reigning line was more firm than any loyalty based merely on the dogmatic assertion of Divine right or hereditary principle. The gentlemen of the clans, or duinhewassels, as they were termed, were attired in the full Highland costume with fire-arm, broad-sword, dirk, target, and pistols; but such complete equipment was the portion of but few of the followers of the Pretender. The lowlier clansmen were glad to be satisfied with some single weapon, as a sword, dirk, or pistol. In spite of all evasions of the disarming act, the law had been so far effectually put in force in the Highlands that many of the clansmen were armed only with scythe-blades, set straight on poles, and some with no better weapons than clubs or cudgels. The scanty and ill-provided appearance of the poorer soldiery gave them an air at once wretched and terrible. Some had no coats and little but a torn cloth tied round their waists. Many were devoid of brogues or shoes. Some had their long and unkempt hair, tied back merely with a leather strap, without bonnet or covering of any kind. Inured to war and hardship, spare and muscular, their variety of costume and weapons gave them a fierceness of aspect which made them rather appear as a formidable collection of brigands than an army disciplined and equipped for modern warfare.

As the Prince came near to Holyrood House the gunners of the castle fired upon him, but without doing any injury. He entered the palace, preceded by James Hepburn of Keith, who drew his sword and marshalled the way up-stairs. In the evening the long-deserted halls of Holyrood were enlivened with a splendid ball; and Charles there won the favour of numbers of ladies of both rank and beauty, who that night danced at Holyrood, the relatives and friends of the gentlemen who were in arms.

More important to his cause, perhaps, were the junctions of the Earl of Kelly, Lord Balmarino, Lockhart the younger of Carnwath, Graham of Airth, Rollo, Hamilton of Bangor, Sir David Murray, and other gentlemen of distinction, who now linked themselves with his fortunes.

The next morning, that of the 18th, attention was turned to more serious matters. From the magazine of Edinburgh about a thousand muskets, the arms of the trained bands which had been lodged in the city stores, were obtained. These served to arm some of the Highlanders, but by no means provided for all. A requisition was laid upon the city for tents, targets, shoes, and canteens. But notwithstanding the ball at Holyrood and the acclamations of the crowd, scarcely one of the common people who pressed in thousands around the Prince's person when he went abroad, to kiss his hands and touch his clothes, could be induced to take up arms in his service. Perhaps the reflection that in a few days a battle must take place between Prince Charles and General Cope was to the prudent citizens of Edinburgh a check upon their loyalty for the Stuart cause. From the north, however, came 500 of the clan MacLachlan; and another reinforcement arrived of Highlanders from Athole. The whole force was reviewed by the Prince in the camp of Duddingston, and Charles announced his resolution to lead his force forward and give battle to Sir John Cope. This step was the wisest probably that could be pursued, as it encouraged the fiery zeal of the Highlanders; and the conduct of the dragoons had already shown that, as far as horsemen were concerned, who are the most formidable antagonists always to mountaineers, the insurgents had little to fear from the attack of the regular soldiery.

Only one entire day, the 18th September, Charles rested at Edinburgh; on the night of Thursday the 19th he came to the village of Duddingston, and the troops lay upon their arms, ready to move. It was agreed that the Highland army should march forward early on the following morning. The Prince asked the chiefs how they thought their men would behave? These desired that Keppoch, who had served in the French army, and was well acquainted both with the Highlanders and continental troops, should answer for them. Keppoch replied that as the country had been long at peace, few or none of the clansmen had ever seen a battle, and it was not easy to say how they would conduct themselves; but he would venture to assure the Prince that the gentlemen would be in the midst of the enemy, and that the private men, as they loved their chiefs and loved their Prince, would be sure to follow them.

Early on the morning of the 20th, the Highlanders broke up from their camp at Duddingston, and began to move eastwards in a single narrow column. As the Prince put himself at their head, he drew his sword and cried to his advanced guard, "Gentlemen, I have flung away the scabbard." This expression was answered by loud cheers. The cavalry of the insurgents scarcely amounted to fifty men, being only some gentlemen with their grooms, or huntsmen on horseback. But the numbers of the whole force together amounted to 2,500 fighting men. To the army there was attached but one single piece of artillery; an iron gun which was fired as a signal for the commencement of the march, but was useless as a piece of ordnance. The Prince had desired to leave this behind him, as a mere incumbrance, but the Highland chiefs interposed, and urged the prejudices of their followers in favour of "the musket's mother," as they termed any cannons. Being carried with them accordingly, it was dragged along in rear of the column by a long string of Shetland ponies. Besides the royal standard, each clan displayed its banner, inscribed with its gathering cry, such as that of Athole, "Forth and fill the fetters."

As the column moved away from Duddingston, three men abreast, with tartans waving and pipes playing, a few straggling shots from the Castle dropped near it; but with a rapid swinging stride the Highlanders soon placed themselves beyond the reach of the guns of Guest.

Meanwhile, on the same day that King James VIII. was proclaimed at the Cross at Edinburgh, and Prince Charles Edward took up his residence in Holyrood, General Cope had commenced landing his troops at Dunbar, anxious to repair the false step which he had made in leaving the military roads from the Highlands to the Lowlands open to the insurgents. The disembarkation of the troops was not completed till the 18th. Cope had been reinforced at Inverness by an addition of Lord Loudon's Highlanders, and was joined at Dunbar by the dragoons who had retreated so precipitately from Colt Brigg. These horsemen numbered about 600, and his whole force was about 2,200 men. This was composed of Gardiner's dragoons, now the 13th Hussars; and Hamilton's dragoons, now the 14th Hussars; which together mustered 567 men; two companies of Guise's, now the 6th regiment of the line: and eight companies of Lascelles', now the 57th regiment. These brought into the field 570 musqueteers and pikemen. There were also under Cope five companies of Lee's regiment, which is now the 44th regiment; with Murray's regiment, now the 46th; making a strength together of 763 men: besides 183 Highlanders, the remnants of Lord Loudon's regiment that had not as yet deserted.

A few gentlemen from the Lowlands joined Cope as volunteers, but brought little except moral support. The principal of these was the Earl of Home, who was attended by only two servants. To the Southern army were also attached six pieces of artillery, a most effective arm against Highlanders; but these were not manned by gunners of the Royal Artillery, but only by seamen, who seem to have been pressed into the service from the transports.

On the 19th Cope marched from the neighbourhood of the place of disembarkation, and encamped that night near Duddingston. Next morning he resumed his advance. He expected that the Highlanders, if they dared to face his approach, would be met along the regular highway; but it was supposed, not only by the country people, but by many of the royal officers, that there would be no battle, but that the clans would melt away at the very appearance of the regular soldiery. The Highlanders, when they left Duddingston, kept in one narrow column towards Musselburgh, where they crossed the Esk by the old bridge. They then advanced to the eminence of which Carbury Hill is the termination on the south-west. There they occupied the brow, the spot famous in former years for the surrender of the unhappy Mary Queen of Scots.

The tactical arrangements of the Highlanders were extremely simple. On the march they formed a column of three men abreast; when required to halt and form line, each individual faced to the right or left as directed, and the column became a line of three men deep, which by simply facing to either flank might again become a column on a single word of command. The handful of cavalry attached to the Highland army, though scarcely amounting to fifty men, was occupied on the march in reconnoitering. They obtained a tolerably accurate report of the strength of the royal army, except as to the number of the guns, which one party exaggerated to twenty field-pieces, and none stated as under twelve, though there were really only six in all. The English General, hoping to obtain early intelligence of the movements of his enemy, had sent forward two of the Edinburgh volunteers, who had joined his camp, and who it was supposed from their knowledge of the country would obtain good information. These however proved hardly more competent for this than for other military duty; and it is said could not resist the temptation of some oysters and sherry in a public-house that they remembered from former days. Here they were surprised, and both taken prisoners by a young lad, a lawyer's clerk. The English General received no report, and on Friday the 20th, after having marched about eight miles, while he continued to feel for the enemy to the west, suddenly found them crossing the ridge on his left to the southward. It appears that Cope had supposed that the Highlanders would advance along the high road, passing from Seaton House to Preston, which was the regular way from Duddingston. But he failed to remember that an irregular army of mountaineers, marching without baggage, would probably by preference cross the country and occupy heights at the bottom of which the public road took its course. The Highlanders, when they crowned the hill immediately above Tranent, perceived on the cultivated plain below them then in stubble the column of the enemy, gorgeous in scarlet uniform, bright with yellow facings, and capped with glittering steel. On finding his enemy crossing the hills and threatening his flank, Cope immediately changed front, drew up his troops in order of battle, his foot in the centre, with a regiment of dragoons and three guns on either flank. The wall of the park of Colonel Gardiner, and the village of Preston, covered the right flank of the royal army, while at some distance on its left stood Seaton House. The sea, with the village of Prestonpans lay in the rear of Cope's right; while at the hamlet of Cockenzie, on the rear of his left, his baggage and military chest were stationed, under the guard of some of Loudon's Highlanders.

When the royal troops first saw the insurgents, they set up a loud shout of defiance, which, with hearts as big and yells as loud, was promptly answered by the Highlanders. The space between the two armies was less

than a mile, and between them lay the little town of
Morant. At the bottom of the ridge occupied by the
insurgents was a piece of broken and swampy ground,
intersected with ditches and inclosures, and traversed
near the foot of the hill by a thick strong hedge running
along a broad wet ditch. It was about three o'clock in
the afternoon, and Charles was anxious to indulge the
impatience of his troops by an instant attack. Before
doing so, however, it was necessary to reconnoitre the
ground, and he sent forward one of his officers, Kerr of
Graden, who coolly examined the apparently impracticable morass, which divided the armies, with great care,
and in various directions, totally regardless of several
shots that were fired at him by the royal pickets. Kerr
deliberately, in several instances, alighted, pulled down
gaps in one or two dry stone walls, and led his horse
over them. He then returned to the Chevalier to inform
him that the morass was too difficult to be passed, so as
to attack the army of Cope in front, without exposing the
assailants on a narrow path, to a heavy and destructive
fire of some continuance, in face and flank. A wagon
road for the conveyance of coal worked in the vicinity
of Tranant, for the use of the salt works at Kinsale did
indeed cross the morass, but it would have been ruinous
folly to have engaged troops on such a narrow front
exposed to be swept at once in front and flank by
artillery and musketry fire. Charles accordingly desisted
from his purpose, to the great dissatisfaction of the
common Highlanders, who feared that the enemy intended to escape from them as before at Corryarrack;

and they were not appeased, till Lord Nairn with 500 men was despatched to the westward, so as to prevent the English General from stealing off towards Edinburgh, had he so wished, unperceived and unopposed.

In the meantime Sir John Cope, having found a position in which he could not be attacked, considered himself fortunate; although, as Sir Walter Scott remarks, instead of seeking safety he should have looked for victory. Colonel Gardiner urged upon him in vain the necessity of the initiative, and of bolder measures. The only offensive movement of the king's troops that afternoon was to fire a few rounds of artillery, which dislodged a party of Highlanders from Tranent churchyard. In the evening it was resolved in the Highland army that at all hazards Cope should be attacked next morning, opposite Tranent, where the morass seemed less difficult. Fortunately for the Chevalier, there was in his army a gentleman named Anderson of Whitburgh, a native of East Lothian, to whom the ground in the neighbourhood of Tranent was perfectly familiar, and who suddenly remembered a path which led from the height on which the insurgent army lay, round the morass, down to the plain below. This important fact was communicated to Lord George Murray, who immediately went and awoke the Prince. Charles received the tidings with much cheerfulness, and immediately the scheme was prepared to be put in execution. An aide-de-camp was sent to recall Lord Nairn with his detachment, the Highlanders were got under arms, and with perfect silence formed ·olumn, and began the march which should place them on the left flank of the royal army, Anderson leading the way. The path was found lonely and unguarded, and the morass was passed without much difficulty; though even by this chosen path some of the Highlanders sank knee keep. The night was dark and cold, and as day began to break a frosty mist covered the plain, and rising high above the morass, entirely concealed the movements of the Highland army from the outposts of the Royalists. But when the leading clansmen gained the plain, the dragoon pickets stationed there heard the sound of their feet and the clatter of their arms, after challenging and shouting "Who goes there?" fired their pistols and galloped off to give the alarm. A signal gun was almost immediately afterwards heard, warning the regular troops to get under arms.

The right of the Highland line was yielded reluctantly to the Macdonalds by the Camerons and the Stuarts, although both supposed that they ought to have held the post of honour. Charles placed himself at the head of the second line, which was close behind the first. The first line consisted of the clans of Clanranald, Glengarry, Glencoe, Macgregor, Appin, and Lochiel; the second consisted of three regiments, Lord George Murray's Athole men, Lord Nairn's regiment, and those of Menzies of Shian. Lord Strathallan with his tiny force of cavalry was ordered to hold the height above the morass, and to do what his numbers would allow to improve the victory in case one should be gained. It is extraordinary that the English army should have placed no sentries or outposts on this important path, by which the morass was passed; and it would almost appear that the vicinity of the royal army was not properly reconnoitred or patrolled, although a deserted embrasure was discovered by the insurgents in their advance, which showed that the fortification of this passage had been contemplated. On reaching the firm ground beyond the morass the Highland column advanced due northward across the plain, in order to gain ground for turning towards the enemy and forming line of battle.

On the alarm being given in the English camp that the Highlanders were close at hand, a gun was fired as a signal for the troops to get under arms. Seeing that the Highlanders had completely turned his left flank, and were now advancing from the eastward, along a level and open plain without interruption of any kind, Sir John Cope lost no time in disposing his troops to receive them. He changed front to his left, and altered the dispositions which he had made the previous evening along the morass; he formed his line facing eastwards, with the walls of Preston Park and of Bankton, the house of Colonel Gardiner, close in the rear of his army. His left flank extended towards the sea; while his right rested upon the morass which had lately been in his front. The infantry stood in the centre; Hamilton's dragoons on the left of the line; and Gardiner's, with the artillery in front of them, on the right next to the morass. This disposition, against which Colonel Gardiner is said to have remonstrated, was found to be very disadvantageous in the course of the action.

The Highlanders had no sooner advanced so far to the northward as to clear with the rear of their column the passage across the morass, and to place the whole of their force on open ground, than they turned to the left, and formed their line of battle of three deep. For an instant there was a pause in the Highland ranks. With uncovered heads the clansmen bent and muttered a short prayer; then pulling sternly their bonnets over their brows, they drew their weapons; the bagpipes screamed forth the signal of attack; and breaking into small bodies, the tartan warriors rushed forward with a slogan cry that gradually rose into a tremendous yell. The first attacking line rapidly closed amongst the guns, and though Colonel Whiteford, who had joined Cope's army as a volunteer, fired five of the pieces on the advancing Highlanders, the Camerons and the Stuarts, running in upon the cannons, stormed the battery. Gardiner's dragoons, who were drawn up in rear of the guns, received orders to charge, but, like the seamen gunners, were seized with panic, dispersed under the fire of the Highlanders, and fled from the field, without even an attempt to advance, riding down the guard of the guns in their flight. Colonel Gardiner himself stood his ground, and encouraging some of the infantry near him to fire upon the advancing Highlanders, was struck a mortal blow and borne to the earth dead. At the same time as the Camerons and Stuarts scattered Gardiner's dragoons on the right of the English line, in the same manner did the Macdonalds drive Hamilton's regiment like chaff before them. The English infantry now remained uncovered on both flanks, but was still steady, and poured upon the Highland centre a close and well-directed fire, before which several of the best clansmen fell. But the fire of the infantry was no more effectual in staying the wild onset of the clans than was the appearance of the cavalry. The Highlanders, not an instant checked by the fire of musketry, charged into the ordered ranks, parried the bayonets of the foot soldiers with their targets, and broke at several points the extended and thin lines of the regulars. By this fierce assault the whole of the centre of the English line was thrown into confusion; while the inclosures and park wall of Preston impeded its retreat. So rapid was the Highland onset, that in five or six minutes the whole brunt of the fight was passed.

Had Cope had any means of rallying his fugitives, the day might have been in some degree avenged; for the first line of the Highlanders dispersed themselves almost immediately in search of booty and prisoners. The second line, headed by the Prince himself, who had followed so close to the first line that to Sir John Cope's army the two lines appeared but as one body, would have probably disbanded in the same manner, had not a report spread that the dragoons had rallied, and had returned into the field. But the dragoons had no intention to look near the enemy again. They retreated in every direction. Some rushed into Edinburgh, and carried the news of the Highland victory to the capital. Others flew in the direction of Stirling and the west country. Some were rallied by Sir John Cope and conducted in a not satisfactory plight to Coldstream, and then to Berwick. At the latter town the unfortunate General himself arrived, as it is said, being the first to bring the tidings of his own defeat. The victory was most complete. The dragoons, being mounted, and there being no cavalry to pursue them, escaped; but not two hundred of the infantry got away. All the rest were either killed or taken prisoners. The total number of slain in the royal army was about four hundred, and of these none were lamented more than the benevolent and pious Colonel Gardiner, who was carried senseless to the clergyman's house of Tranent, and there expired a few hours after the battle.

Great moderation was shown by Prince Charles Edward in his victory. He remained on the field till mid-day, giving orders for the relief of the wounded of both armies, without distinction of friend or foe; and on seeing the bodies of the English soldiers, expressed deep commiseration for what he considered his father's misguided subjects. On the part of the Highlanders the battle, though short, had not been bloodless. Four officers and thirty men were killed; six officers and seventy men wounded. Thus in five or six minutes the whole of the regular infantry in Scotland, except the small detachments which garrisoned the military posts, were swept away, and the cavalry was scattered in retreat, or driven into the southernmost corner of the kingdom. Scotland was thus freed from the troops of the Government, and almost entirely at the mercy of the insurgents. No sooner was the victory decided than most of the Highlanders disbanded for plunder. The standards, and trophies, and the military chest, containing about £2,500, was brought to the Prince, but all other supplies were reserved by the captors for themselves. This plunder was of considerable disadvantage, as a great number of the Highlanders, unaccustomed to luxuries, retreated to the mountains to place their booty in a place of safety. Had at this time the French Government acted with energy, and thrown troops, either on the coast of England, or sent reinforcements to the Forth, it is probable that they might have made the invasion of Prince Charles Edward, commenced with only seven men, successful and have also obtained Flanders as an easy conquest for themselves. As it was, the British troops who were recalled from Flanders in consequence of the rebellion in Scotland, which led to the sudden conclusion of the Convention of Hanover, left a great opportunity to Maréchal de Saxe. That skilful officer invested Brussels in the following winter, and on the 20th February the capital of the Low Countries surrendered, and its large garrison became prisoners of war. As it was, vessels were despatched from time to time from France with money and supplies, though only in small quantities. One of these vessels arrived some time after the victory of Preston at Montrose, with £5,000 in money, and 2,500 stands of arms; a train of six brass four-pounders, was also sent; and some Irish officers came by these vessels. But such aid was not sent either in sufficient quantities, or with a sufficiently organised plan, and after a time, to intercept such communications, Admiral Byng entered the Firth of Forth with four or five royal men-of-war, which forced the cavalry of the insurgents to scour the coasts with patrols, in order to prevent the landing of the English seamen.

In the meantime the Government in London had not been idle. At the news of the progress of the insurrection King George himself had set out from Hanover, and on the 31st August had arrived in London, three weeks before the battle of Preston. He found that the Regency in his absence had not neglected precautions. A requisition had been sent to the Dutch government for the six thousand auxiliaries they were bound by treaty to furnish; and it had been resolved to recall some of the English regiments from Flanders.

Marshal Wade had also been ordered to collect as many troops as he could concentrate at Newcastle; and the militia of several counties had been called out. But the people as a rule in no degree supported the endeavours of the government; but remained cold spectators; not indeed openly favouring the rebellion, but little inclined to struggle against it. Marshal Wade himself, in a letter written early in September, before the battle of Preston, says, that England is, according to his belief, the prize of the first comer; that if anybody could tell whether the six thousand Dutch, and the ten battalions of English from Flanders, or five thousand French or Spaniards, would be here first, the fate of the country would be known. The same officer, writing a few days later, says, "The French are not come, God be thanked; but had five thousand landed in any part of this island a week ago, I verily believe the entire conquest would not have cost them a battle." Parliament was summoned for the 17th October. On the tidings of the first success of Prince Charles Edward, the King of France became better disposed towards him, and the French court took into consideration what, if promptly carried out, might have been a most important diversion in his favour. It was intended to put the younger brother of Charles Edward, Henry of York, at the head of the Irish regiments in the French service, and of some native French troops, and with these attempt to effect a landing in England. Preparations were actually begun with that object in the harbour of Dunkirk, but intrigues sprang up against the intended expedition, pretexts of delay were always found, and obstacles invariably interposed. The French government deferred long, and finally lost the fairest chance that it had ever had since the Revolution of swaying the destinies of Britain into the channel that it so much desired.

The first wish of Prince Charles himself was that the blow struck at Preston should be followed up as rapidly as possible by a bold irruption into England; and that he himself at the head of his army should march immediately upon London. The morning after the action an agent was sent into Northumberland with instructions to stir up the country and prepare the way for the coming of the Prince. Had he been able at this moment to push forward with a body of two thousand or three thousand men, there is reason to believe, from the state of matters in England, the apathy of the people, the terror consequent on the victory at Preston, the want of troops previous to the arrival of the Dutch and the battalions from Flanders, the jealousies and intrigues in the English cabinet, that the Highlanders might have reached London with but little opposition, and succeeded at least in a temporary restoration.

On the road from Scotland to the metropolis beyond the Tweed, there was no fortified town, except Newcastle; and even at Newcastle there was consternation. Though the walls were mounted with cannon, and preparations made to sustain an assault, the townspeople were busy in removing their goods, and most of the best houses were left without either furniture, or inhabitants. This is stated positively by an eye-witness on the second day after the battle of Preston.

In Scotland, where previous to the action at Preston, the heir of the Stuarts could claim control over hardly an acre of land, beyond that occupied by the lines of his clansmen, his victory in Lothian had placed the whole country at his feet. Nowhere, except in the Castles of Edinburgh and Stirling, and the four small posts in the Highlands, was the standard of the government flown.

Yet the Prince could not but be aware that his own army, after the battle of Preston, was reduced by nearly one half, through the number of Highlanders who had returned home to deposit the booty which they had captured in the field. His Scottish advisers were almost unanimous against an expedition into England, and urged with an appearance of force that he might triple or quadruple his army by reinforcements from the Highlands, and also might obtain the advantage of the supplies which were beginning to arrive at the eastern ports of Scotland from France. Such arguments probably were fallacious; for the supplies from France might have been equally directed to the ports of England, and the English Jacobites would probably have furnished as many recruits to the white flag as might be expected from the Highlands; provided that the advance had been made into England, while the government was still unprepared. But the melting away of the clansmen after the victory of Preston left hardly any course open, except to remain in Scotland until larger supplies of men were forthcoming, with which to advance southwards.

It was accordingly determined that the Highland army should take up its headquarters at Edinburgh, and await the reinforcements from the hills, which the news of the victory of Preston would probably cause quickly to take up arms. The Chevalier having passed the night of his victory, the 21st September, at Pinkie House near Musselburgh, returned on the following evening, to fix his residence for some time in Edinburgh. The main body of his army was encamped at Duddingston, where it was with great difficulty that the mountaineers could be persuaded to make use of, as covering, the tents which they had captured from the regular troops, after the battle of Preston. The appearance of the camp was most irregular, the assistance of the quartermaster-general was entirely discarded; clans drew up their own lines and pitched their own camp as best suited their convenience; and regulations of a sanitary nature seemed almost entirely to have been disregarded. As it was, however, it does not appear that any amount of sickness worthy of note broke out amongst the clansmen, who were probably in their native glens fully inured to exposure to the weather, and had been probably bred without much regard to cleanliness. A considerable quantity of troops marched back into Edinburgh with the Prince in triumphal procession, escorting the prisoners, the supplies, and the colours that had been taken in battle. The multitude, as all multitudes, ever eager to side with success, greeted the Highlanders and their leaders with repeated acclamations; while the pibrochs of the pipemen woke up the echoes of the old High-street, with the well-known Jacobite air of "The king shall enjoy his own again."

The battle of Preston made Prince Charles Edward master of all Scotland, except the few posts held by the royal troops. In almost every town his father was proclaimed as King James VIII. while the public cess and the excise were collected in his name and for his service. Circular letters were sent to the magistrates of all towns in Scotland, commanding them to repair immediately to Edinburgh to pay their proportion of the contributions which were imposed on every district.

The collectors and controllers of the land tax and customs were also forced to bring to Holyrood their books and the public money in their hands, on pain of high treason; while the goods in the Customs House of Leith, held for the Government, were sold out for the military chest. On the city of Glasgow, the richest and least friendly to the Jacobite cause, an extraordinary contribution of £5,000 was imposed.

The Prince himself at Holyrood bore all the state of royalty, and made every exertion to confirm and exalt popular feeling in his favour. He prohibited rejoicings for his victory, giving as a reason that the men who had been slain were his countrymen and his father's misguided subjects. The clergy of Edinburgh were, by edict, encouraged to resume the exercise of their functions and assured of the protection of the Prince. The ministers, however, not confident, perhaps, in the security of the protection which even the goodwill of the Prince might afford to them, against the Highlanders and Papists, who composed the bulk of his forces, left their pulpits vacant. It is only recorded that one, Mr. Macvicar the minister of the West Church, continued to conduct his services with boldness and even to pray for King George. It is worthy of notice, however, that the West Church was within easy point-blank range of the guns of the Royal garrison of the castle. The Chevalier was urged to punish the boldness of the clergyman in praying for the reigning king of England; but with wisdom refused to disturb the services of the congregation; and possibly out of gratitude for this immunity, Mr. Macvicar on the following Sunday added to his prayers in behalf of King George, this petition in favour of Prince Charles. "As to this young person who has come among us seeking an earthly crown, do Thou in Thy merciful favour give him a heavenly one."

More inconvenience than was caused by the prayers of the worthy minister arose from the banking companies of Edinburgh having on the advance of the Highlanders withdrawn into the Castle, carrying with them the specie which supplied the currency of the country. A proclamation was issued, which invited these establishments to return into the city, and to resume the ordinary course of their business. But the controllers of money felt no more security against the inroads of the Highlanders than did the majority of the controllers of spiritual exercises, and declined to trust themselves beyond the sentries of the Castle.

This fortress was at first closely blockaded, but the Governor wrote to the magistrates of Edinburgh, that unless communication with the country was re-opened, and means given him to supply food to his garrison, he would fire upon the city and lay the houses in ruins. It is probable that the earnestness with which the Governor insisted upon the communication with the country being kept open, was not prompted by any fear of the starvation of his garrison, for it is believed now that there was a large supply of salt provisions in the place. He was eager, however, that the insurgent army might be induced, by the hopes of a speedy capitulation of the Castle of Edinburgh, to remain before its guns instead of

leaving to march southwards before there were troops of
the government assembled to bar the way. The threat
of the Governor to fire upon the town caused naturally
much alarm among the magistrates and citizens, whose
valour had not been proved to be of the highest order
before the victory of Preston. A day's respite was
obtained from General Guest, in order that his threat
might be laid before Prince Charles at Holyrood.

The answer from the headquarters of the rebel army
was delivered in writing. It expressed surprise that any
officer should be so barbarous as to threaten ruin to the
inhabitants of a city for not doing what they were im-
potent to accomplish, and pointed out, not unjustly, that
the government might with equal reason require the
rebel army to leave the city under threat of reducing it
to ruins, if it were thought that an instrument could be
made of the Prince's compassion for the people. This
answer was transmitted to the Castle, and after entreaty
the magistrates obtained from the general an agreement
to suspend hostilities till the return of the express which
was immediately despatched for orders from London.
General Guest expected that, pending further instructions,
no inconvenience would be given to the garrison, but as
that condition was not understood or promulgated
through the rebel army, a' few days after some Highlanders fired at a party of country people carrying
provisions up the Castle hill ; upon this the gunners
immediately opened fire, the streets of the town were
swept with shot, and several of the inhabitants as well
as many of the advanced posts of the Highlanders were

killed. An earnest appeal was now made to the Prince to interpose and save the city from destruction; and with a moderation which does him infinite credit, the Chevalier himself insisted that the blockade should be raised and free communication allowed between the garrison and the sources of their supply.

Although the inhabitants of Edinburgh were well pleased with the Prince's generosity, his clemency in another matter excited no small disappointment among his followers. It had been proposed that one of the prisoners taken at Preston should be sent to London in order to demand of the Court of St. James that an exchange of prisoners who had been taken or should be taken in the war should be allowed; in fact a demand that the rebels should be treated as belligerents, with the intimation that if this course were declined, and that if any of the Prince's followers fell into the hands of the government and were put to death as rebels, the Prince would be compelled to treat his captives in the same manner. It was evident that a recognition by the government of the rights of the insurgents to be treated as belligerents, and not as rebels, would be of the utmost importance, as many would be willing to face the dangers of war and the field and join the army as recruits who would not be prepared to add to the hazard of battle the subsequent horrors of the gibbet, the rope, and the scaffold. It was urged upon the Prince that in order to induce the English officers to bring pressure to bear upon their government to allow the exchanges of prisoners, some English officers who fell into his hands should be made examples of, so that their own comrades might be anxious that the exchange of prisoners should be allowed. With a moderation which is usually the best policy, Charles stubbornly refused his sanction. "It is below me," he said, "to make empty threats, and I will never put such as these into execution. I will not in cold blood take away lives which I have spared in the heat of action."

In opposition to the advice of those who had urged this barbarous course, great clemency was shown by the Chevalier himself to the prisoners taken at Preston. Within a few days of the battle the officers were liberated on parole, and permitted to live where they chose in the town of Edinburgh. Little more restraint was imposed upon the privates, but as an officer, unworthy of the the English army, broke his parole and escaped into the Castle, both officers and privates were sent afterwards into custody near Perth. Few were persuaded to enlist into the Prince's army; but as it was found expensive and troublesome to confine those who had been sent to Perth, the greater number were released on taking an oath not to serve against the House of Stuart for one twelvemonth—an engagement which, it is alleged, was not respected by the English government. Nor is it unnatural that the government should consider that an oath made to a rebel commander was invalid.

It had been intended by the Prince to summon a Scottish parliament at Edinburgh, but the difficulties of the scheme were found to be insuperable. He published however a proclamation on the 9th of October, denouncing the pretended parliament of the Elector of Hanover, summoned at Westminster for the 17th, warning the English not to attend, and declared the attendance of the same to be high treason on the part of the people of Scotland. On the 10th of October, the following day, an important proclamation was issued by the Prince, in which he announced that his father would never ratify the "pretended union with England," but that with respect to every law and act of parliament since the rebellion, so far as in a fair and legal parliament they should be approved, he would confirm them. He also publicly proclaimed that the King his father would uphold liberty of conscience, and give the most solemn promise to accord whatever a free parliament should propose for the happiness of the people. These proclamations had probably less effect than the victory in Preston in bringing reinforcements to the Prince's standard. But many loyalist gentlemen now joined the ranks of the rebels. General Gordon of Glenbucket led down from the upper part of Aberdeenshire one hundred men; Lord Ogilvie, eldest son of the Earl of Airlie, appeared at the head of six hundred men, from Strathmore; Lord Pitsligo, a still more important accession, being a nobleman of the most irreproachable character, and already in an advanced stage of life, took the field at the head of a squadron of north country gentlemen, amounting to one hundred and twenty in number, while Lord Gordon, brother of the Duke, declared for the Chevalier, and undertook to levy a considerable force in his own country, though his brother declined to join the rebel standard, mindful probably of the result of 1715.

Macpherson of Cluny, who had gone from Perth to levy his clansmen, returned to Edinburgh with about three hundred. Lord Balmerino, a bold, hard-drinking veteran of the old Scottish stamp, took up arms again, as he did in 1715. These new forces were organised in all possible haste. Two troops of cavalry were formed as guards, one of which was placed under the command of Lord Elcho, the other, which was at first intended to be commanded by the son of Lord Kenmure, who declined to join, was subsequently conferred on the unfortunate Balmerino. A troop of horse grenadiers was placed under the command of the equally unhappy Kilmarnock. Mr. Murray of Broughton the Prince's secretary, desirous of military as well as civil command, levied a small regiment of hussars, intended for light cavalry duties, which were commanded under him by an Irish officer in the French service, named Lieutenant Colonel Bagot. The dress of these horsemen is recorded with considerable accuracy. The privates in their ranks were all gentlemen, and were uniformly clothed in blue, faced with red, and had scarlet waistcoats laced with gold.

These accessions were chiefly men from the Lowlands, and from the Lowland counties of the Highlands, and not from the hills. With Sir Alexander Macdonald and the Macleods the Stuart cause found less favour. Three days after the battle of Preston the Chevalier had despatched a messenger to the chieftains of Macdonald and

Macleod, exhorting them, but in vain, to join his standard. These two great chiefs were probably deterred from entering upon any decided action through the duplicity of Lord Lovat. He hesitated even after the battle of Preston, chiefly through the instrumentality of Forbes, President of the Court of Session, who possessed over him that species of ascendency which men of decided and honest principle usually hold over such as are crafty and unconscientious. Had Lovat, the Macdonalds, and the Macleods thrown in their fate with the Chevalier, their united forces would nearly have doubled the numbers which Charles was collecting at Duddingston, and with such a force the Prince might have ventured on an instant march to England after the battle of Preston, where every day's news was now prompting Marshal Wade and the English government to collect troops and make arrangements to bar his progress, as well as to resist the threatened invasion from France. Lovat proposed to form with the Mackintoshes, Farquarsons, and other branches of the clan Chattan, over whom he possessed considerable influence—a northern army at the pass of Corryarrack, which, united with the Macleods and the Macdonalds, would probably have amounted to five or six thousand men. He believed that he could have retained this army, to throw it on whichever side might subsequently serve best to promote his own interests. But the crafty Lovat overreached himself. The chiefs of the Macdonalds and Macleod of Sleat perceived that the mere desire of Lovat was to profit by their services without giving them any share of his expected advantages, and thought it not unreasonable to secure to themselves the price of their own labours. They began to listen to the more sincere and honest counsel of Lord President Forbes, who exhorted them to keep their dependents from joining in the rebellion, and finally induced them to raise their vassals on behalf of the House of Hanover. The President was furnished with commissions which the government had placed at the disposal of this active and intelligent judge, and he distributed these among such clans as were disposed to take arms in defence of the government. Both Sir Alexander Macdonald and Macleod were prevailed upon to accept some of these commissions, and as soon as these chieftains had done so they had committed themselves to the government too far to allow them to retire from their engagement. Other chieftains among whom commissions were distributed were the Lord Seaforth, the Earl of Sutherland, the Master of Ross, and the Laird of Grant. The companies raised under these commissions were ordered to assemble at Inverness, and this northern army of Royalists was there concentrated about the end of October, in the rear of the insurgents, while the increasing forces under Marshal Wade at Newcastle threatened to bar the possibility of an entrance into England.

The defection of Macdonald and Macleod made Lovat's plan of the northern army of Highlanders assembled at Corryarrack altogether abortive, and now, afraid of losing all credit with the Pretender's party, he adopted the dastardly middle course of exposing his son's life to protect his own. It was arranged that his eldest child, the Master of Lovat, should join the Chevalier with seven hundred or eight hundred of the best-armed and most warlike Frasers, while Lovat protested to his neighbour, the Lord President, that the march was made to his infinite sorrow, against his repeated orders, and alleged that the Frasers having by accident come too near the rebel army, were compelled by force to join them. The previous hesitation of Lovat had lasted so long that the Frasers had not arrived at Perth till after the Chevalier had entered England.

Although he was disappointed in receiving the reinforcements which he might have hoped to have expected from the Highlands proper, the army of the Chevalier six days after his victory mustered nearly six thousand men in the camp of Duddingston. Great pains were taken here during the halt to equip and discipline the infantry. Their rations were punctually supplied; all the regiments of foot wore the Highland garb, even those who consisted not of Highlanders proper, but of Lowlanders. The regiments of infantry were sixteen in number, but many of them were very small.[1] The pay of a captain in this army was 2s. 6d. a day; a lieutenant 2s.; an ensign 1s. 6d.; and a private received 6d. a day without deductions. In the clan regiments every company had two captains, two

[1] *Highland Clans.*—Lochiel, Appin, Keppock, Glencoe, Mackinnon, Macpherson, Glengarry, Glenbucket, Macloughlan, Strowan, Glen Morrison.
Lowlanders.—Athole, Ogilvie, Perth, Nairn, Edinburgh.
Horse.—Lord Elcho, Lord Balmerino, Lord Pitsligo, Earl Kilmarnock.

lieutenants, and two ensigns. The front rank of each clan consisted of persons who called themselves gentlemen, and were paid 1s. a day. These gentlemen were better armed than the men in the ranks behind them, and had all of them targets, which many of the others had not. A spy sent from England about the middle of October, who obtained an audience of the Prince, as desiring to become a partisan, and was asked by him many questions as to the number of troops, and the state of public feeling in England, reported as follows : " They consist of an odd medley of grey beards and no beards ; old men fit to drop into the grave, and young boys whose swords are nearly equal to their weight, and I really believe more than their length. Four or five thousand may be very good determined men, but the rest are mere dirty, villainous-looking rascals, who seem more anxious about plunder than their prince, and will be more pleased with four shillings than a crown." The spy, however, cannot have been well informed, because by the middle of October there were hardly more than five thousand men in all in the Highland camp at Duddingston, and in spite of their looks, their discipline was good, and little plunder or pillage was committed against the people of the country. Sometimes a comfortable citizen was stopped by a Highland musket levelled at him with threatening gesture, but the price at which he was allowed to pass free without insult or hindrance was a penny. Some serious robberies which were at first supposed to have been committed by the Highlanders were subsequently traced to have been the work of professional thieves, who took advantage of the prestige of the Highlanders as robbers to improve the occasion for their own benefit.

Money, which is scarcely less necessary in war than men, was obtained in the manner alluded to above by the levying of contributions within the country, and also from a French ship which anchored at Montrose with £5,000 on board. Three other ships coming to the same coast carried £1,000 more, and also brought with them a valuable contribution in the shape of five thousand stand of arms, a train of six brass four-pounders, and several French and Irish officers. With them came over also M. de Boyer, called the Marquis d'Equilles, who was entrusted with a letter of congratulation to Charles from Louis XV. To bear this letter was the real object of his coming; but the Chevalier, with excellent policy, insisted on calling him Monseigneur de Boyer, and received him with studious honours and careful ceremony, affecting to regard him as the accredited agent of the King of France. This, together with a promise of the French landing in England to aid the enterprise, tended in no small degree to raise or sustain the spirits of the warriors of the white cockade.

To consult upon the strategical objects of the campaign, and confer as to the execution of administrative measures both military and political, the Prince formed a council, which met every morning in his drawing-room. This consisted of the two Lieutenant-Generals, the Duke of Perth and Lord George Murray, the Quartermaster-General, Colonel O'Sullivan, the Colonel of the Horse

Guards, Lord Elcho, the Prince's Secretary, Murray of Broughton, Lords Ogilvie, Nairn, Pitsligo, Lewis Gordon, Sir Thomas Sheridan, and the Highland Chieftains Lochiel, Keppock, Clanranald, Glencoe, Lochgarry, Ardshiel, and Glenbucket. This council met every morning at ten o'clock. It was then the practice of the Chevalier first to declare his own opinion, and afterwards to ask that of every other member in their turn. The deliberations were often void of harmony and concord, and were embittered by quarrels and jealousy between the Scottish and Irish officers. The latter appear, with a servility which is not unusual among those attached to the person of a prince, but which is a curse to a prince himself, as it prevents him obtaining the real opinions of those whom he would wish to consult, to have always confirmed what the Chevalier said. It is also stated that his Royal Highness, with a dogmatic idea of his own perception, which cannot be regarded as extraordinary in one trained up as a prince in the doctrines of the Stuarts, could not bear to hear anybody differ in sentiment from him, and took a dislike to everybody that did so. The Chevalier and Sir Thomas Sheridan, who had been his former tutor, an Irishman by birth, but who had lived abroad, were both ignorant of the ways and customs of Great Britain, and both were believers in the doctrine of divine right and absolute monarchy. They would easily have fallen into blunders which must have hurt the cause, had not wiser counsellors interposed and prevented them from adopting measures which must have seriously injured the whole enterprise. Among the most experienced of the officers was Lord George Murray. He was however, unfortunately, endowed with a blunt temper, without tact, which frequently caused considerable offence to the Prince and also to Sir Thomas Sheridan. The Duke of Perth, on the other hand, was courteous, gentlemanly, and affable, and he possessed the advantage, in the Prince's eyes, of being a Catholic. Between Lord George Murray and the Duke of Perth there sprung up considerable differences of opinion, which burst out openly at the council table and also in the camp. These differences were fanned by Murray, the secretary, who calculated that he should gain a stronger influence over the milder temperament of the Duke than over the blunt and soldier-like spirit of Lord George Murray. It appears that the secretary spared no pains to lower the capabilities and devotion of the former in the eyes of the Chevalier.

The Prince created a committee also for providing the troops with forage, which was composed of various gentlemen and officers of the army. Courts-martial also sat every day for the discipline of the army. So strongly was this discipline enforced that some who were found guilty were punished with death.

Before his council met in the morning Charles always held a levee. When the council was concluded he dined in public with his principal officers, and then rode out with his Life Guards, usually to the camp at Duddingston. On returning to Holyrood in the evening a drawing-room was usually held for the ladies of the party, and not unfrequently the day closed with a ball, given in the old picture-gallery of Holyrood. The courtly manners of the Prince and his constant desire to please were neither relaxed through his good fortune, nor clouded by his cares. In the camp he talked familiarly to the meanest Highlander; at the balls he was careful to call alternately for Highland and Lowland tunes, so as to avoid an invidious preference for either. The fair sex in general throughout Scotland, became devoted to his cause, won over either by his gaiety and gallantry, or dazzled by his romantic enterprise and situation.

If it is true, as all accounts seem to lead us to believe, that the Prince was dogmatic and selfish in his council, and listened only with impatience to the advice of the best of the men around him, we can hardly fail to be struck with the wonderful ability and power of administration he showed in the nomination of his council; in the careful tact which led him to please the lowliest of his officers, in the measures which he took for the maintenance of the life, security, and property of the inhabitants of the country, which the majority of his followers occupied only in the position of a hostile army, and the knowledge he seems to have shown of the minute details of Scottish life.

Till towards the end of October the Chevalier lay at Holyrood, and his army at Duddingston. By that time, having collected as large a force as he had any hope to expect would join him, he was eager to move forward into England. He was not inclined to remain at

Edinburgh inactive and aimless, while his difficulties and his enemies thickened around him, and was not unjustly disposed to supply by energy and activity his want of numerical forces. Towards the end of October he informed his council abruptly that he intended to march for Newcastle, and give battle to Marshal Wade, who he was convinced would fly before him. This idea appears to have been entirely his own, and he was strongly persuaded that even the paid soldiers of England would hesitate to lift their weapons against their rightful Prince, the representative of an injured and banished monarch, whom heaven itself would not fail to befriend, if the rights with which providence had invested him were boldly asserted. But the Scottish officers, on the contrary, held that the army now at the Chevalier's disposal consisted still of under six thousand men, and was far beneath the number necessary to force the English nation to accept him as their sovereign; that it would be time enough for him to march to the southern kingdom when he should be invited by his friends there to join them, or to favour their rising in arms. It was also observed that as Marshal Wade had assembled a great many troops lately arrived in England from Flanders at Newcastle, with a view to march into Scotland, it was better to let that officer advance than to move forward to meet him, because when Wade moved into Scotland he must of necessity leave England undefended exposed to any insurrection of the Jacobites, or to the landing of the French expedition which the Marquis d'Equilles confidently promised. Lord Mahon, whose opinions on military matters are worthy of the utmost confidence, and are endowed with the clearest perception, considers that the advice of the Scottish counsellors in this case was founded on traditional feelings rather than upon strong reasons; that the young Prince perceived with better judgment that, in his circumstances, to await attack was to insure defeat, and his only hope of retaining Scotland lay in conquering England. This might be so if it had been intended that as a part of the plan the throne was only to be wrested from the House of Hanover by a small band of Highland marauders, but the essential and the first condition under which the Highlanders had agreed to take up arms, and which the best men in the Scottish camp considered was of vital importance to success, was that a French force should land either in England or Scotland to support the enterprise of the Chevalier. At this time it was confidently expected that the French forces were being formed in the harbours of Dunkirk, Calais, and Bolougne, and would soon be on the southern coast; and it would appear to have been of the utmost importance that the attack on the English metropolis should have been made simultaneously by the army which advanced from Scotland and by the force which descended upon the coast from France.

To attack separately and at different times, allowed the whole bulk of the forces of the government, collected for the defence of the kingdom, to be hurled on either side in their entirety. It was not even supposed or ascertained at the council of Holyrood, that the French force was yet ready to embark in the Channel ports. It would appear that in this instance the author of one of the best, if not the best, histories of England has dealt unjustly with a nation to which on other occasions he has given fair and generous praise.

At three different councils, towards the end of October, the Chevalier accordingly proposed to march into England and fight Marshal Wade, whose army was gathered at Newcastle; as often was his proposal overruled. At length he replied to all the objections offered to his scheme by saying in a positive manner, "I see, gentlemen, you are determined to stay in Scotland and defend your country; but I am not less resolved to try my fate in England, though I should go alone."

It was clear that the determination of the Chevalier was taken, and the Scottish chiefs could not separate themselves from his project without endangering his person and ruining the expedition irretrievably. Lord George Murray and the other leaders reluctantly yielded to his wish; but, in hopes of gaining some middle course between their own plan and that of the Prince for marching directly to fight Wade, proposed that the Highland troops should enter England on the western frontier. They would thus, it was calculated, avoid a hasty collision with the English army, which it was their obvious interest to defer, and would at the same time afford their partisans in England an opportunity to rise, or the French to land their troops, if either were disposed to act upon it. If neither should so act, and Wade, being left unimpeded, should march across the country towards Carlisle in order to give the invaders battle, he would be compelled to do so at the cost of a fatiguing march over a mountainous country; while the Highlanders would fight to advantage among hills not much unlike their own. The Chevalier reluctantly gave up his plan of a direct attack against the main force of the enemy at Newcastle, and rather acquiesced in than adopted the views of Lord George Murray. To mislead the English General as long as possible by the idea that an attack would be made upon his cantonments, the Chevalier adopted another suggestion of Lord George's, that the army should proceed in two columns, which should be concentrated on an appointed day near Carlisle. The first with the baggage and artillery was to march by the direct road of Moffatt; but the second, with the lightly equipped-division, was designed to move under the Prince in person, and make a feint on Kelso, as if with the design of pushing into Northumberland.

On the 31st October, 1745, Prince Charles Edward, the heir of all the Stuarts, marched out of the ancient capital of his race at the head of his Life Guards and of Lord Pitsligo's horse. The rendezvous was at Dalkeith, where they were joined by other corps of their army from the camp behind Duddingston, and from their various cantonments. There the two columns suggested by Lord George Murray were formed. The first of these, which consisted chiefly of Lowland regiments, was commanded by the Duke of Perth; in it marched the Athole brigade of Highlanders, the men of Perth and Ogilvie Roy Stuart and Glenbucket, the horse of Kilmarnock, the hussars of Murray, with all the baggage and artillery. This division was commanded by the Duke of Perth, and took the western road towards Carlisle. Though intended to act as a kind of escort to the baggage, the troops were compelled at Ecclefechan, by the badness of the roads, to abandon part of their train, which after they had marched on was seized by the people of Dumfries.

The second and lighter column of the army consisted chiefly of the three regiments of Macdonalds, of Glengarry and Pitsligo, with the remainder of the clansmen. This division was commanded by the Prince in person. That night Charles slept at Pinkie House, the same as he had occupied on the evening after the battle of Preston. The following morning the army began its march toward England.

At this period however the government at London was no longer, as immediately after the battle of Preston, unprepared or defenceless. The regiments which had been recalled from Flanders, in consequence of the convention of Hanover, had left the camp at Vilvorde in the middle of September, embarked at Wilhelmstadt about the 20th of that month, and arrived in England about the 1st of October. Among these were a battalion of the First Foot Guards, a battalion of the 2nd Guards, a battalion of the Coldstream or 3rd Guards, and seven regiments of infantry of the line. The Blues, the King's

Horse, now the 1st Dragoon Guards, Ligonier's Horse, now the 7th Dragoon Guards, and the 1st Dragoons, also crossed, while the Greys, the Enniskillens, and the 7th Dragoons embarked, but were driven back by bad weather. The regiments in Ireland on the Irish establishment were moved up towards Dublin. Among these were the regiments now known as the 4th, 5th, and 6th Dragoon Guards, which then were called from the colour of the facings and the arms borne by them, the Blue and Green Horse and Carabineers.

The army of Wade at Newcastle already amounted to near ten thousand men. Under his command there were the Queen's Horse, now the 1st Dragoon Guards, Wade's Horse regiment which is now the 3rd Dragoon Guards, the 8th, or St. George's Dragoons, and the 8th Hussars, Montague's Horse, now the 2nd Dragoon Guards, 2nd battalion 1st Regiment, 3rd battalion 1st Regiment, and other battalions of foot.

The Duke of Cumberland, who had been recalled from Flanders, and had arrived on the 18th October, was mustering another force in the midland counties. To it were attached, among other regiments, Ligonier's Horse, now the 7th Dragoon Guards, and some companies of Guards. Troops were scattered through the country to oppose the intended invasion. The Blues were cantoned at Aylesbury, Andover, and Weybridge. To the same duties were also assigned the King's Horse, now the 1st Dragoon Guards, the 1st Dragoons at Windsor, Reading and Colnbrook, and the 4th Dragoons. The militia had been raised under the acts which still did not sanction the employment of this force without its own county.

The Duke of Bedford, with thirteen other noblemen favourable to the reigning line, had undertaken to raise a new regiment of his own, but the Duke of Kingston's, known as Kingston's Horse, the first light cavalry ever adopted in the British service, and the Duke of Montague's Carabineers were the only corps so raised that did effectual service.

The 2nd Dragoons, or Scots Greys, the Enniskillen Dragoons, and the 7th Dragoons embarked at Wilhelmstadt for England, but were driven back by bad weather, and with Wolfe's Foot, now the 8th Regiment, Graham's the 11th, Pulteney's, the 13th, Howard's, the 19th, Semphill's the 25th, the 32nd, and 33rd Regiments, encamped behind the Dyle.

The House of Commons had voted not merely a loyal address, but, what was of much more practical importance, liberal supplies. The regiments on the establishment were ordered to beat up for recruits; and an order was promulgated that no Irish, Scottish, or vagabonds (the terms appear to have been regarded as synonymous) should be enlisted. In order to throw no discredit on the auxiliary forces, a strict injunction was issued to the Guards that they were not to laugh or make game of the militia when reviewed, under pain of military penalties. The House of Commons, usually so jealous of what is regarded almost as much a bulwark of the British constitution as trial by jury, consented to suspend the Habeas Corpus Act. The statesmen on both sides of the House had begun to open their eyes to the importance of the impending danger, and the Chancellor awakened to a sudden study of geography, remarked, that although he had hitherto thought nothing of the Highlanders, he had now discovered that in the map of the island they formed a third part. Every means that could be used to stimulate the people were exerted; and with a true perception of the tastes of the multitude, appeal was made to the feelings which mostly sway them. The butchers were reminded that the Papists eat no meat in Lent, and hence it would be bad for trade if London were captured by the supporters of the Catholic Stuarts. The most absurd and exaggerated stories were spread with regard to the Highlanders. It was asserted that these were cannibals, and that the children of the citizens of London, should the invasion be successful, would probably be eaten, but if rescued from such a fate, would certainly be torn from home and country, and forced to endure slavery in the French galleys and the Spanish Inquisition. The just appeal which might have been made to the danger of the religion and liberties of the people was not so much insisted upon; it was probably justly believed that the people took much more interest in the probable results to trade, than to religion, through a conquest by the Stuarts.

But the exertions of the government and of a few leading noblemen, and the exaggerations of pamphleteers, do not seem to have produced much patriotism among the great body of the nation. The county of York, where property must have been imperilled by the immediate advance of the Scotch, appears to have been the only one where the gentry and yeomen, headed by the Archbishop, made a public and zealous appearance. The fourteen regiments which were promised mostly vanished into air, or dwindled into jobs, as the colonels would name none but their own relations and dependants to hold the commissions of officers of any rank. But if the supporters of the government did little, the supporters of the Jacobite cause did less. These seem to have remained inactive and palsied, and took no apparent measures to rise in arms or to assist to overcome the immense numerical superiority of regular troops which the Chevalier would have to encounter.

The force divided by Prince Charles at Dalkeith did not muster six thousand men in all. Four hundred or five hundred were horsemen, and of the whole number not quite four thousand were real Highlanders of the mountains, who formed the clan regiments, and were the true strength of the insurgent army. A march into England was extremely distasteful to the common clansmen, who attached some superstitious idea of misfortune to the movement, and believed that evil fortune must necessarily fall upon them after their crossing the border. Desertions rapidly increased, and although the army when it marched off from Dalkeith consisted of nearly six thousand men, ere the border was crossed it is estimated that at least a thousand combatants had melted away from the ranks. The weather too was most unfavourable, and added to the difficulties and hardships of the advance.

The light column commanded by the Chevalier in person moved from Dalkeith for Kelso, where it halted for two days, and sent orders forward to Wooler to have quarters prepared in England. Thus Wade was alarmed, and his attention was diverted from Carlisle, the real objective point. Turning from Kelso by a sudden march to the westward, and down Liddisdale, this column entered Cumberland, on the evening of the 8th November, and having passed by Hawick, took post at the village of Brampton in Cumberland, to cover the other column against an advance by Wade from Newcastle, in case he should make such a movement. In the meantime the column of the Duke of Perth, which consisted chiefly of Lowland regiments, horse, and artillery, had advanced by the western road and reached Carlisle. On the following morning both columns united and proceeded to the investment of the place.

Carlisle had long been the principal garrison of England upon the western frontier, and many a Scottish army had in former days recoiled from before its walls. It was now surrounded by only mouldering defences, which had been raised in the reign of Henry VIII., and slightly improved in the time of Elizabeth. The Castle, upon a slight eminence and surrounded by deep ditches, was old and out of repair, but respectable on account of the massive nature of its walls, and strong from its situation. It was, however, little qualified to stand a regular siege, though it might have resisted the efforts of an enemy who possessed no ordnance of larger calibre than four-pounders. In the Castle there was only a garrison of one hundred invalids, commanded by Colonel Durand, of the 1st Guards, but in the city there had been mustered a considerable body of the Cumberland militia. The commandant of the Castle and the mayor both took measures for the defence of the place, and returned no answer to Prince Charles's summons; while the mayor issued a proclamation to inform the townsmen that his name was not "Paterson," nor was he a native of Scotland, but Pattison, a true-born Englishman, and determined to hold the town to the last.

The Chevalier determined upon a siege, and already orders had been given to open trenches. But a false report that Marshal Wade was marching from Newcastle to relieve the city held the Prince in person at Brampton, although he had detached a considerable portion of his column under the Duke of Perth to assist in the attack upon the place. On the 13th November a battery was raised on the east of the town, and the Scottish noblemen worked in the trenches with spade and pickaxe to encourage their men. As the battery rose, the courage of the brave mayor, born Englishman as he was, began to ooze away. A white flag was hung over the mouldering wall of the city, and a capitulation was requested. An immediate express was sent to the Prince, who with true military knowledge refused to grant any terms, unless the Castle was included; and the result was that both the town and the Castle surrendered. The defence cannot have been extremely serious, as but one man was killed and another wounded in the besieging army; and as the defenders had the advantage of cover, it is not probable that their loss exceeded much that of their assailants. The conditions of capitulation were that the garrison and militia might retire where they pleased on surrendering their arms and horses, and engaging not to serve against the Stuart cause for the space of one twelvemonth. It was also agreed that the privileges of the community should be respected. The capitulation was signed by the Duke of Perth and Colonel Durand, and by it about three months' provisions for the militia, and nearly two hundred horses with their furniture were gained. In the Castle were found a thousand stand of arms, a hundred barrels of powder, and a large quantity of military stores. The military chest was not the worse either for the occupation of the Castle of Carlisle, as the inhabitants of the country, for several miles round, had there secured their money, plate, and valuable effects, as in a place of safety. In the town and neighbourhood the cess, excise, and land tax were exacted, under severe penalties, and a contribution was extorted from the inhabitants upon pain of military execution.

On the 17th November the Chevalier himself made a triumphal entry into Carlisle ; but the inhabitants, who entertained no affection for his cause, and were probably smarting under the application of the contributions and the loss of their effects, received him exceedingly coldly, though they could not help expressing gratitude for the clemency with which they had been treated by the Duke of Perth on their surrender.

As for Marshal Wade at Newcastle, the feint on

Kelso had completely blinded him as to the real point of attack. This general was already of considerable age, and his military movements seem to have partaken of that tardiness which is so often concomitant with advanced years. He did not move from Newcastle until the 9th November, the day after Carlisle had surrendered.; and hearing of that fact at Hexham, and finding the roads across the mountains very difficult on account of a fall of snow, he considered that he was too late to avert a disaster, and thought proper to return to his cantonments at Newcastle, leaving the insurgents at liberty to push forward if they pleased.

The fall of Carlisle added no small lustre to the arms of the Chevalier, and terror to his name. But the advantage derived from the occupation of the fortress which covered the road into Scotland was balanced by a quarrel that it produced amongst his generals. Lord George Murray, angered by the expressions of gratitude and the favour which the Prince thought himself obliged to bestow upon the Duke of Perth, considered these as an encroachment upon his own pretensions; he also made an excuse of the Duke, being a member of the Roman Catholic faith, to consider that he should be disqualified from holding such an important post as one of the chief commanders in the expedition. Lord George, influenced by these feelings, wrote to the Prince, resigning his commission as Lieutenant-General, in no very courteous terms. At the same time a petition was presented from several officers, praying that the Prince would be pleased to dismiss all Roman Catholics from his councils, and to reinstate Lord George Murray in his command. The Chevalier at ·first accepted the resignation of Lord George Murray, and was disposed to support his own friends and his own faith ; but Perth, seeing the danger that discord might bring upon the cause, at once professed his willingness to serve in any capacity, waived his pretensions to command, and the Chevalier thus continued to benefit by the far superior military skill of Murray.

Nor was the success achieved at Carlisle unalloyed by bad news from Scotland. On leaving Edinburgh the Chevalier had appointed Lord Strathallan commander-in-chief during his absence ; and directed him to collect as many reinforcements as he could at Perth. Strathallan had, by the arrival of the Master of Lovat, of the Earl of Cromarty, and of Macgregor of Glengyle, and other detachments from various clans, mustered between 2,000 and 3,000 men. Three battalions had also been raised by Lord Lewis Gordon in Aberdeenshire. But as we have already seen, the clans friendly to the government under the Earl of Loudon and the Lord President were gathered in considerable force at Inverness. The populace of the towns of Perth and Dundee had intimated their dislike of the Stuart cause, and their adherence to the House of Hanover, by assembling on the birthday of King George to celebrate the festival with the customary demonstrations of joy. Glasgow, Paisley, Dumfries, and Stirling had resumed their allegiance to the reigning line, and had called out their militia in support of the government. At Edinburgh the troops from the Castle had resumed possession of the city, which had been deserted on the march of the Highland army towards England. The lords of session and the government officers who had quitted the town on the approach of the insurgents, had re-entered the city in a solemn procession, and had ordered a thousand men, formally voted to the government, to be immediately levied. General Handiside had also marched to the capital of Scotland on the 14th November from Newcastle, with the regiments of Price and Ligonier, as well as with the two regiments of dragoons which had fled from Colt Brigg, and been defeated at Preston, and already had an unfortunate experience of the country on the banks of the Forth.

Colonel John Campbell, heir of the Argyle family, and representative of the chief of that powerful clan, had arrived at Inverary, and was raising, in the interest of the government, the whole of the feudal array of his house, as well as the militia of his county. These were symptoms that showed the frail and brief nature of the influence of the Chevalier in Scotland, and that the cause of his party was not likely, in the Lowlands at least, long to endure after the absence of his army.

The forces of the Highlanders which had been levied in favour of the Stuart cause, lying at Perth, Doune, and other towns on the road between the extreme north and the Lowlands, now amounted in all to perhaps 4,000 men. Under these circumstances the chief of Maclachlan was sent back from Carlisle to Scotland with orders to Lord Strathallan to march and join the Chevalier in England with his whole force and with the utmost speed. Strathallan, however, cautious as to an advance, pled some of those excuses that are never wanting to those who wish to excuse inaction, and delayed an immediate advance until a time when a movement to the front was far less useful to the cause, and much more dangerous to himself and to those under his command. So true is it that in war more is ever lost by timidity than by temerity.

While these reinforcements from the Highlands were being waited for, a council was held, at which the sanguine Chevalier proposed that his army should without delay pursue its march to London. Lord George Murray objected that the Scottish gentlemen engaged had consented to the invasion of England in the hope of being joined by the English friends of the Prince, or in the expectation of a descent from France. He held that without one or other of these events it was hopeless to undertake to effect the restoration of the Stuart family. The Chevalier replied that he was confident of gaining the junction of a strong party in Lancashire, if the Scots would but consent to march forward; and d'Equilles vehemently affirmed with oath and wager his immediate expectation of a French landing; while Murray of Broughton, who was financial controller as well as Secretary, assured the council that it was impossible to stay longer at Carlisle for want of money. On hearing these urgent reasons for an advance southwards the council acquiesced.

The little army was now reduced to about 4,400 men; out of which a garrison of 200 or 300 had to be left in

Carlisle, to keep open the communication with Scotland. With the remainder it was resolved to march on London by the road through Lancashire, although, including militia and newly-raised regiments, it was to be expected that they would encounter upwards of 6,000 men under arms upon the side of the government, lying directly on the line of the advance. The better course would probably have been to have awaited at Carlisle the reinforcements that were expected to arrive from Perth; but this proposal was made and overruled.

In two divisions, on the 20th of November, the insurgents marched out of Carlisle. The first was commanded by Lord George Murray, the second by the Prince in person. The divisions moved about half-a-day's march from each other. At Penrith the whole army reunited on the evening of the 21st, and hearing that Wade was advancing from Newcastle to attack, halted there one day; but ascertaining that the English general had retired from Hexham towards Newcastle, the invaders pursued their progress southward. The line of march lay by Shap, Kendal, and Lancaster to Preston; where the whole army again concentrated on the 26th and rested on the 27th. The column which Lord George Murray commanded was composed of what were called the Lowland regiments; that is to say, the whole army, except the clan regiments; although the greater part of the so-called Lowlanders were Highlanders by language. The Prince himself, at the head of the clans, properly so called, each of which formed a regiment, led the way on foot at the head of his column, with his target on his shoulder, sharing all the fatigues of the march. On arriving at Preston Lord George Murray had to contest against the superstition of the soldiers whom he commanded. There was a belief among the Highlanders, based upon the defeat of the Duke of Hamilton in the great civil war, and the later misfortune of Brigadier Mackintosh in 1715, that Preston was a fatal barrier, beyond which a Scottish army could not pass. To allay this feeling, Lord George, on the first night of arrival at Preston, led his advanced guard across the bridge over the Ribble, a mile beyond the town. The fatality which was supposed to arrest the progress of Scottish troops beyond the fatal river was thus thought to be broken. The rubicon was crossed, and the road to London was believed to lie open. At Preston Charles was received with cheers, the first which had greeted him in England; but on sending out officers to beat up for recruits, those who had been willing to cheer did not testify any eagerness to enlist. The Prince, however, was still sanguine that he would be joined by large numbers of friends at Manchester; and M. d'Equilles renewed his protestations that the French had either already landed, or would certainly land within a week. Thus the murmurs which were beginning to rise amongst the men against a further progress were once more reduced to silence.

From Preston the army pushed forward to Wigan. The road was thronged with people anxious to see the Highlanders pass by, who goodnaturedly expressed their good wishes for the Prince's success, but shrank with horror from the arms which were offered to them, when they were invited to enlist, and urged, perhaps with truth, that they did not understand fighting. On the 29th November the Prince entered Manchester, and bonfires, acclamations, and a display of white rosettes, greeted his arrival. A considerable number of persons came to kiss his hand and to offer their services; but only 200 of the populace, and that of the lowest class, were enlisted; and being embodied with the few English who had already joined the standard of the Chevalier, were formed into what was termed the Manchester regiment. This was placed under officers, in general respectable men, enthusiasts in the Jacobite cause, but the common soldiers were the very dregs of the population. Such reinforcements were much inferior to what might have been expected from the results of 1715. At that time nearly the whole of Lancashire was devoted to the cause of the Stuarts; but it is clear that the lapse of thirty years had quenched the flame of affection for James among the common people, and that even in the minds of the Catholic gentry it burnt only with a fitful and flickering light. Still these symptoms were construed favourably by those who wished that they should be favourable; and although disturbing news arrived of the movements of the enemies around them, it was determined by Lord George Murray that the expedition should not now be renounced, but that the army should advance as far as Derby, on the understanding that if there the Chevalier was not joined in considerable numbers by the English Jacobites, he would propose a return.

The military situation was indeed becoming formidable. On the left rear of the advancing columns, which numbered now but little over 4,000 combatants, Marshal Wade had begun to move against them through Yorkshire. In their front lay the Duke of Cumberland, with his headquarters at Lichfield, and with a force of scarcely less than 8,000 men. A third army for the immediate protection of London was being formed at Finchley, composed in part of newly-raised troops, which King George declared, with the lion courage that ever distinguished him, that he would in case of attack command in person. At Finchley there were gathered as a nucleus of this force the Grenadiers of the Foot Guards, the Horse Grenadiers, and the Life Guards, with thirty field-pieces. To prevent the French descent, or even supplies being forwarded from France, Admiral Vernon was cruising up and down the Channel, while Admiral Byng with a smaller squadron blockaded the east coast of Scotland, and held the entrance to the Firth of Forth. The militia had been levied in force in several counties; and close in front of the advance the Earl of Cholmondley had secured Chester; while the town of Liverpool was securely held by the energy of its own inhabitants. News too came in that the bridges over the Mersey and other rivers in front had been broken down by the order of the Duke of Cumberland.

On the 1st December the Chevalier resumed his march by the road to Stockport, forded the Mersey at the head of his division, though the water rose to his middle, and pushed on southwards. The other division with the baggage and artillery passed lower down at Cheadle on a kind of rough bridge made by choking up the channel with the trunks of poplar trees. Both divisions concentrated that evening at Macclesfield. Near this town Lord George Murray, by a skilful stratagem, succeeded in completely misleading the enemy. His column of the army was pushed forward to Congleton, where he dislodged and drove before him the Duke of Kingston and a small body of English horse, which his vanguard under Colonel Kerr of Graden pushed some way on the road to Newcastle-under-Lyne. This movement made the English head-quarters believe that the whole rebel army was on its march in the direction of Newcastle, either to give battle or to join their partisans in Wales. Accordingly the Duke of Cumberland rapidly pushed forward with his main body to Stone, ready either to intercept the insurgents or to fight them, as circumstances might require. Lord George, however, in the skirmishes at the outposts, had captured a man named Weir, one of the principal spies of the Duke of Cumberland. The Highland chieftains were anxious to hang this prisoner; but Lord George Murray saved him, and obtained in return some valuable information, which caused him to turn off to the left, and by a forced march gain Ashburn. There the Prince's column also arrived along the main road. Next day both columns pushed forward and entered Derby, Lord George in the afternoon, and the Chevalier himself in the evening of the 4th December, having thus skillfully gained two or three marches upon the Duke of Cumberland, and interposed between his army and London.

At Derby Prince Charles was at a distance of 127 miles from the capital. The Duke of Cumberland, having been deceived by Lord George Murray's feint towards Newcastle, was at Stone with the greater part of his troops, although it is probable that some of his infantry was still at Lichfield. Marshal Wade, whose movements showed much of the tardiness of advanced age, was in the rear of the Highland army, but at too great a distance to be of any effect in impeding its advance upon the metropolis. As far as the positions of the two contending forces went, the Chevalier had the advantage. He was already nearer to London than the troops with which it had been intended to bar his progress, and the army which had been collected for the immediate defence of the capital at Finchley was inferior numerically to the number of men who had marched into Derby with the Pretender on the night of the 4th December. It was not likely that the troops of Wade or Cumberland would be able to interpose now between the Highland advance and the metropolis. Nor would it have been of much effect on an army such as that which followed Prince Charles, that the forces of the enemy should operate on its line of communications. In a rich country such as England was even in those days, an army of invasion required no organised commissariat to feed it, unless indeed it had consisted of far larger numbers than those which rallied round the heir of the Stuarts. The only supplies which it was necessary for such a force to carry consisted of ammunition, as the country itself would supply from its granaries, its barns, and the bakeries and butcheries which were to be found in every town, sufficient resources for the subsistence of the soldiery. In rapidity of movement the Highland army had a great advantage over the regular troops; and the advance into England is certainly a wonderful instance of rapid marching. On the 20th November Prince Charles left Carlisle, and on the 4th December reached Derby, thus marching a distance of 160 miles in fourteen days, inclusive of halts. While we find from the records of the Duke of Richmond, who commanded the royal cavalry, that he considered a march of twenty miles on two days consecutively was an impossibility even for his mounted men in the then state of the roads. The same officer considered at this time, or at least in a letter written early on the morning of the 5th December, that it was out of his power to send out guards or outposts after two days' march, such as would lead him from Lichfield to Northampton, a distance of about fifty miles, and that the rebels, having passed the Trent, there was no pass left now for the royal army to defend, and the Highlanders, if they pleased, might cut off the Duke of Cumberland's horse from his main body, or give the whole of his Royal Highness' army the slip and march upon London.

At this moment too, when the clansmen had already occupied a town in the centre of England, it appears the British cruisers were only feebly watching the coasts of Kent and Essex, and the French ministers had already completed their preparations at Dunkirk for a descent on our southern shores. Had the court of Paris only then launched its blow, it is more than possible that the invasion might have been crowned with success. Probably too had Charles decided on pushing forward, the French expedition might have been ordered to sail. The Jacobites in England, palsied as they hitherto had appeared, were now beginning to think of rising, and Sir Watkin Wynn and Lord Barrymore had sent a letter to him at Derby to assure him of their support. Despatches also arrived at Derby on the morning of the 5th December to say that Lord John Drummond had already landed at Montrose from France with the regiment of Royal Scots and some detachments of the Irish brigade in the French service. These, joining Lord Strathallan at Perth, raised his force to nearly 4,000 men.

Yet the whole serious success of the expedition depended upon the invasion from France. The invasion from the north could only be regarded as a subsidiary and auxiliary movement. And as far as the advisers of Prince Charles at Derby could see, the invasion from France appeared indefinitely postponed. Failing this support and diversion of the royal troops, they found that the Duke of Cumberland, although passed by for the moment, might come within striking distance of them with a force much superior to their own, while Marshal Wade was closing up on their rear with another force of greatly superior numbers. In front of them lay the camp at Finchley, barring the direct road to the metropolis. The total strength of the royal troops combined could hardly be less than 30,000 men. Even if the insurgents, favoured by the best possible fortune, could slip away from Cumberland and Wade, engage the army under the King in person at Finchley, and drive it in flight into the streets of London, their losses in the engagement must be severe, and they could hardly hope to occupy the city with a strength of much over 3,000 men. It would be utterly impossible for such a force to maintain itself in London amidst a hostile population and to restore the line of the Stuarts to the throne and maintain it there. Had rapid means of communication existed in those days; had it been possible, as at present, to flash the exact position of Prince Charles from Derby to his base of communications in Scotland, and from Scotland to France in a few moments, the French expedition would assuredly have set sail, and it is probable that the House of Stuart would have, at least temporarily, been restored to the throne of England.

That King James could have long remained king of England can hardly be believed. His son, with every necessity of showing a conciliatory temper, and with every need to profit by the warning of his ill-starred race, showed even at this time, when tact and temper were particularly necessary, that his education had imbued him with the ideas of divine right and despotic and arbitrary kingly authority, which would have rendered his maintenance on the throne of England an anachronism and an impossibility. His counsellors, unable to hear anything of the French expedition, and clearly perceiving the preparations of the government, and the dangers of the position which their army held between Wade, Cumberland, and the camp at Finchley, determined that it was hopeless to push forward to the metropolis, and that it was necessary to retire into Scotland.

Accordingly, on the following morning, the 5th December, Prince Charles, who the previous evening had dwelt in conversation on his intended journey to London, and had seriously considered whether he should enter the city on horseback or on foot, in the costume of the Highlands or in that of England, was astounded and mortified by an unexpected deputation from his followers. Lord George Murray, with all the commanders of battalions and of squadrons, waited upon the Prince, and, a council being called together, the earnest and unanimous opinion of the chieftains and leaders was submitted to him, that an immediate retreat to the north was necessary. They pointed out that they had marched into the heart of England on the understanding that there should either be a rising of the Jacobites in England or an invasion of the French on the south coast. Neither had yet occurred. Time for both had been allowed in plenty, and it was dangerous longer to trust to either. Their own force, which amounted to considerably less than 5,000 fighting men, was totally insufficient to maintain a conflict with any one of the armies by which they were surrounded even separately, and in case they should suffer a disaster, not a single man in the army would be able to escape.

Lord George Murray, who spoke in the name of the remainder of the leaders, added to these causes for retreat a proposal for a plan of a campaign in Scotland which he thought might be advantageously carried out by a retreat to that country. Charles had the advantage of retiring upon his reinforcements, which included the body of Highlanders lying at Perth, now strengthened by the French troops under Lord John Drummond. Murray strongly requested in conclusion, in the name of all present, that they should go back and join their adherents in Scotland, and live or die with them.

Many of the council expressed similar opinions. The Duke of Perth and Sir John Gordon, however, proposed as an alternative to penetrate into Wales and give the partisans of the Jacobites in that principality the opportunity of joining the standard. This idea was abandoned on reflection that to do so it would be necessary to fight the Duke of Cumberland, who occupied at Stone the passages of the Trent between Newcastle and Lichfield, and barred the way towards the west.

Prince Charles listened to the arguments put forth by his followers with the utmost impatience; he expressed his determination to push forward to London; he announced his firm reliance on the justice of the cause, and in Providence, which had hitherto so signally favoured him. In vain he urged upon his council the probability that the French would still land in Kent or Sussex, that the Jacobites would not fail to rise in proportion as his army pushed forward, and that the officers and soldiers even of the royal troops would not fight against their anointed king. But the council remained firm, though some of the Irish officers were willing to proceed. The Scots observed that these did not run equal risk; still holding French commissions, they were certain at the worst of being treated honourably, as prisoners of war, instead of being tried and hanged as traitors. No impression being made on the Scottish chieftains, after several hours of stormy debate, Charles broke up the council without having formed any decision, and the army halted that day for rest at Derby. The subaltern officers and soldiers, ignorant of what was passing in the council, eagerly expected a forward movement on the morrow, and spent the day, some in taking the sacrament at the various churches of the town, others in having the edges of their broadswords sharpened at the cutlers' shops.

During the whole of the day the Prince continued to entreat and expostulate with some of his officers individually; but finding he could make no impression upon them, by the advice of the two he most trusted, Sir Thomas Sheridan and Secretary Murray, consented reluctantly to yield to the prevailing sentiment. Accordingly, at the second council convoked in the evening, the Chevalier, with sullen resignation, declared his consent to return to Scotland. At the same time, however, he informed the chiefs that in future he should call no more councils, since he was accountable to nobody for his actions excepting to Heaven and his father, and therefore would no longer either ask or accept their advice. Here broke out the true ring of the dogmas which had driven the line of Stuarts from the throne of the country. It is doubtful whether the unhappy princes of his family were more unfortunate in holding doctrines of so pernicious a nature, or unlucky in choosing their opportunities for promulgating them.

Thus terminated the romantic march to Derby, and with it every chance of the success of the invasion. Had at this moment, when the Highland troops were in the centre of England, the French government boldly pushed its forces on to the southern coast, very different might have been the fate of the expedition.

Early next morning, before the break of day, the Highland army began to retreat northwards. The columns moved out of the town in the first dawn; and those who from their lower rank were ignorant of the opinions of their chieftains, still believed that they were pressing forward to fight the Duke of Cumberland; but when the late daylight of a December morning gradually grew so clear that the clansmen were able to perceive in what direction they were moving and to find that they were returning along the road traversed two days previously, sounds of regret and of lamentation rose from the saddened ranks.

In the meantime the news of the approach of the insurgents at Derby had created the greatest fear in London. A writer favourable to the government, who was in the city at the time, states that, when the Highlanders by a most incredible march got between the army of the Duke of Cumberland and the metropolis, they struck a terror into it scarcely to be credited. An immediate rush was made upon the Bank of England, which it is said only escaped bankruptcy by paying in sixpences to gain time. The shutters of the shops were put up; public business in great part was suspended; and the restoration of the Stuarts was regarded as not an improbable or far-distant possibility. It is said that the King himself ordered some of his most precious jewellery to be embarked on board his yachts, and that these were ready at the Tower quay, to sail at a moment's warning. For long afterwards, the day on which the advance on Derby became known in town was remembered under the name of Black Friday. What might be expected if. the invading army were not an irregular body of Highlanders, but a well-disciplined mass of trained soldiers, occupying a position not at Derby, but at Croydon or Blackheath ?

The army of the Chevalier, on its retreat, retraced the road by which it had pushed forward ; but the fact of a retrogade movement broke the charm which had bound the Highlanders to discipline and steadiness on their advance. As they returned they committed numerous acts of outrage, some from hunger, others for the sake of plunder. Violence on their part induced the people of the country not only to regard them with wonder and awe as outlandish strangers, wearing a wild and unwonted dress, speaking an unknown language, and with much of the appearance of barbarians, but to hate them as robbers and murderers. Near Stockport, where the inhabitants fired upon a Highland patrol, some of the clansmen in revenge set the village in flames. Such acts naturally incensed the people of the country, and consequently the stragglers or the sick who dropped behind were killed or molested by the natives. Those who, during the advance, when it was possible that the invasion might be successful, had shown little active malevolence, when success appeared to have declared against the enterprise, flew to arms, and with the ferocity which usually distinguishes an armed and undisciplined mob, vented their indignation and cruelties against the weary or the exhausted.

On the 9th December the heads of the columns closed up to Manchester. In this city, which had been so friendly a few days before, a violent mob opposed the vanguard, and though driven away by the main body, again annoyed the rear as it marched out of the town, and fired upon the rear-guard. The Prince himself, by his behaviour, tended to dishearten the soldiers. Instead of leading the vanguard on foot, or taking the post of honour, as might have been expected, with his rear-guard, he now lingered behind his men, so as to retard the rear in marching off, and rode dejectedly behind his columns.

Charles had intended to halt his army for a day at Manchester, but Lord George Murray strongly opposed this idea, and argued that the men had no occasion to rest, and that to pause would only give time for the enemy to overtake them. The Duke of Cumberland, who, as has been already said, was lying at Lichfield when Prince Charles approached Derby, and then had pushed forward detachments to Stone, fell back as soon as Derby was occupied to Meriden Moor, close to Coventry, to cover the capital. He did not hear for two days after the retreat had begun that the Prince had left Derby for Ashburn on the 5th December. His pursuit was not begun until the 8th, when he marched northward with the whole of his cavalry and a number of infantry mounted upon horses which were supplied by the gentry of the neighbourhood. The spirit of his troops was high. The retreat of the Highland army, the advance of which had been regarded by the comrades of those who had been swept away at Prestonpans with a vague apprehension of terror, was naturally regarded as a signal of success. The regulars believed that they had merely to push the flight of a disorganised and disheartened band of rioters, who had confessed the failure of their desperate project. In proportion as they anticipated little opposition, and as they were encouraged by the retreat of the enemy, their own valour rose.

On the other hand, the Highlanders retreated with speed and in unabated courage; and their acts of violence did not throw that disorder among irregular ranks which they would have caused in a more perfectly military machine. Lord George Murray himself took charge of the rear-guard, a post of danger and of honour, and great was his difficulty in bringing up the baggage and the artillery, which from the bad weather and the bad state of the roads in a winter that was more than usually severe, was perpetually breaking down. Although the Duke of Cumberland pushed forward only mounted men, he found on arriving at Macclesfield that his enemy was full two clear days' march ahead of him. But pushing forward, he was joined at Preston by another body of horse, that had been detached from the army of Marshal Wade and sent across country in hopes of cutting off the retreat of the Highlanders. Again the royal troops pushed onwards, but they did not come up with even the rear-guard of the retreating army until on the most northern confines of the county of Westmoreland.

Towards the evening of the 17th December, Prince Charles, with the main body of his army, had cantoned for the night in the town of Penrith. Lord George Murray, who had been much delayed by various accidents to his artillery and baggage, was forced to pass the night six miles further south, at the village of Shap. The Glengarry regiment at this time formed the rear-guard, and at Shap a small detachment of 200 men had been left by the Prince, under the command of Colonel Roy Stuart. Prince Charles resolved to await at Penrith the junction of his rear-guard, which was separated from him by a distance further than prudent with so small a force.

Early next morning Lord George Murray accordingly resumed his march before daybreak, but when the light became clear he perceived in front of him, at the village of Clifton, about three miles before he could arrive at Penrith, several parties of mounted men drawn up between Shap and the village of Penrith, and crowning the heights beyond it. The Highlanders, who since the battle of Preston had no fear of charging horsemen, and had learnt to despise this branch of the service, of which formerly they stood in considerable awe, were ordered to attack. The Macdonalds, stripping off their plaids, without hesitation rushed upon the military, shouting the slogan and brandishing their claymores. The cavalry, who were volunteers that had assembled more for the purpose of harassing the rear of the Highland army, and for giving time for the Duke of Cumberland to come up, than with the intention of encountering serious opposition, immediately galloped off. They left however several prisoners in the hands of the Macdonalds. Among these was a footman of the Duke of Cumberland's, who told Lord George Murray that his Prince was coming up in the rear of the Highlanders with 4,000 horse.

Lord George sent the prisoner to Penrith to be examined by the Prince, asking for orders, and also suggesting reinforcements. Charles, with considerable courtesy, dismissed the servant to his master, and sent back, for the support of the rear-guard, the two regiments of the Stuarts of Appin and the Macphersons of Cluny.

It does not appear clear why Lord George Murray did not, immediately after the defeat of these volunteers, draw off to Penrith, as there seemed to be no object in standing his ground. Possibly time may have been required to evacuate the town of Penrith, or to allow of the march of the baggage or artillery train. Certain it is that although it appears the volunteers were driven away at daybreak, or shortly after daybreak, the sun was just setting when the Duke of Cumberland's advanced troops first came in sight of the Highlanders. His whole force was slowly formed across the high road upon the open moor of Clifton ; while beyond the moor the retreat of the Highlanders to Penrith must lie through large plantations of fir-trees on the property of Lord Lonsdale. It appears that Lord George Murray objected to be attacked while retreating through these plantations, although it does not seem clear why irregular forces, accustomed to mountain warfare, should not have preferred to fight in inclosures against men who had advanced on horseback, than to face an action on an open moor. However that may be, Lord George drew up the Glengarry regiment upon the high road, and placed the Stuarts of Appin in some inclosures bounded by stone fences on their left. The Macpherson regiment stood again to the left of the Stuarts. On the right of the line he placed the men of Roy, covered by a wall.

The troops that came up to attack the Highlanders were detachments both from the armies of Wade and of the Duke of Cumberland, which had united, and were under the command of Major-General Oglethorpe. They consisted of the Queen's Horse (now the 2nd Dragoon Guards), Wade's Horse, Ligonier's Horse, Montague's Horse, the 3rd Dragoons under Honeywood, and the 8th Dragoons.

The dispositions of the English were not completed till the shadows of night were gathering over the little village of Clifton, but the moon soon shone out at intervals from among the clouds, and in one of the glimpses of light about a thousand dismounted dragoons were seen creeping forward along the fences, with the intention of attacking the Highlanders on the flank, while the rest of the army of the Duke of Cumberland was held massed upon the moor. These men seen gliding forwards, while objects were scarcely discernible, were the 3rd Dragoons dismounted. The cry of "claymore" was immediately raised by the leader of the Highlanders, and the Macphersons and Stuarts, sword in hand, rushed on their assailants with so fierce an assault that many Highlanders broke their swords on the steel caps of the dragoons. Lord George Murray himself lost his bonnet and wig in the fray, and continued to fight bare-headed. In a few moments, by the bold rush of the clansmen, the English were completely repelled, their commander, Colonel Honeywood, was left severely wounded on the field, and the total number of their killed or wounded exceeded a hundred men,[1] while the Highlanders lost but twelve. At the same time, or nearly so, that the dragoons on the left were thus driven off with considerable loss, and forced back to their main body on the moor, another body of dismounted dragoons pressed forward upon the high road, and were repulsed by the Glengarry regiment and that of Roy. The Highlanders with difficulty were recalled from the pursuit, exclaiming that it was a shame to see so many of the King's enemies standing fast upon the moor without attacking them. A few of the men who

---

[1] The regimental records say only twelve. Of such materials is history compiled!

ventured too far were either killed or taken. Lord George Murray now sent a message to the Prince, proposing that a further reinforcement should be sent back from the main body, with which he offered to engage and defeat the whole of the mounted men opposed to him. The Prince, doubtful of the event, or jealous of his General, declined to comply with his request. On receiving an answer to this effect, Lord George Murray returned to Penrith. The rear-guard united with the main body, and it seems that the bearing of the Highlanders impressed the royal leaders with the idea that some risk might be incurred by a too precipitate attack on the northern army. Certainly the experiment was not repeated, the retreat was continued, and early on the morning of the next day, the 19th, the Highland force arrived at Carlisle.

Here it was considered necessary to leave a garrison, so as to secure the key of the road into England, in the event of the Highlanders making, as it was hoped they would soon, another invasion in greater force. The road might, however, have been left perfectly open, without risking the loss of a detachment, had the walls and castle been blown up. A few French and Irish, some men from a Lowland regiment, and Mr. Townley with the English volunteers, remained at Carlisle. It appears to have been believed that the Duke of Cumberland had no siege train with him, and it is probable that this small detachment was merely left with the view of holding the place against the assault of the dragoons and mounted infantry, whom it was known were with the Duke of Cumberland. A siege train was, however, suddenly obtained from Whitehaven. As soon as the Highlanders had retreated, the garrison was invested. Two batteries were raised— the one against the English, and the other against the Scottish or North Gate. The new battery was completed during the night of the 29th December, but on the first platoon of the old battery firing against the Castle, the white flag was hung out. The Duke of Cumberland ordered Lieutenant-Colonel Lord Bury, of the Coldstream regiment, and Colonel Conway, his aides-de-camp, to go in and deliver two messages in writing. In about two hours they returned. The rebels capitulated, on which Brigadier Bligh was immediately ordered to take possession of the town with 400 footguards, who appear to have come up on horseback, 700 marching foot, and 120 horse to patrol the streets. The only conditions of capitulation granted were that the garrison should not be put to the sword, but should be retained for the King's pleasure.

Having left a garrison in Carlisle on the 20th, the Prince's birthday, the Highland army left the town, and crossed the Esk at Langtoun into Scotland. The river was swollen, but the Highlanders, wading in arm-in-arm, supported each other against the force of the current, and got safely through, though with some difficulty. Marching in three divisions, they arrived that day at Annan and Ecclefechan. The next night the main body was at Dumfries. This town had always been remarkable for its attachment to the Protestant succession, and a report having lately reached it of some defeat or disaster of the Highland army, a general rejoicing had ensued. When the Highlanders marched in, they found the candles of the illumination yet in the windows, and the bonfires still unextinguished. A fine of 2,000*l*. was put upon the place as a punishment for this ill-timed joy; and as the whole could not be obtained, the Provost and another magistrate were carried away as hostages for the remainder.

The state of Scotland had considerably changed during the absence of Charles and his army upon the expedition to Derby. Inverness was in the hands of Lord Loudon, with an army composed of the Macdonalds of Skye, the Macleods, and other loyal northern clans. This force in all numbered about 2,000 men. Edinburgh was again in possession of the authorities of the government; and was occupied by a garrison of a portion of Wade's army, which had been pushed forward from Newcastle for the purpose. The peasantry in many parts of the western counties had taken up arms, but showed little inclination to use them when they found the Highland army return in complete order and with unbroken strength.

After crossing the border, the Chevalier divided his forces into three bodies. The first, consisting of the clans, moved, with Charles in person, by way of Annan and Hamilton. Lord George Murray took the road by Ecclefechan with the Athole brigade and the Lowland regiments; while Lord Elcho with the cavalry passing by Dumfries, and having carried off the magistrates of the refractory town, pushed forward by the western route. On the 26th Charles entered Glasgow. This city was even yet more objectionable in the eyes of the Highlanders than the town of Dumfries. During the absence in the south Glasgow had raised a body of 600 men, called the Glasgow regiment, in the cause of the Protestant dynasty. Many of the soldiers of this corps served without pay under the command of the Earls of Home and Glencairn. This force had been sent to Stirling to reinforce General Blakeney, the Governor of the Castle, in his defence of the passes of the Forth. When it was known that the Highlanders were advancing on Glasgow, the Glasgow regiment fell back with the other troops, which had concentrated on the Forth, to Edinburgh, with a view to the defence of the capital. Glasgow was thus left open; and while the citizens of London were suffering from the apprehension of the arrival of the Highlanders, those of Glasgow paid the penalty attached to their presence. But this did not cool the obstinacy of the burghers against the Pretender; and one fanatic fired a pistol at him as he rode along the Saltmarket. Clothing for the troops and stores for their supplies were demanded from the town to the value of more than 10,000*l*., which the citizens were compelled to pay, under the threat of military execution.

The stores demanded on requisition from the magistrates of Glasgow to furnish the Highland army, were— 1,200 shirts, 6,000 short coats, 6,000 pairs of shoes, 6,000 bonnets, 6,000 pairs of stockings; the value of these, added to the 5,500*l*. paid on the 27th September, amounted to 10,000*l*. Parliament, in 1749, after the peace of Aix-la-Chapelle, granted 10,000*l*. to the Corporation of Glasgow as reimbursement for this expense.

It was not till his arrival at Glasgow that Prince Charles Edward became aware of the succours sent to him by France. These consisted of his own regiment in the French service, the Royal Scots, detachments of the six regiments of the Irish brigade, and about two squadrons of Fitzjames's light-horse. The French expedition against the southern coast, which it was intended should be under the command of the Duke of Richelieu, and numerically to muster 9,000 infantry and 1,350 cavalry, was abandoned on the news of the retreat of the Highlanders from Derby. Charles did not, however, for a long time either hear or believe that the scheme had been given up; and his confidence that the French intended to persevere in it led him into more than one error.

Having arrived at Glasgow, the question now for the Prince and his advisers to decide was, in what way his forces could be best employed. Some held that an advance ought to be made direct upon Edinburgh. Part of the troops which Wade had concentrated at Newcastle were now preparing to hold the capital of Scotland; and the rest of his forces were pushing forward towards that city under the command of General Henry Hawley. This officer had been appointed in place of Marshal Wade, whose talents had become torpid beneath the advance of age, and of whose inactivity just complaints had been made during the late movements in England. General Henry Hawley was an officer of some experience; he had served in the battle of Sheriffmuir as a major of dragoons, but seems to have possessed more of the power of detail of a sergeant-major than of the capacity of a captain. He was hated by his own soldiers for a cruel, violent, and vindictive temper. One of his first measures, on arriving at Edinburgh to take the command-in-chief, was to order two gibbets to be erected; and he had a staff of several executioners attached to his army on its march. Such ferocity is fortunately as alien from as it is rare in the military character.

It was believed that although Edinburgh was thus likely to be strongly held, the Highlanders could in the winter season distress the English troops, by forcing them to concentrate, and preventing them from separating to obtain quarters; thus causing them to undergo hardships which would be most severe to the southerners, but would be little regarded by the men of the Highlands.

Charles, however, although this scheme might have promised considerable advantage, both political and strategical, was tempted by the fact that Lord John Drummond had brought with him from France some engineers and a train of artillery. He considered that with these the first measure which should be undertaken must be the reduction of Stirling Castle, in order to promote a free passage of the Forth and a clear communication between the Highlands and the Lowlands. This view cannot be considered wrong. Indeed throughout, the military capacity which Prince Charles Edward showed in his campaign appears to have been underrated by historians. The Highland army, in their advance into the low countries in summer, had crossed the Forth by the fords of Frew. This passage was easy for the clansmen, unencumbered by horse, artillery, or baggage. In the Lowlands, however, they had been joined by the horsemen of Pitsligo, Balmerino, Elcho, and Kilmarnock. They had also now with them a small train of artillery; certainly the pieces were light, but it must be remembered it was more difficult in those days to drive artillery of four-pound calibre along roads rendered difficult by a Scottish winter than it would now be to move heavy siege ordnance. On the other hand, at Montrose, Lord John Drummond had landed with the forces from France, consisting partly of cavalry. The continental troops were accustomed to supplies of baggage and camp equipage, which were totally unnecessary for the Highlanders. It appears tolerably clear that if the campaign was to be prosecuted in the Lowlands, and if any idea of a future invasion of England was adhered to, there must be a free communication over the Forth, especially in the winter season, by which waggons and artillery could move. The fords of Frew —especially in a winter which was exceptionally rainy and severe—did not permit of this. Stirling Castle, on its craggy height, covered the passage of the Forth. Beyond it lay the forces of Lord John Drummond and Strathallan. The Castle was held by an experienced governor, General Blakeney, and a sufficient garrison.

To afford an easy access for troops of all kinds, it was advisable that this fortress should be reduced.

On the 3rd January, 1746, Prince Charles Edward evacuated Glasgow, after a halt there of eight days, and marched towards Stirling. On the following day his headquarters were fixed at the House of Bannockburn, while his troops occupied St. Ninian and other villages in the neighbourhood of the Forth. The town of Stirling was summoned, and not being fortified, was surrendered by the magistrates, although there were about six hundred militia within it. Some of these left the place, and others retired to the Castle. Those who read carefully the accounts of this invasion must derive some benefit from considering the position which the militia and volunteers are seen at this time to have held. We see in this instance at Stirling, as in other similar cases, that the militia appear to have acted solely under the orders of the civil authorities, and to have been independent of the commandant of the troops. In the cases of Edinburgh and Stirling, the commandant of the garrison appears to have held no control over the militia, nor to have leavened the auxiliary forces with any detachments of the regulars. On the contrary, the governors of the castles seem to have considered that their sole duty was to defend the fortress with the regular troops at their disposal, and to leave to the magistracy the defence and care of the towns with their own auxiliaries. The castle was summoned, but the general gave a resolute refusal to surrender, and the Chevalier resolved to open trenches without delay.

Although an order had been sent by Charles through Colonel Maclachlan for the forces from Perth to follow him into England, Strathallan had found excuses for delay, and demurred to obey the command. From Dumfries another order was sent, summoning the body at Perth to push on to Stirling. When this order arrived at Strathallan's quarters, there were assembled at Perth the Frasers, the MacEwans, the Mackintoshes, the Farquharsons, together with the troops which had come over from France, under the command of Lord John Drummond, besides a regiment of men from the low country of Aberdeenshire, under the command of Lord Lewis Gordon, These forces amounted to about 4,000 men. They came down to the Forth when the Prince appeared on its southern side from Glasgow, and the total force under the banner of the Chevalier amounted now to about 9,000 men. This was the largest number which had ever united under his command, and it is to be regretted by those who wish well to the cause of the Stuarts, that it was necessary to employ an army eminently calculated for an active campaign in the field on the slow and trying operations of a siege.

On the 10th January trenches were opened before the fortress of Stirling ; but the siege operations were soon interrupted by the advance of a relieving army.

The Duke of Cumberland, who had obtained the capitulation of Carlisle on the 29th December, occupied that fortified town, and made his entry on the 31st. But his movement towards the north was here stayed by an order which arrived for him to return to London, in order to be ready to take the command against the expected invasion from France. The greater part of his infantry, which had been concentrated at Lichfield when the Highlanders were advancing southwards, was now marched to the coast of Kent and Sussex, in order to resist the threatened descent ; but that part of the Duke's army consisting of dragoons and mounted infantry which he had carried with him to Newcastle, was ordered to continue its march northward and to join the troops which General Hawley took the command of at Edinburgh. These amounted in all to about 8,000 men, of whom two-thirds were veteran regulars ; the remainder consisted of about 1,200 men of Argyle, commanded by Colonel Campbell, heir to the house of Argyle, and of the Glasgow regiment. They were also joined from Yorkshire by a body of volunteer light horse called the Yorkshire Hussars, who had taken up arms for the House of Hanover and the Protestant succession. General Hawley himself, on account of his experience in the campaign of Sheriffmuir with Evan's dragoons, was believed to have a special knowledge of Scotland, and of the mode of fighting adopted by the Highlanders, and therefore to be extremely well fitted to cope with the insurgent army.

With such a strength concentrated at Edinburgh, Hawley not unnaturally concluded that he was about to raise the siege of Stirling. He accordingly formed his force into two divisions, and the first, which consisted of five battalions of the line, a corps of militia, and some dragoons, marched out of Edinburgh on the 13th January under the orders of General Huske, Hawley's second in command. The Highland army before Stirling was naturally, by means of country people and Jacobite informants, regularly apprised of the movements of the enemy. On the 13th January Lord George Murray, who, covering the siege, occupied Falkirk, heard that the people of Linlithgow had received orders from Edinburgh to prepare provisions and forage for troops, which were instantly to advance in that direction. He determined to move with a sufficient force and anticipate the advance of the royal army, and to destroy or carry off the provisions that might be collected in obedience to their requisition. With the three Macdonald regiments, and those of Appin and Cluny, and the horse of Elcho and Pitsligo, Murray marched to Linlithgow. Patrols of cavalry were pushed out to beat the road towards Edinburgh for intelligence. About noon these sent back information that a small body of dragoons, forming the scouts of Huske's division, which had marched from Edinburgh that morning were in sight. Orders were sent to the patrols to drive back the dragoons upon the main body, and to obtain information without retiring, unless they saw themselves in danger of being overpowered. In the meantime the infantry was formed in line of battle in front of the town of Linlithgow. Lord Elcho, who was in command of the cavalry, pushed back the scouts of Huske upon a detachment of sixty dragoons, and then forced these also to retire upon a village where both horse and foot were massed in strength. Elcho reported the amount of force which he had in his front as far as he could make it out, and then received orders to retreat, leaving a small corps of observation. It was not Murray's purpose to fight an army of a strength which, though unknown to him, was obviously considerable; he therefore determined merely to remain in Linlithgow, make his adversary show his force, and then retreat. This object was accomplished, and on passing Linlithgow bridge, so little distance was there between the advanced guard of the royal troops and the rear-guard of the Highlanders, that abusive language was exchanged between the men, though without any violence. Murray continued his retreat to Falkirk, where he halted for the night. On the following day, falling back before the enemy, he again retreated to the villages in the vicinity of Bannockburn, where he heard that Huske with the government army had arrived at Falkirk, and that Hawley in person had also arrived there on the 16th with a second division ; and that besides the regular troops of the government there were more than a thousand Highlanders of the clan Campbell in the enemy's ranks.

Upon the 15th and 16th of January the Chevalier, leaving a thousand or twelve hundred men under Gordon of Glenbucket, to protect the siege works and continue the blockade of Stirling Castle, drew up the rest of the army on a plain about a mile to the east of Bannockburn, expecting an attack. His horse reconnoitered close to the hostile camp, but could perceive no appearance of movement. On the 17th the same operation was repeated, the Highland army being drawn up on the same open ground near Bannockburn, while that of the government still remained inactive in Falkirk.

Hawley meanwhile, filled with a vain and ignorant contempt for the Highland rabble, as he termed his enemy, believed that they would disperse at the mere news of his approach. He neglected the most ordinary precautions of sending out patrols or scouts, and had accepted an invitation from Lady Kilmarnock, whose husband was in the insurgent army, to Callender House. Here, under the influence of the wit and gaiety of the lady, he remained from the time of his arrival at Falkirk till his visit was disagreeably interrupted on the afternoon of the 17th January.[1]

A council of war was held on the field where the Highland army was drawn up, and it was determined, since the English general did not move forward to attack, that he should be saved the trouble, and that an immediate advance should be made against him. A distance of only about seven miles lay between the two armies, and the absence of patrols in front of the royal troops gave the insurgents an opportunity which proved eminently successful. Lord John Drummond

[1] It must be remembered in the account of this campaign that the Old Style of date is used, by which the date of any particular day is eleven days earlier than it would be according to the present calendar. Thus what occurred on the 17th January, according to Old Style, would by New Style have happened on the 28th.

with his own regiment, the Irish detachments, and all the cavalry of the insurgent army, was ordered to advance upon the straight road leading from Stirling and Bannockburn towards Falkirk. With this detachment were to be carried the royal standard and other colours, and of these a great display was to be made in front of the old forest of Torwood. This march, and the position to be occupied by Drummond in front of the forest, were however only intended as a feint, in order to lead the royal generals to suppose that the whole insurgent army was advancing from that direction. While Drummond was moving forward, the Prince with Lord George Murray and the main body was to march by the south side of the Torwood, cross the river Carron near Dunnipace, and advance to the southward of the high ground called Falkirk Moor, which then was an open and unincloscd common, swelling into a considerable ridge or eminence that lay on the westward, and to the left of the royal camp. About eleven o'clock Drummond's division was seen from the English camp, and as had been intended, attracted the exclusive attention of General Huske, who during Hawley's absence was in command.

Between one and two o'clock, when the English soldiers were preparing to have their dinner, some peasants, hurriedly running in, told that the Highlanders were close at hand, and were only separated from the flank of the Royal army by the swelling upland of Falkirk Moor, which lay on the left of the English troops. The report of the country people was quickly confirmed by two officers, who, climbing a tree, were able with a glass to discover the advance of the clans. The drums instantly beat to arms, but Hawley, whose task it peculiarly was to remedy the dilemma, was still absent at Callender House. An orderly galloped off for him, and Huske hurriedly formed line of battle in front of the camp; but in the absence of his senior had it not in his power to direct any movement of importance, either toward the division of Drummond, who threatened him in front, or against that which was pushing up the heights of Falkirk Moor against his left. The royal regiments remained tied to their ground in wonder, impatience, and anxiety, while murmurs rose from both officers and privates; for little can be so trying to brave men as to be hopelessly tied down by the laws of discipline, and to see themselves without an order sacrificed through the neglect of superiors. Hawley, startled by the tidings which had been brought to him at Callender, soon galloped up in hot haste, having left the house so rapidly that he had forgotten his hat. He suddenly appeared in front of the camp and immediately ordered his three regiments of dragoons—Cobham's, now the 10th Hussars, on the left, with Hamilton's, now the 13th Hussars, and Ligonier's, now the 14th Hussars on the right—to advance up the hill called Falkirk Moor. With his sword drawn he placed himself at their head, and pushed up the acclivity, trusting by a rapid movement to anticipate the Highlanders, and before them to gain the summit of the eminence. The infantry, which consisted of the 1st battalion of the Royals, the 3rd, 4th, 8th, 13th, 14th, 27th, 34th, 36th, 37th, 48th, and Batecrean's regiments, with the Glasgow and Paisley militia and the Argyle Highlanders in reserve, was ordered to follow as fast as possible with fixed bayonets. The royal troops pushed forward in a storm of wind, to which heavy rain was now added, beating full in the faces of the soldiery. The Highland movement had been calculated so as to give the clansmen the advantage of both the weather and the ground.

In the meantime the portion of the Highland army with which it was intended to seize the heights of Falkirk Moor had marched in three divisions, keeping along the ground in such a manner that first the thickets of Torwood, and afterwards the swell of the ground of the moor itself, hid them in great measure from the royal camp. In this movement they kept their columns parallel to the ridge of the moor; and when the heads of the columns had pushed as far southward as was necessary to gain room for their formation, the men in each column, turning to the left, formed line of battle, and then began to climb the hill. The first Highland line had the clans of the Macdonalds on the right, and Camerons on the left; in the second marched the Athole brigade on the right, the men of Aberdeen, under Lewis Gordon, on the left, with Lord Ogilvie's regiment in the centre. The third line, or reserve, was weak in numbers, and consisted chiefly of cavalry and the Irish detachments. Lord John Drummond, who had made the demonstration in front of the Torwood, remained with his troops on the high road, until the whole of Murray's division had passed the Carron, and then, moving to his right, fell into their rear, and joined the cavalry who were with the Prince; thus reinforcing the third line of the insurgent army.

When Hawley, from the opposite side to that up which the Highlanders were quickly climbing, pushed up the hill with his three regiments of dragoons, the infantry of the King's army followed in line of battle, having six battalions in the first line and five in the second, while Howard's Buffs (now the 3rd regiment) marched in the rear of the right and formed a small reserve with the militia.

It seemed a race between the dragoons and the Highlanders, which first should gain the summit of the hill. The mountaineers were the first on the top of the moor, and Hawley, seeing that they had gained the vantage ground, halted, and drew up his men on a somewhat lower level. There was a rugged ravine which separated the two armies, and dipped towards the plain, on the left of the King's forces. The whole position thus forced upon the English General was far from favourable to the movements of regular troops. The English artillery, consisting of 3-pounders and 6-pounders, also stuck fast in a morass which formed part of the plain. It could not be extricated in time for the battle; but as the Highlanders had also left their guns behind, neither force had in this matter any advantage. On line being formed, the English horse showed a front, which occupied as much ground as half of the first line of the Chevalier's army. Charles himself took his station, as at Preston, in his second line, or rather close behind it, on a conspicuous mound still known by the name of Charley's hill, and now overgrown with wood. Hawley commanded in the centre of the English infantry, with Huske on the left. The cavalry was under Colonel Ligonier, who on the death of Gardiner had succeeded to his regiment.

The Highlanders, with hardly a moment's pause, pressed their advance towards the enemy. Down the ravine between the two armies they swept, and up the opposite slope in high spirits, and with their natural ardour further increased at the sight of the enemy. The mountaineers kept their ranks close, and, advancing shoulder to shoulder, hurried on at a tremendous rate towards the ridge occupied by the red coats. The dragoons in vain endeavoured to stop this movement of the clans by one or two feints. Seeing their rapid approach, Hawley sent orders to Ligonier to charge with all the horse upon the hostile right. The Macdonalds, who were on that flank, rested on a morass, which prevented the horseman getting round into their rear. The dragoons came on towards their front at a full trot with their sabres drawn and raised high, as if to charge and cut down the Highlanders, who kept still pushing forward. The clans, seeing the threatened charge, reserved their fire, with the utmost steadiness, until the horsemen were within ten yards' distance. Then, only at Murray's signal, the Highland muskets went up to the shoulders, close and well levelled by the skilled marksmen of the mountains. A rolling volley was poured in, a number of hostile horsemen reeled and fell from their saddles; numbers of the horses came down; the ground was covered with gasping dragoons and struggling animals; and about 200 red coats were lying in an instant on Falkirk Moor. The greater part of those who were unwounded belonged to the dragoon regiments which had fled at Colt Bridge and at Preston, and now repeated the military manœuvre that they had performed so effectually at both those places, with an aptitude which showed considerable skill and experience in this evolution. The 3rd regiment, Cobham's (now the 10th Hussars), stood firmer for a while, but was soon compelled to retire after heavy loss.

This defeat of the cavalry began the battle well on the side of the insurgents, but they well-nigh paid dear for their success. At the instant the attack commenced a violent storm of rain came on, which, carried by a fierce and gusty wind, blew straight in the faces of the royal troops, greatly annoyed them, and so wet their powder that they could barely give fire. Lord George Murray wished to bring the victorious Macdonalds back into the regular line. He cried to them to stand fast and pay no heed to the flying horsemen, but to keep their own ranks and to reload. His care was fruitless. The Macdonalds, in their usual manner, rushed on sword in hand and dropped their muskets. The insurgents' left wing at the same moment fell furiously with the claymore on the right and centre of Hawley's foot, broke them, and put them to flight. But the extreme right of Hawley's first line considerably overlapped the left of the Highlanders. Here, on some low ground in rear of the right, the Buffs were seen standing "firm as the rocks of their own native shore." They became a rallying point for the Royals, who were forced back, and these two regiments joined by the 4th, 14th, and 48th, under Brigadier Cholmondeley, with some of Ligonier's dragoons, stood fast on the extreme flank, having the advantage of the ravine in front, which prevented the Highlanders from attacking them sword in hand, according to their favourite mode of fighting. These troops gallantly maintained their position, and by repeated and steady volleys repulsed the Highlanders from the opposite side of the ravine. One of the three routed regiments of dragoons rallied in the rear of this infantry, which stood firm. The other two, who had been at Preston, followed up the course of action pursued by them at that battle.

The battle was now in a curious state. On the royal left all was disorder and confusion. In vain did the General attempt to animate his troops in this quarter by his personal courage, with his white head uncovered and conspicuous in the front rank of the combatants. But the three regiments who held their ground on the right had a decided vantage over the Chevalier's left, and many Highlanders quitted the field under the impression that the day was lost, and spread disastrous tidings of defeat in their rear.

Charles, who had seen from his commanding position the state of affairs, had put himself at the head of his second line, and advancing against the enemy's right, arrested their temporary triumph. The three regiments of the royal army who had remained firm like their comrades, were compelled to withdraw from the field, and in their retreat covered the flight of their companions. These drew off in steady order, with drums beating and colours flying; and Cobham's dragoons also retreated in tolerable condition. Had the Highlanders pursued, there seems little doubt that Hawley's army must have been utterly destroyed. But the Prince, from the want of discipline among the troops he commanded, and through the extreme severity of the weather and the darkness of night, which was rapidly falling, could hardly ascertain the real position of affairs. It was considered imprudent to push forward in the darkness, in case of some stratagem or ambuscade. On account of the want of horses in the insurgent army also there were few mounted orderlies or aides-de-camp, so the troops on the extreme right of the line hardly knew what had occurred to those on the left.

For some time the victors remained upon the field irresolute and ignorant of their own success. But Lord Kilmarnock, who was well acquainted with that portion of the country, where part of his estate lay, being sent forward to reconnoitre, approached the road to Edinburgh beyond the town of Falkirk, and saw a great part of the English army panic-stricken and flying in the greatest disorder. Charles having thus ascertained that the English had already retreated beyond Falkirk, made his entry, late in the evening, and in torrents of rain, into the town. He was conducted by torchlight to a lodging which had been prepared for him. Hawley, pausing in the camp which he had taken possession of with so much anticipated triumph, caused the tents to be set on fire, and withdrew his broken troops to Linlithgow. On the night of the 17th the remains of his army were billetted in the palace there. They began to make such great fires as to endanger the safety of the edifice. A lady of the Livingstone family remonstrated with the General, who treated her fears with contempt. " I can run away from fire as fast as you can, General," was the answer of the lady, who with this sarcasm departed for Edinburgh. The palace of Linlithgow did during the night catch fire, and was burnt to the ground.

Next morning Hawley retreated to the capital with his forces in a state of considerable disarray and dejection. He relieved his wounded vanity by an execution of several of his soldiers, who had misbehaved themselves in the action. The loss to the royal troops was about 400 killed or wounded, with a large proportion of officers, as was to be expected when corps broke and it was the duty of the officers to rally them. The loss of the insurgents was estimated at only forty men, though it probably considerably exceeded that number. About 100 prisoners were taken from Hawley's army, amongst whom was John Home, afterward the historian of this conflict. Most of these were sent to Doone Castle. Three standards, all the artillery, ammunition, and baggage fell into the hands of the Highlanders; while the attempt made by Hawley to fire his tents before he left them was baffled by the rain, and these were placed at the disposal of the insurgent army.

During the night, notwithstanding the violent wind and rain, the Highlanders employed themselves in plundering the camp of the English, and stripping the dead bodies. This work they performed so effectually that a citizen of Falkirk, who next morning looked over the field from a distance, said he could only compare the corpses to a large field of white sheep at rest on the face of the hill. The Glasgow regiment were taken prisoners, and were rather roughly treated, as the Highlanders considered that their case was different from regular soldiers, who were forced by duty into the campaign.

The defeat at Falkirk struck consternation and terror into all parts of Britain. In England men had considered that the rebellion was ended when the Highlanders withdrew across the border. Hawley's swaggering assumption had prepared the nation to expect tidings very different from those which had to be forwarded to London. There the news of the result of the battle were received with general alarm, and at a drawing-room held at the Court of St. James's, on the day they came in, it is said that only two persons appeared with countenances unmarked by signs of trouble ; one of these was George II. himself, whose lion heart was impervious to any sentiment of fear ; the other was Sir John Cope, who was radiant with delight in the belief that Hawley's misfortune might efface his own from public recollection.

It would have been natural that the victory at Falkirk

should have been immediately improved, and that a rapid advance should have been made upon Edinburgh by the Highland troops. The capital probably would have again fallen a ready prey, and the royal army in Scotland might have been destroyed or dispersed. As it was however, the victory brought the Chevalier little fruit, and proved rather baneful than advantageous to his cause. Among the officers it raised angry dissensions. Murray and Drummond each accused the other of not having completed the destruction of the enemy. Many of the private clansmen, having secured their plunder, slipped away to their mountains to store it. Thus the army was for a time deprived of some thousands of men. An unhappy accident the day after the action tended to increase this desertion. One of the men of Clanranald was examining a musket which formed part of his booty, when the piece went off and unfortunately killed a son of Glengarry who was passing along the street. The tribe of Glengarry loudly demanded life for life, and Clanranald reluctantly had to surrender his follower, and saw him shot dead with a volley of bullets; the man's own father aiding in the fire, to terminate sooner the sufferings of his child. But even this savage vengeance did not suffice to satisfy the offended clan, and the greater number forsook the Prince's standard and withdrew to their mountain glens.

The evening after his victory Charles again encamped at Bannockburn, and there issued an account of the battle, which was the last of his Scottish proclamations or gazettes. He then resumed the siege of Stirling

Castle, appearing to consider it derogatory to his dignity to abandon an enterprise of danger once commenced. Thus the royal troops in Scotland were left full leisure to recover from the confusion consequent upon their recent defeat.

In London it was thought that Hawley had suffered his misfortune through want of proper precautions, and the Duke of Cumberland expressed a willingness to attack the rebels with the men that Hawley had left. He speedily had the opportunity of proving his readiness to do so, as it was considered that now no one was of sufficient consequence to be placed at the head of the army but his Royal Highness himself, and he was appointed to the chief command. The Duke set out from St. James's on the 25th January, 1746, and, travelling day and night, arrived most unexpectedly at Holyrood House on the morning of the 30th January— a day of ill augury to the House of Stuart. His arrival restored the drooping spirits of the members of the government at Edinburgh; and to the army the appointment of the new Commander-in-Chief was very grateful, since his presence closed the course of cruel punishments which Hawley had instituted, to rectify a disaster due in great measure to his own neglect of military prevision.

The army placed at the disposal of the Duke consisted of twelve squadrons of horse and fourteen battalions of infantry. Several of these had suffered much in the late action, and all were far from being complete. Every effort had however been made to repair as far as possible the losses of Falkirk Moor. His Royal Highness remained but thirty hours in the capital, and on the 31st he set out with his army to give the insurgents battle. Hawley still acted under him as one of his Lieutenant-Generals, and the Earl of Albemarle held the same situation. Officers and soldiers were in high spirits, and confident of victory under their new commander. In a council of war held at Edinburgh it had been determined that the troops should march towards Stirling to raise the siege of the Castle, and give battle to the rebels, if they should dare to accept it, while the dragoons of Hamilton and Ligonier, now the 13th and 14th Hussars, patrolled the roads leading towards the west, to prevent the rebels from obtaining information. Great pains were taken to explain to the soldiers in general orders the mode in which the clansmen fought. It was stated that the Highlanders could be surely demolished by diagonal fire of ranks within ten or twelve paces, or by bayonet thrusts, delivered, not against the man exactly opposite, when the point would be caught in the target, but against his comrade; but that if a soldier fired at a distance, or gave way, he might give himself up for dead.

On approaching Falkirk the Duke was informed that the rebels, so far from being ready to accept battle, had already commenced their retreat.

The Chevalier had reaped little advantage from the battle of Falkirk. The confusion into which part of his own forces had been thrown, the want of mounted men, as the great body of the horses had been lost during the retreat from England, and the consequent ignorance of the condition of the enemy, prevented the pursuit of Hawley's army, which ought to have been an easy victim.

Charles, who had adhered to his resolution of convoking no councils since the assembly of that which had caused him to retreat from Derby, with the exception of a council of war held on the battle-field of Falkirk, acted only by the advice of his secretary, Mr. Murray, his Quartermaster-General, and Sir Thomas Sheridan.

In the siege of Stirling, under the advice of these officers, a French engineer, M. Mirabelle, had been employed, who had come over from France with Lord John Drummond. This officer, with the assumption which sometimes is found amongst his countrymen, opened the fire from his batteries when only three guns were mounted. The heavier ordnance of the Castle soon silenced them. A siege was of all operations of war that least suited to the capabilities of a Highland army. The force of the clansmen had also suffered great diminutions since the battle of Falkirk, not so much from losses sustained in action, as from the effects of the victory, which caused many of the privates to retire to their homes to place their plunder in safety.

The superior officers of the army, marking this diminution of numbers, angered at not being consulted upon the campaign, and mortified by the fact that the enemy had not been more severely pursued after the battle, drew up a memorial, signed by many influential names, and sent it to the Prince by the hands of Lord George Murray. This memorial is still preserved. It, after lamenting the number of clansmen gone home, and the unequal chances of another battle, advised the Prince to retreat with his army to the Highlands, where it could be usefully employed during the remainder of the winter in taking the forts of the north, while there would be no doubt that in the spring 10,000 effective Highlanders could be got together to follow the Chevalier where he thought proper.

This petition, which under the circumstances had the force of command, struck Charles almost with despair. He passionately exclaimed, "Good God, have I lived to see this!" And dashed his head against the wall with so much violence that he staggered. He then sent Sir Thomas Sheridan to Falkirk to reason with the chiefs against their resolution, but he found them impenetrable, and had no alternative but sullenly to acquiesce in their decision.

The sick and wounded, with the followers of the camp, had already been sent to Dumblane in order to clear the army from incumbrances, under the idea that a battle would be fought against the advancing troops of the Duke of Cumberland. The retreat was resolved upon, and it was arranged by the Prince, in concert with Lord George Murray, that on the 1st of February the army should cross the Forth at the fords of Frew. Early in the morning the cannon employed in the siege operations were to be spiked, and the ammunition which could not be carried with the army was to be destroyed. A strong rear-guard composed of 1,200 picked Highlanders and Elcho's force were to protect the retreat of the army. The powder magazine at St. Ninian's was blown up, but in such haste and confusion that the explosion destroyed, together with the magazine, the neighbouring church, and caused the loss of the lives of several country people.

The precautions which were arranged for the retreat were not, however, observed. Haste and disorder was the consequence; and so nearly did the retreat degenerate into flight, that at the passage of the Forth nowhere were there more than 1,000 men together. The river was passed in small bodies and in great confusion, while abandoned carts and cannon strewed the road behind the columns. The infantry of the rear-guard did not appear to take up its position, and Lord Elcho's troop, which had been ordered to wait at the bridge over the Carron till further orders, was totally forgotten, and was nearly cut off by a body of troops from Stirling before they received orders to retire.

Yet the insurgents, not being pursued, retreated without much loss. The line of march lay by Dumblane and Crieff; and on the 3rd of February the headquarters halted at Fairnton, near the latter town, where the discussion as to the necessity of a retreat from Stirling was renewed with bitterness and acrimony.

At Crieff the army of Charles divided into two portions : one division, which chiefly consisted of the Highlanders of the west, marched northwards by the great high road. A second division, under Lord George

Murray, consisting mainly of the Lowland regiments, and the cavalry, who had lost many of their remaining horses on account of the forced marches over bad roads in that season of the year, took the coast route by Montrose and Aberdeen to Inverness. A small part of the army which belonged to the Highlands of Aberdeenshire went by Braemar.

The Duke of Cumberland followed, but could not overtake the enemy, who was able to carry off with him in retreating the garrisons left on the advance at Montrose and other towns in the north, and safely effected his movement to Inverness, in front of which town the various columns of the army again united together. Here it was thought that Charles would obtain recruits from Caithness and Sutherland. His only enemy in the north was a small force which Lord Loudon had raised from the Grants, the Monroes, and the Rosses, and a few smaller northern clans who had united with the Macdonalds of Skye and the Macleods. Their number was not sufficient to prevent the troops of the Chevalier from spreading everywhere through the country; and the little army of Lord Loudon, which amounted to less than 2,000 men, was couped up in Inverness, where it had rudely fortified itself with a ditch and palisade. It was easy for the Chevalier to attack and capture the barracks at Ruthven, which had successfully resisted his assault before his descent from the Highlands. After this he halted ten miles in front of Inverness, at Moy Castle, the seat of the chiefs of the Mackintoshes. The chief himself was serving in the ranks of Lord Loudon, but Lady Mackintosh raised the clan for the Chevalier, and rode at their head as their commander.

The vicinity of Moy Castle, and the lax manner in which the Highland soldiers were kept together, induced Lord Loudon to make a sudden night march, in hopes of seizing the person of the Chevalier, who had only a few hundred men round him as a guard. For this purpose Loudon employed the Highlanders of Macleod's clan as well qualified to execute a swift and secret enterprise. They were accompanied by several volunteers, but a scheme which promised success was baffled by six or seven of the Mackintoshes, who, meeting the royal troops, dispersed themselves in different parts of the heath and forest that fringed the road from Inverness to Moy, fired from various points upon the advancing columns, and at the same time shouted from various quarters the slogans of Lochiel, Keppoch, and other well-known clans, while two or three bagpipes played furiously their gathering tunes. Thus, those who were attempting the surprise conceived themselves to be surprised, and thought that the whole Highland army was around them. Astonished, and doubtful from the darkness, they hastily turned back to Inverness, where they arrived in so much confusion, that their retreat is known still in the Highlands as the rout of Moy.

On the following morning, the 17th of February, Charles assembled his men, and on the 18th advanced to Inverness to repay Lord Loudon his intended visit. Neither the strength of the place, nor the number of

Loudon's forces, entitled him to make any stand against an army so much superior to his own; he therefore did not await the arrival of the Highlanders, but embarked with the Lord President and his army in boats, and rowed across the Moray Firth to Cromarty. He was afterwards pursued by the Earl of Cromarty and some Highland regiments, who marched round the head of the inlet and forced him to cross over the Great Ferry into Sutherlandshire. Still pursued by Cromarty, his army was forced to disband; but the latter in his turn, too confident in his first success, was surprised and taken prisoner with his officers at Dunrobin Castle by a band of the Sutherland militia. This last event, however, did not occur till the day before the battle of Culloden, and had therefore no influence upon the main events of the campaign.

The Highland army took possession of Inverness on the 18th February, and immediately commenced the siege of the citadel called Fort St. George, which on the 20th capitulated. Another of the Chevalier's parties was sent against Fort Augustus, which it reduced and destroyed.

While the Chevalier in the north was pushing his petty and unimportant advantages against the few garrisons held for King George, the Duke of Cumberland, advancing in the rear of his army, occupied successively the districts which the Highlanders abandoned. He was also bringing up important reinforcements, by which he hoped to narrow the country still left free to the rebels, and finally to destroy their troops. Following the track of the Highlanders, he had arrived at Perth on the 6th February, and sent Sir Andrew Agnew, with 500 soldiers and a hundred of the Campbells, to take possession of Blair Castle; while Colonel Leighton, with a considerable force, occupied Castle Menzies. These garrisons were intended to prevent the Highland army from drawing reinforcements from the countries in which they were stationed.

About the same time a body of auxiliaries, consisting of 6,000 troops of Hesse, subsidised by the English government, had disembarked at Leith, under the command of Prince Frederick of Hesse Cassel; as the 6,000 Dutch troops, which were originally destined to assist the King of England, had perforce been withdrawn from the fighting ranks. These troops had been captured in the Low Countries by the French, and had been liberated on parole not to serve against France. So soon as Lord John Drummond arrived with the French auxiliaries, a message had been despatched to the Dutch commandant, formally acquainting him that the colours of France were displayed in the camp of Prince Charles. The Dutch were thus called upon to withdraw themselves from the war. They recognised the summons, and retired from Britain accordingly. To replace these auxiliaries the government concluded a subsidiary treaty with the Prince of Hesse Cassel; and in consequence of this engagement, 6,000 Hessian troops had now arrived at Leith. The Duke of Cumberland paid a flying visit to Edinburgh, where he held a conference with the Prince of Hesse and the principal officers. Most supposed that the Highlanders would break up and disperse, and never venture a battle against the Duke of Cumberland, who was now about to collect his forces in the Highlands, leaving the Hessians to garrison the Lowlands and the posts on the line of communication. Lord Milton, a Scottish judge, was of a different opinion. He, well acquainted with the Highlanders, declared himself persuaded that they would again unite in a large body to make another final struggle for the accomplishment of their enterprise. This opinion of Lord Milton made a deep impression on the Duke of Cumberland's mind. He resolved accordingly to be prepared for battle, and to move northwards slowly, but with an overpowering force. Having made this determination, he returned to Perth, and sent three regiments of infantry to Dundee, pushed forward with the main body of his army northwards, and reached Aberdeen on the 27th February. The English fleet along the coast kept him supplied with the stores and provisions that were required. The Hessian troops, as the Duke of Cumberland moved forward, spread their garrisons through the Lowlands, and advanced to Perth. Their moustaches and blue uniform occasioned some surprise to the Scottish people, who were accustomed only to soldiers dressed in red and shaved close, as was then the fashion with all troops in the British service, except hussars. But the Scotch Calvinists were greatly edified by the quiet and orderly behaviour of the Germans, which was a strong contrast to the horrible language and profligate bearing of the soldiery of

England. Thus the country between Perth and Aberdeen, including Blair, and some parts even further north, were occupied by parties of the royal side.

The Highland leaders supposed that the Duke of Cumberland would remain at Aberdeen till the summer, and determined during the remainder of the winter to push their operations against Fort William, the last of the chain of forts still held by the English. This post was however provided with everything necessary for a siege, and the garrison was reinforced by some of the Campbells; so that it amounted to about 6,000 men. Lochiel and Keppoch formed the blockade, but could not cut off the communication of the garrison with the sea. So two sloops of war were able to support the fort with their guns. Some of the French detachments came up and formed a regular battery against the place, but to little purpose. Supplies from France to the Highland troops occasionally came in, but several ships carrying reinforcements were captured by the British cruisers, and others forced back to French ports. One, which had 150 soldiers and 10,000$l.$ in gold on board, ran ashore on the north coast of Sutherland, and both crew and specie were captured by the Mackays, who were favourable to the government. This loss was of great importance to the Chevalier, as it reduced his treasure to 500 louis-d'or, and he was forced to pay his troops in meal, which caused the desertion of many, and the discontent and grumbling of the others. Nor were even these meagre supplies certain. The men were often pinched with hunger, and were ferced to disperse over the country, to seek for subsistence, while even the best officers were glad when they could procure a few leaves of raw cabbage from the kail gardens of the peasantry. A few troops from France, consisting of a portion of Fitzjames's dragoons, and a detachment of Berwick's regiment, were landed; but no other troops of the French armada which was promised reached after this period the army of the Chevalier. The remainder of Fitzjames's cavalry were captured by Commodore Knowles, and sent into the Thames.

Still the Highland troops did not view the occupation of Perthshire and Southern Inverness-shire without endeavouring to annoy the enemy. Various attacks were made on the posts held by the royal troops. Blair Castle, where Sir Andrew Agnew commanded, was blockaded; but the blockade was raised, owing to the advance of a body of Hessians from Perth, together with the Earl of Crawford.

The Highlanders were now cooped up, notwithstanding some partial and petty success, in a bare and mountainous country, and pinched for supplies. The armies of the king's government, on the contrary, had abundance of subsistence, and had been powerfully reinforced. On the 8th April, the Duke of Cumberland, deceiving the expectations of the Highland leaders, who supposed he would rest in Aberdeen till the summer, broke up from that town in command of about 8,000 infantry and 900 cavalry. As the royal troops advanced northwards they were joined by Generals Bland and Mordaunt, and the whole army concentrated at the town of Cullen, about ten miles from the banks of the Spey, intending to move forward upon Inverness, where were the Chevalier's head-quarters. The Highland outposts were extended along the river Spey, and seemed disposed for a time to dispute the passage of the deep and rapid stream. They were apparently not well informed of the strength of their enemy, as the royal troops on their advance had seized and hanged, at Banff, two Highland spies, who, in primitive fashion, were obtaining reports of the strength of the army by marking their numbers with notches upon a stick.

A few earthworks seemed to show that resistance was here purposed, and a considerable division of the troops of the Lowlands were drawn up under Lord John Drummond, with the apparent purpose of holding those defences. The final orders of Charles were, however, that Lord John should retreat to Elgin as soon as the enemy should approach in force the south-east bank of the river. He did so, and the Duke of Cumberland forded the Spey on the 12th of April, in three columns, with the bands of the regiments playing a tune which was calculated to insult the Highland enemy.[1] The main body of the Duke's army crossed the Spey at the ford of Gormach; the second division at a ford close to Gordon Castle; and the third passed near the church of Bellie. The Duke himself was the first to plunge into the water at the head of his cavalry, who pushed through it with some difficulty; and the infantry found

---

[1] "Will you play me fair play,
Bonnie laddie, Highland laddie?"

that the water rose above their waists. Thus was one of the strongest passes of Scotland, over a deep and rapid stream, abandoned by the Highland army, and given up to their assailants, who got over with no other loss but that of one dragoon and four women, camp-followers, who were carried down by the stream. In this pass 2,000 men might easily have kept back an army of 20,000. It was a sure prelude of disaster when a Highland force thus abandoned one of the natural fastnesses of the country, which it was so well adapted to defend.

On the 14th the advanced guard of the troops of the government seized Nairn, having halted on the 13th on the moor of Alves. Beyond Nairn there were several skirmishes between the outposts of the two armies. The Highlanders, in falling back from the town, were supported by Charles himself, with his guards and a Mackintosh regiment. On this force appearing in the opposite line, the advanced guard of the Duke's army retreated upon their main body at Nairn.

On the night of the 14th Prince Charles Edward and his staff lodged at Culloden House, the seat of his most able and determined enemy in Scotland, President Forbes. His troops lay out upon the moor of Drummossie, about a mile to the south of Culloden, where they suffered much from the severity of the cold and scarcity of fuel. The royal army, on the other hand, was well provided with camp equipage, and was for the most part cantoned in the town of Nairn. Provisions were abundant in the quarters of the Duke of Cumberland, but the insurgents were so ill supplied that only a single biscuit could be served out to each man during the whole day of the 15th. On the morning the Highlanders were drawn up in battle array, and expected an attack. The enemy however did not appear, and Lord Elcho was pushed forward with his cavalry to reconnoitre. He brought in a report that the Duke of Cumberland was halting for the day at Nairn, and that his troops were passing the day, which was the birthday of their leader, in festivity and mirth.

In their advance from Aberdeen the 8,000 infantry and 900 cavalry of Cumberland had suffered little. The roads were indeed bad, and the weather was severe; but they were amply provided and supplied from the fleet. The sick seem to have been few in number. In the Highland army, on the other side, numbers were deficient. Notwithstanding every exertion, the unexpected advance of the Duke of Cumberland prevented the outlying Highland detachments from having returned in time to concentrate with the main army. Thus Macpherson of Cluny, Lord Cromarty, and the Master of Lovat were away. So that barely 5,000 insurgents could be mustered for the battle now impending.

The spirit of their leader was however undaunted. During his stay at Inverness he had employed himself in hunting in the forenoon, and in the evening with balls, concerts, and parties of pleasure, in which he appeared as happy and gay as after the battle of Preston. This exterior show of confidence appears not only to have been assumed in order to impose upon his followers, but to have rested on the idea in Charles's mind that the army of the Duke of Cumberland would not seriously venture in battle to raise their arms against their lawful Prince—an idea which he found it difficult to impress upon such of his followers as were acquainted with the temper of English soldiers. While he lay at Inverness, bad news arrived from France. Two gentlemen came to him from that country to state that the Court of Versailles had entirely laid aside all thoughts of an invasion on a large scale, and that his brother, the Duke of York, who had been intended to be placed at the head of the expedition, had left the coast, being recalled to Paris. This news put a final end to the most reasonable hopes of the Pretender, which always rested, as they justly should have rested, upon a grand exertion of France in his favour.

The rapid advance of the Duke of Cumberland had prevented a large number of Highlanders from returning to the camp, as several of the clans had been dispersed through the country, in order more easily to obtain subsistence; but General Stapleton, who had been engaged in the attempt to reduce Fort William, together with Lochiel and the other Highlanders who had assisted him in the enterprise, were enabled to regain Inverness before the time of the battle. The cavalry of the Prince had suffered greatly. The corps of Lord Pitsligo might be said to be entirely destroyed by their severe outpost duty on the retreat from Stirling, and was converted into a company of foot-guards. The loss of the horses of these gentlemen was a great misfortune to the army, as from the spirit and ingenuity of such educated troopers, they were of the greatest service as light cavalry. The Highland clansmen were discontented from want of pay, and from the absence of provisions; and, goaded by hunger and misery, were guilty of repeated mutiny and disobedience to orders. For all these evils Charles Edward saw no remedy but a general action, to which he was the more inclined by the memory of his former successes, which almost appeared miraculous, when he had come off victorious against all ordinary expectations. It would have been more prudent to have withdrawn his forces into the uttermost regions of the Highlands, and there have maintained them in such force as he could, had he been able to do so. But want of provisions, the worm that gnaws out the heart of any army, forbidding him from following such a course, he had no alternative, and was forced, with troops mutinous for want of pay, half starved from want of food, and diminished in numbers by the absence of 3,000 or 4,000 men, to risk an action against a well-organised, well-disciplined, and well-conducted body of royal troops.

On the night of the 14th the Highlanders lay upon their arms on the moor of Culloden; and on the next morning were drawn up in order of battle. On their right there were some park walls; on their left a slow descent which slopes down upon Culloden House. The order of battle was formed in two lines. The Athole brigade held the right, and next them Lochiel, the clans of Appin, Fraser, and Macintosh, with those of

Maclaughlan, Maclean, and Farquharson ; while on the left were ranged the three divisions of Macdonald's, called after their respective chiefs, Clanranald, Keppoch, and Glengarry.

These preparations for the engagement were not made with prudence. By a singular fatality, which now seems to have fallen over the councils of the Pretender, the disposition of this order of battle involved the point of honour esteemed of the utmost importance in this singular army. The Macdonalds had claimed from the beginning of the expedition, as being the most powerful and numerous tribe, the privilege of holding the right of the whole army. At the battle of Preston Lochiel and Appin had waived any claim to this idle precedence. At the battle of Falkirk the Macdonalds had also been upon the right. But now, when the left was assigned to them, the men of the clan regarded the arrangement as not only an evil omen, but also as a personal insult. The second line of the Highlanders, or the reserve, was divided into three bodies, with an interval between each. On the right were the horse of Elcho, Fitzjames, and Strathallan ; with the infantry regiments of Abbachie and Ogilvie. The centre was formed of the Irish detachments from the French army, the regiment of Lord John Drummond, and the horsemen of the Earl of Kilmarnock ; while the left wing consisted of the hussars, with the Lowland battalions of Sir Alexander Bannerman and Moir of Strongwood. The number of the whole first line was possibly about 4,700 men ; that of the second 2,300, of which 250 were cavalry. But the numbers that formed up in order of battle on the morning of the 15th, were considerably diminished before the subsequent action took place.

The commissariat department of the Highland army was apparently totally incapable, as during the whole of the 15th the men received no provisions, except a single biscuit per man, as the ration for the whole day. Thus if the army had been victorious upon the 16th it must have been broken up immediately, to disperse through distant quarters from the mere necessity of supply. Soon after mid-day, on the 15th, Lord Elcho brought in his report as to the position of the enemy's troops. Upon this Prince Charles assembled the chief officers of the army and held a council of war. There was a diversity of opinion as to the best course to be pursued. The want of provisions, however, was an imperative cause for an action, and rendered a battle inevitable; the place and mode alone were matters for discussion. With justice, Lord George Murray asserted that the strength of an irregular army such as theirs depended in its power of surprising its adversary. Regular soldiers, he said, depended much on their discipline, an advantage of which they were deprived by darkness and confusion; Highlanders, on the contrary, had little discipline, but that which was of a natural kind, independent either of light or regular formations. This officer gave his opinion that the right division of the first line should march in two divisions at the dusk of the evening, move round the town of Nairn, and attack the Duke of Cumberland's camp in the rear; at the same time he proposed that the

Duke of Perth, with the left division of the first line, should attack the camp of the Duke of Cumberland in front; and he did not doubt the confusion occasioned by the sudden onset on both points, joined to the effects of the past day's festivity, would throw the regulars into total confusion, and afford the Highlanders a complete victory. The whole of the second line, or reserve, was to move forward under the command of Charles Edward himself, to support the front attack. The Prince, who had already formed the same scheme, rose and embraced Lord George Murray on his proposing it; and orders were immediately given for its execution. The moor on which the army was lying was set on fire at night, so that the light might convey an idea of the troops still holding the same position; the watchword given out by Prince Charles was "King James VIII." During the day, however, the army had been still further diminished, for many stragglers, worn out by want of food, had left the ranks and gone to Inverness and other places to seek for something to eat, and they told the officers sent after them to shoot them if they pleased, rather than compel them to starve any longer. In the hopes of getting back some of these stragglers the movement was deferred, and it was not till eight at night that every preparation was complete. Lord George Murray then started at the head of the first column; Charles put himself at the head of that which followed, and gave the signal to march.

The distance from Culloden was about twelve miles. The night was dark, and so far favourable to the purpose of surprise ; but for the same reason the guides were deceived, and the progress of the troops in consequence of losing their way was considerably delayed. The men, too, were exhausted with privation, and could not display their wonted energy. The columns slowly and painfully toiled through the heathery waste or marshy hollows, while many men dropped from the ranks, and the rear fell away considerably from the van-guard. In order to cross the Nairn, it was necessary to take advantage of the passage near Kilravock House ; and in order to get to their intended points of attack, the whole of the army was forced to follow one road as far as this point. Thus a long and straggling column was formed, and as the march proceeded, the van which could push forward without impediment drew away considerably from the rear. Messages were frequently sent forward to Lochiel, who was in front, and to Lord George Murray, who was at the head of the advance, begging them to halt until the rear of the columns could make up their lost ground. Fifty of these messages were brought to the van-guard before they had marched over the eight miles to Kilravock Castle.

At this point the Duke of Perth himself, who commanded the second division of the first line, came up to Lord George Murray, and insisted that the rear could not come up unless the van was halted. Here a halt was made accordingly, and several of the principal officers came to the head of the column to consult what was to be done. Many of the Highlanders had straggled from the ranks and lain down to sleep in the wood of

Kilravock. It was now two o'clock in the morning, the hour at which the attack had been intended, but the head of the column was still four miles distant from the English camp. It seemed doubtful then if the assault could still be made in the dark, and to come within striking distance of the enemy's camp after the dawn would expose the columns to his observation. While a discussion was still going on the sudden roll of the drums from the royal army told that the king's troops were on the alert, and that all possibility of taking them by surprise was gone by. Messages came up from the Prince to say that his Royal Highness would be glad to have the attack made, but that as Lord George was in the van, he could best tell whether the assault could be carried out or not. With these powers Lord George gave orders for the retreat, and Charles, afterwards riding up, was convinced of the unavoidable necessity of retiring.

Meanwhile the Duke of Cumberland's army, neither by means of patrols, nor scouts, nor spies, was alarmed on the advance of the enemy; and it appears probable that but for the unfortunate circumstances which delayed the movement, the attacking column would have had a great chance of success.

The retreat was carried out with much more rapidity than the advance, as it was unnecessary to take any precautions for concealing the movements of the troops, and the road was also well known to the guides. At five o'clock in the morning the whole army had regained the heights of Culloden, and had resumed its former position. But the Highlanders were now harassed and hungry, without any neighbouring stores of provisions. Even for the Prince himself no refreshments beyond a little bread and whisky could be found. It was the wish of Lord George Murray and other officers that the army, thus unfitted for exertion, should retire and take up a position behind the river Nairn, where high and inaccessible hills would give them a post where they could not be attacked by cavalry. Charles, however, was imbued with the chivalrous idea that he ought not to take advantage of the ground in action, nor enable his enemies afterwards to say that his victory had not been owing to valour. This was a romantic absurdity for any leader of men in war. In war there is no chivalry; it is the duty of every man who has the lives of troops and the happiness of a country in his hands to take every advantage he possibly can of his enemy, and the science of war is but to place by every means one's enemy in the most disadvantageous position possible.

The weary clansmen threw themselves on the burnt heather to rest, while many started away towards Inverness in order to seek for provisions. From their repose they were roused about eleven o'clock by the news that the outposts had seen the advancing scouts of the Duke of Cumberland's army in the distance. The chief officers immediately mounted their horses, the drums were beat, and the pipes were ordered to bray out the gathering pibrochs. This sudden summons to arms caused much hurry and confusion among the men, who, half dead with fatigue, were suddenly roused from the sleep which they so much needed. The chiefs in charge did what they could to get them together, but as the men were dispersed in all directions as far as Inverness itself, nearly 2,000 of the Highlanders who had been in line of battle on the preceding day were absent from the action on the 16th.

The Duke of Cumberland's army now appeared about two miles off, advancing straight against the front of Charles's line of battle. The royal force consisted of for the most part the troops which had been worsted by the same enemy at Falkirk; but they were commanded by a very different leader.

The order of battle was in two lines, of which seven battalions formed the first, and eight the second. The second line was supported by two squadrons of horse on the right, and four squadrons of dragoons on the left. On the left of the whole line were the Campbells, with the dragoons. There were two pieces of cannon ranged between every battalion in the first line, while three guns were on the right and three on the left of the second.

Had the whole insurgent army been concentrated, there would have been little if any numerical difference between the contending parties, each of which amounted to about 9,000 men. But, as has been seen, Prince Charles was deprived of above 2,000 of his troops who had not yet come up, and the stragglers who had left his standard amounted to at least 2,000 more, so that at the decisive battle of Culloden only 5,000 of the Highland army were opposed to 9,000 of the King's troops. The men who were absent also were chiefly true Highlanders, who formed the particular strength of the army of the Chevalier. To obviate the effect of the Highland target, the soldiers of the royal troops had been drilled to direct in action their bayonet thrusts, not at the man directly opposite, but against the one who fronted his right-hand comrade.

Both armies were apparently full of spirit. On the royal side an appeal made to the troops by the Duke himself was answered by loud cheers and repeated shouts of "Flanders, Flanders." On the Highland side there was no want of loud huzzahs and slogan cries, and the mountaineers seemed as if they had lost all sense of fatigue at the sight of the enemy. On the left of the field the Macdonalds, alone sullen and discontented, stood silent and morose, offended at the post which had been assigned to them.

The battle began with a cannonade from the artillery on both sides, in which the royal army was little harmed; but the insurgents suffered considerable loss. The staff of the Chevalier himself as he rode along his ranks to animate the men, was a conspicuous mark for the royal gunners. Several of his guards fell, and a servant who held a led horse was killed by his side, while Charles himself was covered by the mud thrown up by the ball. Without being discomposed, he coolly continued his inspection, and then, as at Falkirk, stationed himself on a little height close behind the second line.

The Duke of Cumberland took up his position between

his first and second lines. During the preparations for action a bitter storm of snow and hail had begun to fall; but, unlike the day at Falkirk, the storm now blew full in the faces of the Highlanders.

On the right, Lord George Murray, finding his division lose so much more than they inflicted from the cannonade, sent Kerr of Graden to the Prince, requesting permission to attack; this was allowed. The right wing and the centre of the Highland first line, with one loud slogan cry, rushed forward, firing their muskets, and then dropping them, came on furiously, sword in hand, against the red lines of the enemy. They were received with a rolling fire of musketry, and were ploughed into by grape-shot and cannon-balls. But, like waves dashing up against a wall of sand, with a resistless onset, they dashed aside the bayonet points of their opponents, broke through Munro's and Burrell's regiments in the first line, and captured two pieces of cannon. The Duke of Cumberland, however, having foreseen the probability of this event, and in order to provide against its results, had carefully strengthened his second line. It was drawn up three deep, with the front rank kneeling, so as to afford three lines of fire. These, reserving their discharge till the enemy were close upon them, poured in then a volley so well sustained and destructive as completely to disorder them. Before the Highlanders, shaken by this withering fire, could recover or rally, the royal troops advanced, and with the bayonet point, driving the clans together till they became one mingled mass, turned them into fugitives. Many of the best chiefs were borne down, killed, or wounded, and trampled upon. Lochiel himself fell seriously hurt, but was carried away from the field by two retainers; and in vain the other chiefs cried to their men to attack again, who were being forced back by bayonet and musketry fire. In a very few minutes the whole right and the centre of Prince Charles's force was in irreparable disorder, and was being pushed back across the moor by superior numbers of fresh troops, while they themselves were dropping from previous fatigue.

On the left the Macdonalds, sulky because they thought themselves aggrieved by their exclusion from the post of honour, stood motionless and irresolute. In vain did the Duke of Perth, who commanded, tell them that he would in future make a right of the left, and call himself Macdonald, if they behaved with their usual bravery. In vain did Keppoch charge against the enemy's line with a few of his kinsmen; his clan, with a carelessness for their chieftain almost unknown in Highland history, refused to follow, and without emotion saw their chief brought down by the bullets of the enemy. Thus they remained, while the right and centre of the army was put to flight; and then, falling back in good order, with colours flying and pipes playing, joined the remainder of the second line. Another danger was already threatening the rear and right flank of the line so formed. By this time the Argyleshire Highlanders, supported by some English horse, had broken gaps through the park walls on the right of the insurgents, had passed through the breaches so made, and formed up on the open moor beyond. Had these been reinforced in time, the retreat of the defeated army might have been cut off.

The remnant of the insurgent army, with which perhaps an effectual endeavour might still have been made to restore the fight, did not long remain compact and united. It was pressed by the royal troops in front and flank, and was forced into two divisions. Of these the smaller, composed of the French auxiliaries, and some of the Lowland troops, who were naturally tempted to trust more to roads than rugged pathways across the hills, were driven back towards Inverness, where they were forced to lay down their arms. The other, preserving some degree of order, but thinned every moment by men who quitted the ranks to hasten singly to their homes, made its way to Ruthven and Badenoch. Fourteen stands of colours, 2,300 muskets, and all the cannons and baggage of the insurgent army fell into the hands of the King's troops. It was reckoned that the loss in the Royal ranks amounted to 310 men, while that of the insurgents was about 1,000, or a fifth of their army. Quarter was seldom given to the stragglers and fugitives, except to a few who were kept back for public execution. The wounded were most of them put to death on the following day. At the close of the battle the horse and the dragoons had closed in upon the insurgents upon both wings. They were cruel in the moment of success, and only too eager to avenge the previous defeats of their comrades at Preston and Falkirk against the unhappy victims who now fell into their power. A general carnage ensued; the moor was covered with blood; and the men, according to an eye-witness, what with killing the enemy and dabling their feet in the blood, and splashing it about one another, looked like so many butchers. The road from Culloden to Inverness was everywhere strewed with dead bodies. The wounded insurgents were permitted to be left among the dead on the field of battle, stripped of their clothes, in bitter weather, from Wednesday, the day of the engagement, till the afternoon of Friday, when detachments were sent to knock on the head those who were still alive, and some who had resisted the effects of the continual rains which had fallen till this time, were then despatched. A barn, where many of the wounded Highlanders had taken refuge, was set on fire, and the unfortunate wretches burnt together with the walls. Soldiers were stationed round the building, who with fixed bayonets drove back any miserable men who attempted to save themselves. The conduct of the generals who commanded in the royal ranks was certainly most severe, and much of the severity is said to have been due to the counsels of General Hawley, whose character for ferocity has been certainly thoroughly established.

From the field of Culloden Charles rode with a few followers to Gortuleg, where Lord Lovat was residing; but the latter was far too much engrossed with the danger that might ensue to himself to bestow any sympathy or compassion on the Prince. He accordingly passed on, and on the morning of the 17th, with his little party, gained Glengarry's castle of Invergarry before daybreak. The battle of Culloden decided the campaign and the invasion. France had already abandoned all idea of an expedition against the southern coast when the retreat from Derby commenced. The news of the defeat of the Highland army at Culloden confirmed this resolution of the Court of Versailles. The further efforts of the French government were confined to sending two vessels to aid in the escape of the Chevalier, who, after many months of wandering, privation, hardship, and danger amidst the Highlands and islands of the western coast, was enabled to embark on the 20th of September, five months after the battle of Culloden, at Lochnanuagh, the same point at which he had landed at the time of his descent on the coast of Scotland. With Lochiel and about 100 more fugitives, he embarked, and landed at the small port of Roscoff, in Brittany, on the 29th September.

After the battle of Culloden the Duke of Cumberland fixed his head-quarters near Fort Augustus, in the centre of the insurgent districts, whence parties were detached, who laid waste the rebels' country, plundered their houses, burnt their cabins, carried away their cattle, and reduced the people to such misery and destitution, that the women and children sometimes followed the bands of soldiers, praying for the offal of their own cattle to sustain the sparks of a flickering life. Every brutality seems to have been perpetrated in the camps and the expeditions of the conquerors; for which, if truth is told,

General Hawley appears to have been personally responsible. Matrons and maidens suffered from the brutal and profligate soldiery horrors which to the women of the Highlands must have been worse than death; while races of naked native women on horseback were held at Fort Augustus for the amusement of the troops.

It is beyond the province of this work to go further into the history of the rebellion. The battle of Culloden decided the fate of the invasion. Penal steps were taken for the punishment of the chiefs, the clansmen, and the soldiers who were implicated in this last effort to place the House of Stuart on the throne of these islands; while legislative measures were soon after enforced, which broke down the feudal power of the mountain chieftains, disarmed the clansmen, and destroying the military character of the Highlands, prevented these districts in future from being a hotbed for a rebellion in the cause of the Stuarts, which might be made use of by a hostile government, at any time, to create a diversion for an invasion of England.

The war between France and England was terminated two years afterwards by the peace of Aix-la-Chapelle, which was signed in 1748. One of the conditions of the treaty was that the government of France should no longer afford an asylum to the family of the Pretender to the throne of Great Britain. Prince Charles Edward was reluctantly compelled to quit France and to take refuge in Italy, where he gradually sank into a life of dissipation, which alienated many of his supporters from him, while the moderate policy of the English government and the glories which the country gained under the subsequent administration of Pitt, linked the great majority of the nation firmly in a loyal bond of affectionate union to the House of Guelph.

CHAPTER XVII.

INVASIONS IN CONNECTION WITH THE AMERICAN COLONIES.

AUTHORITIES.—Lord Mahon's "History of England;" Regimental Records of the British Army; Allan's "Battles of the British Navy;" in Carlyle's "Frederick the Great" will be found a picturesque description of the actions of Quiberon; the "Annual Register" commences in 1758, the first part of this work is attributed to Burke; the "Life of Pitt," by Stanhope; and Lord Macaulay's two Essays on him; together with the "Life of Pitt," by Thackeray; Duncan's "History of the Royal Artillery;" Bancroft's "History of the United States;" Massey's "History of England, from the Accession of George III.;" Walpole's "Memoirs of the Early Reign of George III.;" Mr. Green's excellent "History of the English People;" may be consulted with advantage.

By the peace of Aix-la-Chapelle both parties to the quarrel which had raged between France and England restored their conquests. In England it was considered, with the usual want of foresight which distinguishes our insular administration of military affairs, that now peace was secured, immediate retrenchment must begin in the military and naval establishments. Regiments were disbanded, and those that were maintained were reduced to a strength of 285 men, including officers; while in each battalion the numbers of companies were diminished. Multitudes of half-pay officers and soldiers were thrown upon the country. These had no occupation or employment, and many of the soldiers turned to a mode of life which little, if at all, differed from that of highwaymen. The consequence was that public indignation was aroused, and a new clause was inserted in the Mutiny Bill for 1749, by which half-pay officers and privates were rendered amenable to military law. A wiser and more merciful method of dealing with the disbanded soldiery was, on the instigation of Captain Coram, found in establishing a military colony on the coast of Nova Scotia, which was named Halifax, after Lord Halifax, who was the President of the Board of Trade, and which has now grown into the thriving commercial port of that name.

Although the English ministry reduced the military force of the crown with no sparing hand on the conclusion of the peace of Aix-la-Chapelle, it was soon seen that this treaty had only been under pressure of force agreed in by some of the continental powers; war between France and England soon again threatened. The quarrel now was not on account of any increase of territory in Europe. The squabbles of a few colonists in the distant mountains of America led to this war between the mother countries. The French settlers in the valleys of the St. Lawrence and the Mississippi desired to connect their settlements in Canada and Louisiana by a chain of forts, and, determined to check the spread of the English colonies, declared that our countrymen should not fix their settlements beyond the Alleghanies. To enforce this command, and as a link in the chain of military communication to extend from the St. Lawrence to the Mississippi,

Fort Duquesne was planted on the waters of the Ohio, amidst pathless woods and swampy marshes, where now rises the busy and smoky city of Pittsburg, encircled with furnaces and factories. The Fort of Niagara, also on the St. Lawrence, and that of Ticonderoga on Lake Champlain, supported by a chain of less important posts, threatened to sever the English colonies on the coast from any possibility of extension over the prairies of the west. In 1755 General Braddock was sent against Fort Duquesne with a small force of regulars and of colonial militia. A part of this latter was under the command of Colonel George Washington, who is now well known throughout the world as the great and good Washington, the first President of the United States. Contemptuous of the auxiliary force and of the Indians who marched in his train, and who might have been utilised as spies, Braddock fell into an ambush, and was repulsed with great slaughter and loss to his men. It was now necessary for the English government to take serious measures, as war between France and England was inevitable, both on account of America and India too, where a Frence adventurer was founding a French empire and planning the expulsion of English merchants from their settlements along the coast. In the war which then ensued between England and France the true alliance which naturally should exist between England and Prussia was first commenced. The Queen of Hungary, by a startling change of policy, had as early as 1752 secretly drawn to the alliance of France and Spain, while Saxony and Russia, in league with her, had formed a secret agreement for the partition of Prussia. In 1755 the league of these five Powers was silently completed. So secret were the negotiations that the Duke of Newcastle, who was at the head of the English ministry, was not aware of any intention of the kind. But the keen eye of Frederick of Prussia had detected the secret alliance from its origin. He proposed to England an alliance between himself and the King of England. War was soon after imminent, and as it was evident that Hanover lay exposed to the attack of the French, and would suffer on account of its connection with England in the quarrel that was about to ensue, it was only natural that the English ministry should gladly welcome an alliance with the King of Prussia, the first soldier of the age. The conclusion of this alliance at the close of 1755 gave the signal for the Seven Years' War.

The struggle threatened to be gigantic; but with such sweeping retrenchment had the military establishments of our country been reduced on the conclusion of the peace of Aix-la-Chapelle, that only three regiments fit for service were in England at the commencement of 1756. France, on the other hand, was well prepared, and she opened the war with vigour and energy. Fort Mahon in Minorca, the key of the Mediterranean, which was then in the occupation of the English, was besieged by an expedition under the Duke of Rochelle and forced to capitulate. A fleet sent to raise the siege under Admiral Byng retreated before the French, to the rage and mortification of the English people. In Germany, Frederick had grasped Dresden at the commencement of the war, and forced the Saxon army to surrender at Pirna. In 1757 his victory of Prague laid Bohemia at his feet; but a defeat at Kolin drove him back again into Saxony. In this year the Duke of Cumberland, who had occupied the line of the Weser with an army of 50,000 men, to defend Hanover, was forced to retire before a French army to the mouth of the Elbe, and compelled by the Convention of Closter-seven to disband his forces. A despondency such as perhaps never either before or since possessed our country, fell upon it on the news of this reverse, and Chesterfield groaned in despair, " We are no longer a nation."

But at the moment that the people were raging, and some statesmen were despairing, our country was on the eve of its greatest triumphs. The early disasters of the war drove the Duke of Newcastle from the direction of affairs before a storm of popular anger, and in November, 1756, the great genius of William Pitt undertook the government of England. In a few months Pitt was forced to resign and Newcastle returned to office. But in July, 1757, it was seen that Pitt was the only man who could save the country. His genius roused in the nation a temper which made ultimate defeat impossible, and though there were many errors and many failures in his earlier military operations, yet Pitt seems to have been the only minister who ever combined the power of diplomacy and of military energy which causes a ruler to make his nation great and triumphant. Probably from the time of Pitt till the time of Bismarck, no single man has, in his own mind, embraced so many of the qualifications necessary for the statesman as distinguished from the politician, and the general as distinguished from the sergeant-major. Frederick of Prussia, afterwards recognising a genius parallel with his own, exclaimed, "England has long been in labour, but she has at last brought forth a man."

The French government had been a good deal surprised at the treaty between Prussia and England, but affected to take little notice of its importance. They declared quietly, hinting at an invasion, that perhaps there were places nearer home where the French troops could be employed to more advantage than in Germany, the neutrality of which was guaranteed in the treaties of the alliance of our country with Prussia. And the danger of an invasion was not slight. There had been great diligence in French dockyards, many troops had been moved to the coast, and it was tolerably clear that an invasion of England was likely to be attempted.

Both England and France were alike fiercely determined on war. But the state of preparation of the two countries was widely different. The French, although their navy had suffered much in the previous war, had now got war-ships again, and seriously meant to try the question of supremacy at sea once more. In England, as has been before remarked, there were only three regiments in the country, and the Duke of Newcastle, the first minister of the crown, did not dare to have colonels, still less higher officers, appointed, because the Duke of Cumberland would claim the privilege of naming them, and he was hostile to the ministry, and would name political enemies to his Grace.

The country was seized with terror. Cries arose that Hessians should be hired and Hanoverians subsidised to defend our country from the French; that application should be made to the Dutch for the 6,000 men which they were bound by treaty to furnish us. But the Dutch piteously proclaimed the dire necessity that they themselves should guard their country against France, and that they must keep their men in Holland. The English government had no power to enforce the treaty, and the Dutch auxiliaries remained at home. Hessians and Hanoverians were sent for to guard against the invasion. About 10,000 from each country did land. The native population immediately became disgusted with them, and refused to billet them. The following extract from Carlyle's "Frederick the Great" describes graphically the state of affairs at this time:—

"The native population very sulky on them (the Hessians and Hanoverians). We will not billet you, not we; build huts and be ——. With much parliamentary newspaper commentary going on of a distressful nature. Saturday, 15th May, 1756, Hessians disembark at Southampton, obliged to pitch camp in the neighbourhood. Friday, 21st May, the Hanoverians at Chatham, who hut themselves Canterbury way, and have what is the sum total of their achievements in this country, a case of shoplifting. Pocket-handkerchief across the counter in open day, and the fellow not to be tried by us for it, which enrages the constitutional heart. Alas, my heavy-laden constitutional heart; but what can we do? These drilled soldiers will guard us should this terrible invasion land."

But there was no need for the Hessians and Hanoverians, because the movement of troops towards the coast, as if for an invasion of England, was a feint to cover the departure of the expedition against Minorca, which succeeded in taking that place. On the 2nd December, 1756, the session of Parliament was opened with Pitt as Secretary of State. Under his energetic hand, immediate measures were taken for the increase of the military forces; and the scheme of a national militia was in the Speech from the Throne recommended to the care and diligence of Parliament. Already in the previous year, when war was seen to be likely, in order to obtain light horsemen, whose value had been proved in the previous war, measures were taken permanently to establish light dragoons in the British service. A troop of light dragoons was ordered to be added to the 1st, 2nd, and 3rd regiments of Dragoon Guards; and to the 1st, 2nd, 3rd, 4th, 6th, 7th, 10th, and 11th regiments of Dragoons, as well as to the 1st, 2nd, 3rd, and 4th Irish Horse, which now form the 4th, 5th, 6th, and 7th Dragoon Guards; but the 5th, 8th, 9th, 12th, 13th, and 14th Dragoons, being on the Irish establishment, did not receive the same addition. These troops of light dragoons were mounted, armed, equipped, and trained, according to specific instructions, calculated to render them available for the services for which they were designed. Several of them were reviewed in Hyde

Park in 1756 by His Majesty, and their neat appearance, celerity of movement, and the exact manner in which they performed their evolutions, were much admired by the populace. At the same time we find the regiments of foot-guards practising the Prussian pike exercise in Hyde Park, so the military preparations apparently began to be seriously made. It was also announced that the unpopular foreign soldiers should be ordered to return to Germany. During the summer the Hessians were encamped near Winchester, the Hanoverians near Maidstone. When the cold season came on, and the magistrates refused to billet foreigners in the public-houses, the wretched soldiers were left in their camps, exposed to the wind and rain, until the transports were ready for their return. Under all circumstances, during their stay in this country the conduct of these German troops was not only free from all exception, but most exemplary. Their discipline, good conduct, and sobriety were very different from the conduct of the profligate and immoral English soldiery such as we find it, not at the now spoken of time, for there were almost no soldiers, but in the previous war. The case of shoplifting to which Mr. Carlyle so graphically alludes is now clearly allowed to have been due to a mistake, by which the foreigner, buying handkerchiefs in a shop, took away erroneously the whole piece, containing six, having paid only for four, through misunderstanding. A robbery was sworn against the man, and he was committed to gaol. The action of the commanding officer caused, however, hot clamours amongst the constitutional people of England, as Count Kilmansegge, ignorant of our law, applied to the Secretary of State, who signed an arbitrary warrant for the soldier's release. This despotic action of an English minister raised a popular uproar, and was avenged upon Count Kilmansegge, who was ordered to leave the country immediately, and upon the unhappy soldier, who atoned for the sin of the minister by receiving 300 lashes. It is hardly necessary to point out that this occurred before Pitt was associated with the ministry, and while the pusillanimous Duke of Newcastle alone held direction of affairs. The foreign troops which had been summoned to England by the King at the express request of both Houses of Parliament were accordingly sent away as soon as the popular mind recovered from the terror of invasion, and lampoons and diatribes were hurled against the Sovereign for his supposed partiality for his Hanoverian subjects. The gratitude of the English nation is indeed wonderful.

Although Pitt himself, almost from the day of his appointment, became bedridden with gout, and could take but little part in the parliamentary campaign, the vigour of his nature was seen in the preparations for carrying on the war. 55,000 men were voted by the House of Commons for sea service, and 45,000 for land service. Reinforcements were despatched to the Earl of Loudon, the new Commander-in-Chief in the American plantations, while fresh regiments were rapidly raised at home. The total supplies granted for the year amounted to 8,300,000*l.*, the national debt being at the outset of the war about 72,000,000*l.*, having decreased but 6,000,000*l.*, notwithstanding all the retrenchments in the military and naval service in the seven years since the conclusion of the treaty of Aix-la-Chapelle.

But Pitt was not content to rely on the ordinary methods or usual system of raising soldiery. With the originality of true genius, he commenced at this period his bold, but, as it was afterwards proved, most safe and wise policy, of raising regiments of Highlanders from the lately disaffected clans. We who have read of and seen the gallant actions of the Highlanders in Egypt, the Peninsula, the Low Countries, and the Crimea, can hardly realise that any should have doubted of the success of this experiment. Yet there were grave fears expressed by even far-seeing statesmen, and it was only with a due sense of pride that Chatham himself, in after years, recalled the memory of the House of Lords to the boldness of his step in the following words:—" My lords, we should not want men in a good cause; I remember how I employed the very rebels in the service and defence of their country; they were reclaimed by that means; they fought our battles; they cheerfully bled in defence of those liberties which they had attempted to overthrow but a few years before."[1]

Another measure of public defence was the new modelling of a national militia. Pitt had already brought in a bill for this object in a previous session, but it was rejected by the Lords, chiefly through the

[1] Speech in House of Lords, December 2nd, 1777.

instigation of Lord Hardwicke. This nobleman objected to the establishment of the militia on the curious ground that their being exercised on Sunday, as was proposed, would lead to constant fairs and scenes of jollity in the several parishes where those exercises might be held, notwithstanding an injunction being given to the men to previously go to church; and he considered that if this was permitted, the face of religion would soon be abolished from the country. On account of this supposed danger, the idea of creating this force for the defence of the nation was abandoned. It would appear that at this time the militia were intended to be of much the same character as the present volunteers, and to be formed of men engaged in civil pursuits, and in ordinary avocations of life, and only to be embodied and called out in case of actually being required to take the field.

As soon as Pitt took office a bill was again brought into the House of Commons by Colonel George Townshend, eldest son of Lord Townshend, to form a militia. After many discussions in the Commons, it underwent several amendments, and notably the number of militiamen proposed in the Lower House was reduced to half, namely, 32,340 for England and Wales. During the progress of the bill through Parliament its objects had been most popular with the nation at large. No sooner had it passed, however, than the people who had clamoured for it found that it pressed heavily upon themselves; and, as is usual with the populace, which ever desires to make others fight its battles and become soldiers, but objects very much to any military hardships thrown upon itself, the Act became highly unpopular.

Although the invasion from France, which had been threatened at the beginning of 1756, had been diverted to Minorca, there was a constant danger of invasion during the time that the military preparations of this country were in such a backward condition. The great genius of Pitt from the beginning perceived that the true defence against an invasion of this island is the power of taking the offensive against an enemy, and of compelling him, through fear of his own dominions, to retain at home those troops which might be launched against our shores. In 1758, accordingly, expeditions were sent by the English ministry against the coasts of Brittany and Normandy, and against Rochefort, and did some damage to French towns and villages. But as there was not force sufficiently available to furnish a large army, these expeditions were little more than buccaneering descents, and were not pushed with sufficient strength to enable them to threaten the enemy's capital; though such must be ever the true objective point in war. It is manifest that when the French were threatening English interests on the Ohio and in India, if the English government had been able to push an army into France, defeat the French troops under the walls of Paris, and dictate a peace in the capital of the French government, it would have been absolutely necessary for the King of France to consent to any terms which might have been insisted upon. In the same way, at the present time, when there is public anxiety in

England lest Russia may advance through the sterile deserts and over the trackless steppes of Central Asia against our Indian Empire, it seems to be entirely forgotten that if Russia seriously contemplates the annexation of our Indian dominions, it would be much more easy for her to attempt an invasion of England, and to settle the question of supremacy in the Orient by a battle on the banks of the Thames. Should an action in front of London go against the British arms, there would be no resource for our government but to accede to any terms which a victor might demand, and to hand over, if required, without a blow being struck out of Europe, the entire control over the rich plains of Hindustan.

In 1757, as soon as Pitt returned to office at the beginning of July, although the session was too far advanced for him to exert much influence on that year's campaign, which was so unfortunate for English arms in Germany, he applied himself to the fitting-out of a secret expedition against France, which was intended to make a descent on Rochefort, and capture there one of the chief French naval magazines. This blow was calculated as a powerful diversion for the armies of the Duke of Cumberland and the King of Prussia. The opportunity was favourable for such an enterprise, since over 100,000 French troops had marched to Germany, and scarcely 10,000 remained to protect the coast of France itself from St. Valéry to Bordeaux. The expedition was unsuccessful, but it is well worthy to be remembered, as in it Colonel Wolfe, afterwards the conqueror of Canada, first attracted the notice of the great minister who was directing the affairs of the country. In 1758 British expeditions were directed against Cherbourg and St. Malo, but these were only on the buccaneering scale; while the French were gradually pushed back to the Rhine by Prince Ferdinand in Germany, through his victory at Crafeld. He had, however, subsequently to retire into Westphalia. In the course of that year the British navy reaped some of its brightest laurels. It captured or destroyed 16 French men-of-war, 49 privateers, and 104 merchant ships. The enemy had in the latter respect the advantage, for their capture of merchant ships exceeded 300, while of our privateers they took only 7, of our men-of-war only 3.

Early in 1759 the court of Versailles, stung with the success of the allied Prussians and British in the previous year, determined in good earnest on a descent upon the shores of England. At Havre and several other ports flat-bottomed boats were built to assist the projected invasion, and large fleets were equipped at Toulon and Brest, besides a small squadron in Dunkirk, under the command of a brave and skilful seaman, named Thourot. In England preparations were made to resist the invasion. All the country squires were in regimentals. The militia was embodied, while a British fleet, numerically superior to the French, swept up and down the Channel. At this time the first attempt which is found upon record was made to render the militia a force available for the general defence of the country, instead of, as hitherto, only of their own counties. In May powers were taken to enable the government to march the regiments of militia out of their several shires. In July Admiral George Rodney, under the instructions of the ministry, cast anchor in the roads of Havre, and began a bombardment, which continued for fifty-two hours without intermission, destroying many of the newly-constructed flat-bottomed boats intended for the conveyance of troops, and causing considerable damage to the town itself. In August the fleet which the French had assembled at Toulon put out to sea in order to join the fleets assembled in the northern ports. It was pursued immediately by Admiral Boscawen from Gibraltar, and attacked off Lagos, in Algarve. Of its largest vessels two were captured and two others run ashore. In the Downs an English squadron watched the preparations for invasion which were being made at Dunkirk, while an English fleet, under Sir Edward Hawke, blockaded Brest.

But with a true appreciation of the advantage of assuming the offensive in order to provide for defence at home, an expedition was despatched against the French islands in the West Indies, consisting of six regiments and several ships of war. A still more important enterprise was undertaken, the conquest of Canada, which remained a French colony in North America, although the other dominions and dependencies in that continent, which had been formerly French, had already fallen into our hands. To command the expedition against the French colony of Canada, Wolfe was selected. It is hardly necessary to recall the bold attack upon Quebec, or the heroic death of its designer. The surrender of Quebec gave Canada to England, and led to the annihilation of the French power in America.

On the very day (the 20th November, 1759) that Pitt was speaking in a debate in the House of Commons upon a monument to Wolfe, a great victory was achieved by the British navy. We have seen that the preparations for the French expedition against England from Havre had been interrupted by the bombardment of Rodney in July, while Thourot was blockaded in Dunkirk, and the French fleet from Toulon was rendered *hors-de-combat* by Boscawen off Lagos.

During the whole summer the Brest fleet had been closely blockaded by Admiral Sir Edward Hawke, while some frigates under Commodore Duff cruised along the coast to the southward, from Orient to Oléron. Within Brest Admiral Conflans had the supervision of many preparations for the invasion. At Vannes, where the ships of Duff were watching, preparations were also being made. 18,000 troops were massed at these two places, and large numbers of flat-bottomed boats were ready for their embarkation. While Hawke watched the outlets of his harbours, Conflans, however, dared not go to sea with convoys of transports. On the 9th November a wild gale of wind drove Hawke from the coast of France to Torbay. The French admiral rapidly seized the opportunity, and put to sea on the 14th November, with twenty-one ships of the line and four frigates. He intended to attack and overpower the squadron of Duff before the larger fleet could come to its assistance. But Hawke had weighed anchor from Torbay immediately he could profit by the slightest variation of the weather; and hearing that the French fleet was out of Brest, crowded every stitch of canvas that the wind would allow him to carry. At break of day on the 20th November the English admiral signalled "a fleet in sight;" and soon after, "the French fleet in sight." The day of trial had come.

The French admiral was of about the same strength as Hawke, and much was expected of his fleet by France. But, with the addition of the squadron of Duff, the English admiral was superior in strength to the French. He had a stronger force by two ships of the line and six frigates. At the moment that Hawke came in sight Conflans was endeavouring to open the way for the convoy from Vannes, and was in hot chase of Commodore Duff and his small squadron, which had been blockading the troops there. These were running with all their canvas available, while the French fleet followed in hot pursuit. On a sudden the little squadron, aware of the appearance of Hawke, whirled round, and with a sky-rending cheer commenced advancing towards the French. The French admiral, astonished, perceived that Hawke was coming down from windward at his highest speed, and that now he must prepare to be chased, and give over chasing. About eleven o'clock Hawke was close down upon the French, and eight of his foremost ships were sweeping on for action.

The French admiral at first determined to fight, formed line-of-battle, and made an attempt to resist, but seeing the whole British fleet closing up, he decided to draw his ships close in shore towards the mouth of the Vilaine, and to take shelter along the shoaly coasts in nooks guarded by granite rocks and craggy islets, and dangerous with shoals and quicksands, which were naturally unknown to the English masters. The weather was extremely bad, and almost a gale of wind was blowing. But neither the terrors of an unknown coast, nor those of a winter storm, even on an early closing winter day, prevented the English admiral from engaging. Probably, had Newcastle still held the reins of power in England, excuses would not have been wanting for the fleet not coming into action, but the energy of Pitt communicated itself to all of those who served under him. Under his administration the leaders both of the land and sea services viewed obstacles and dangers only as a spur to exertion, and as an additional stimulus to fame. Such is always the case when great men guide the destinies of a nation. The same has been seen under Frederick of Prussia ; under Napoleon ; in the camp of Wellington ; and at the present day under the ruler of Germany.

The English admiral gave the signal for immediate action, but it was two o'clock before he, with his vanguard of eight vessels, could close with Conflans. Hawke himself, passing by the rest of the hostile fleet with his own vessel, the *Royal George*, reserved his fire for the *Soleil Royal*, which bore French admiral, and was at this time the largest vessel in the French navy. The navigating officer represented to Hawke the dangers of the coast and the perils of the navigation; but the admiral answered, "You have done your duty in this remonstrance; you are now to obey my orders: lay me alongside the French admiral."

Conflans waited and exchanged a couple of broadsides with the *Royal George*, but then sheered off, finding the fire too heavy. The French vice-admiral also poured a broadside into Hawke's vessel, and then also moved away, satisfied with the return. Some four other vessels in succession also poured their broadsides into him, so that the *Royal George* seemed swallowed in volcanoes of fire and smoke, and the blue flag of the admiral flying from her mast was invisible for some time. But although the smoke was great, and the *Royal George* seemed buried in its heavy clouds, the firing of the French gunners was very bad, and various British ships were crowding all their canvas to come to the aid of their commander. A fifth vessel, *La Superbe*, a seventy-four, that came up against Hawke, was answered by all the guns of one side of the *Royal George* together, which sent *La Superbe* to the bottom in a hideously sudden manner. One other, the *Thisbé*, had already sunk in fighting, and the *Soleil* and the *Héros* were running shoreward. By the close of the action four French vessels were sunk, while two others had struck. The rest of the French squadron sought refuge, more or less damaged, by running up the Vilaine; and the country people, to the number of 10,000, who had been crowded on the shore to watch the battle, disappeared into the interior, sad at heart and sorrowful at the disgrace which had fallen on the white flag.

Such a night as followed had seldom been witnessed before. Walpole says, the roaring of the elements was redoubled by the batteries from our ships, and both concurred in that scene of horror to put a period to the navy and hopes of France. During the whole night Hawke heard guns of distress, but could not tell whether from friend or foe, nor yet, on account of the weather, offer any assistance. Seven French ships of the line, which got into the shoals, lay there fourteen months, strictly watched by British vessels; thumping against the shallow bottom every tide, till their backs were broken, and only three liners, with three frigates, ever got out again. Eight more escaped into the river Charente; the French admiral's own ship and another were run on shore and burnt; one was captured by the English, two, with their crews, were sent to the bottom. Lord Howe, who attacked *La Formidable*, bore down on her with such violence that her prow forced in his lower tier of guns. Captain Digby, in the *Dunkerque*, received the fire of twelve of the enemy's ships; but so unskilful were their gunners that he lost not a single man. Keppel's vessel was full of water, and he thought her sinking, when a sudden squall emptied his ship. But he was informed all his powder was gone; then said he, "I am sorry I am safe." They came and told him a small quantity was undamaged, " Very well," said he, " attack again."

Not above eight of our ships were engaged in obtaining

this decisive victory. In the morning it was found that besides the French ships stranded, two British, the *Resolution* and the *Essex* had been lost, having become entangled in the shoals; but all their men and part of their stores were saved. The number of our killed had been but forty, of our wounded but 200. Such was the entire loss attending this important victory, won in the midst of storm and tempest, which ended all thoughts of the threatened invasion in force from France, and gave the finishing blow to the naval power of that country during the whole remainder of the Seven Years' war. This brilliant result seems to have been almost entirely due to the superior gunnery of the British seamen; surely when gunnery has become more scientific than it was one hundred years ago, it is more than ever necessary for our country to nurture and foster a similar superiority.

Hawke continued watching the mouths of the Vilaine and Charente rivers for a good while after the action, and without interruption henceforth. Supplies of fresh provisions had come to him from England all the summer, but had latterly been stopped by the wild weather.[1] The British seamen, with sarcastic appreciation of the gratitude which the British people usually feel towards their

[1] Walpole's "George II. and III." 232. Here is the list of ships accurately made out, according to Mr. Carlyle:—"First, *Formidable*, struck about 4 p.m.; second, *Thisbé*, sunk by a tumble it got while in action under an unskilful captain; third, *La Superbe*, sunk; fourth, *Héros*, struck, could not be boarded, such bad weather, and recommenced next day, but had to run and strand itself, and be burnt by the English; as did also fifth, the *Soleil Royal*, flagship of Conflans; Conflans and crew, like those of the *Héros*, getting out in time."

soldiers and sailors, the moment that the terror of an enemy is removed, passed round the fleet the following stave, which, as Carlyle says, has "a wrinkle of briny humour grinning through it."

> "Till Hawke did bang Monsieur Conflang,
> You sent us beef and beer;
> Now, Monsieur's beat, we've naught to eat,
> Since you have naught to fear."

This stave is worthy to be placed in the same rank as the more modern one, which says—

> "When danger's near, and foes are nigh,
> On God and the soldier is all our cry;
> When the enemy's beat, or the danger righted,
> God is forgotten, and the soldier slighted."

The invasion that had been contemplated from France at this time was on a grand scale. It had been intended through the means of 500 flat-bottomed boats and other transports, to carry over and land in England more than 54,000 men. Many regiments had already been ordered on the expedition, and a number of the king's guards were also to go. The Prince de Conti had been designated as the Commander-in-Chief of the expedition, and with him were associated as generals the Prince de Soubise and an Irish Jacobite of the name of Thourot.

The same gale which drove Hawke away from the front of Brest had driven the British blockading squadron from before Dunkirk. There the brave and able Thourot seized the opportunity to make his escape; but his force did not consist of more than five ships; and with these, in order to give time for a general and simultaneous attack on the English coasts, he at first sought shelter along the shores of Norway and Sweden. It appears that he had as his instructions a descent on the north coast of Ireland, in order to act as a diversion, and to prevent the regiments of the Irish establishment being taken over to England, in order to assist in the defence of the country against the main invasion. On his escape from Dunkirk Thourot first steered for Gottenborg in Sweden, and thence to Bergen in Norway. Here he remained some weeks, and then, sailing round the north of Scotland, attempted to land near Londonderry. The vessels with which he left Dunkirk consisted of the *Maréchal de Bellelisle*, of forty-four guns ; the *Bégon*, the *Blonde*, the *Terpsichore*, each of thirty guns, and *Le Marente*, of twenty-four guns, having on board 1,270 soldiers and 700 seamen ; 200 of the troops were disembarked on account of sickness before they sailed, and at Gottenborg and Bergen. During a violent storm, as Thourot was about to attempt a landing in the vicinity of Derry, the wind became tempestuous, and blew him again out to sea. Then the *Marente* parted company, and never again joined. Blown away from the coast of Ireland by this storm, he steered north, and anchored off the Island of Isla, where he was forced to put in for fresh provisions, of which he stood greatly in need. For these he punctually paid, instead of plundering, as he so easily might have done, the defenceless people. As Lord Stanhope says, indeed throughout the expedition the honour and humanity of this brave adventurer are warmly acknowledged by his enemies.

At Isla, Thourot obtained the first tidings of the defeat of Conflans; but as he could not be sure that this intelligence was not invented for the purpose of deceiving him, and as he felt unwilling to return without making an effort, he adhered to his resolution of descending upon Ireland. The weather no sooner permitted, after he had obtained his provisions, than he steered for the Bay of Carrickfergus, and on the 28th of February, 1760, effected an unopposed landing with 600 men; his ships at this time having been reduced to three.[1] The garrison of Carrickfergus consisted only of four companies, chiefly composed of recruits under the command of Lieutenant-Colonel Jennings. The town itself was defended only by a ruinous wall; nevertheless the gates were shut, and a sharp fire of small arms was kept up against the French. The French prisoners in custody at Carrickfergus had previously been sent to Belfast. A regular attack was soon commenced by the French, and sustained by the British, as a French author says, "with their usual spirit," until all the English ammunition was expended. Then the little garrison retired to the castle, which was in all respects untenable, not only on account of the wall having a breach fifty feet in width, but also from the total want of provisions and ammunition. It is stated, that notwithstanding the want of cartridges, the assailants were repulsed in their first attack, even after the gate was burst open, the "enthusiastic heroism of

---

[1] Lord Stanhope makes this descent the 28th of February, the French authorities assert it to have been accomplished on the 21st; but the difference is of slight importance.

Britons supplying the want of shot with stones and rubbish." This is, however, only from an English account, written in order to prove to England the improbability of the success of a French invasion against this country, and appears a little exaggerated by patriotism. Finally, Jennings was forced to surrender, though not unconditionally, as it was arranged that his men were not to be sent prisoners to France, but to be ransomed by the exchange of an equal number of French prisoners in their places.

Thourot demanded a supply of fresh provisions from the magistrates of Carrickfergus, which they were imprudent enough to refuse. The town was accordingly plundered, and a contribution levied. He had now received certain news of the defeat of Conflans at Quiberon, and also ascertained that several thousand men, regulars, militia, and volunteers, were being assembled at Belfast to act against him. He therefore hastily re-embarked his soldiers and sailed away. But about nine o'clock on the morning of the 28th, when he had not been many hours out of Carrickfergus, he was brought to by Captain John Elliott with three English frigates. These had been lying in the harbour of Kinsale, when orders came from the Duke of Bedford, the Lord-Lieutenant, for them to go in search of the French expedition. A hot engagement ensued. The vessels were equal in number, being exactly three frigates to three. Thourot displayed his usual courage, and fought his ship until she was nearly filled with water, and the deck was covered with killed and wounded. At length he himself was slain. The fall of so gallant a chief disheartened not only his own, but the other French crews, and Elliott was cannonading them hotly. The whole of the three French frigates struck their colours. Captain Elliott's lieutenant boarded the *Belleisle*, and these vessels were carried captive to Ramsey Bay, in the Isle of Man, to be repaired. The loss of the English in killed and wounded did not exceed forty men, but the French lost over three hundred. This, and the relative proportion of loss at Quiberon, shows conclusively that at this time the naval battles between the French and the English were mainly decided by the superior skill of gunnery shown by the English sailors. Probably that skill in gunnery was considerably aided by the skill in seamanship, which allowed the guns to be advantageously placed, worked and pointed.

Thus ended the invasion which was attempted during the Seven Years' War against the coasts of England. This war was brought to a close by the peace of Paris in September 1762. By no war has England's fame, glory, or gain been so increased as it was during this contest. By it she obtained possession of India and America. In the first the French abandoned all right to any military settlement; in the second they yielded up Canada and Nova Scotia. Never has our country played so great a part in the history of mankind as in the latter years of that war. Three of its many victories were decisive for many years to come of the destinies of the world. " With the victory of Rossbach, gained by the brilliant strategical genius of Frederick, began the restoration of Germany, and its political union under the leadership of Prussia and her kings. With that of Plassey the influence of Europe told for the first time since the days of Alexander on the nations of the East."[1]

"The world," in Burke's gorgeous phrase, "saw one of the races of the north-east cast into the heart of Asia new manners, new doctrines, new institutions. With the triumph of Wolfe on the heights of Abraham, began the history of the United States of America."

INVASION IN CONNECTION WITH THE INDEPENDENCE OF AMERICA.

The very colonies on account of which England had originally embarked in the Seven Years' War were about twenty years later forced by British misgovernment to shake off their allegiance to and connection with the mother country, and to declare themselves an independent nation, under the style and title of the United States of America. The independence of the United States was recognised by France in two treaties of commerce and alliance, that were signed at Paris on the 6th February, 1778. But for some weeks it was endeavoured to keep these treaties secret so as to afford further time for the coveted accession of Spain to the alliance. During some weeks, accordingly, the official announcement of the treaties to the Court of St. James's was postponed, but the negotiation between the American

[1] Green's "Short History of the English People."

commissioners and the French government did not long remain a secret to the British ambassador at Paris, nor even to the British public. On the 13th March, in the same year, however, the French ambassador in London, the Marquis de Noailles, delivered to the Secretary of State, Lord Weymouth, a note formally announcing the treaty of friendship and commerce as lately signed between France and the United States. The note was couched in terms of irony, almost of derision, and stated that the United States " are in full possession of independence, as pronounced by them on the 4th July, 1776." As at this moment the troops of the King and the troops of what was regarded by the English government as the rebellious colonists were in open arms against each other, this French note could only be regarded as an insult. The British ambassador was ordered to return from Paris forthwith, and the Marquis de Noailles likewise took his departure from London. A war with the Court of Versailles was now impending, though not as yet avowed or declared. Measures were taken at this juncture by means of the lord-lieutenants to call out and assemble the militia in several counties. It was expected that Lord Chatham, the Mr. Pitt of the Seven Years' War, would be called into office. If called upon he was ready to obey the summons. His blood was again roused, as it had been before against the House of Bourbon, and although he deprecated the measures which had alienated the colonies of North America from British rule, and also the civil war which was raging between men of English blood, he considered that the war with France, if it could not be averted, should be most vigorously conducted. On reading the French note recognising the independence of America, he had given his eldest son, Lord Pitt, permission to re-enter the army, a permission that was necessary, as he had insisted on his son resigning his commission rather than bear arms against our colonists and fellow countrymen in America.

An invasion of Great Britain or Ireland from France was already under consideration at Paris, and it may be gathered that it was the intention of Lord Chatham to place at the head of the army Prince Ferdinand, under whom British arms had been so successful in Germany in the Seven Years' War. General dismay prevailed among all ranks and conditions of society, arising from an opinion that the administration of Lord North was not equal to the necessities of the times. This opinion was so universal that it prevailed amongst those who were most dependent on and attached to the ministry, and was current even amongst the ministers themselves. King George III. was strongly averse to Lord Chatham, but notwithstanding his aversion, his Majesty would probably have yielded to the pressure of public opinion. It seems beyond doubt that had Lord Chatham's last and fatal illness been delayed a few weeks, nay even perhaps a few days, he would have been called to the helm of public affairs, and have had the opportunity of endeavouring to solve the problem which he had himself propounded, to regain the affections while refusing the independence of our American fellow-subjects. But before a summons was received from St. James's, on the 7th April, 1778, Lord Chatham, while speaking in the House of Lords, fell down in a fit, and to all appearance lay in the very agonies of death. Without its being certain whether he ever recovered full consciousness, he died on the 11th May.

In 1779 Spain also joined the league against England, and on the 16th June of that year the Spanish ambassador delivered to Lord Weymouth a state paper which amounted to a declaration of war. Projects of invasion were now loudly vaunted by both France and Spain, and appeared near and impending. It was necessary to provide most vigorous measures for defence. The ministry proposed and passed, though not without some criticism in the Upper House, an Act for augmenting the militia. The government had prepared a much more stringent measure, namely, to suspend for six months all exemptions from impressment in the royal navy. This was practically an attempt to give the government the power during the period to man the fleet with any portion of the people at their discretion. This unprecedented measure, which was tantamount to the establishment of conscription in these realms, was brought forward in a no less unprecedented manner. On the night of the 23rd June, at twenty minutes past twelve o'clock, as the House of Commons was on the point of adjourning, the Attorney-General, Wedderburn, rose, and, without any previous notice, moved for leave to bring in this Bill, with a retrospective effect from the 17th. He did not attempt to disguise its arbitrary character, but defended it on the ground of necessity. He urged that when an invasion of the country was threatened by perfidious foes, it was necessary to remove all legal impediments from the path of the State in calling every man to its aid. He also argued that it was a necessity to encourage the willing and to compel the reluctant to join in the defence of the country. He stated that there were at Portsmouth six or eight ships of the line ready for sea, but useless through want of seamen, and that they could not be manned if the power of impressment continued to be fettered by common law and statutory restrictions.

So much was an invasion probable at this moment that the Attorney-General in his speech asked the House of Commons, " Will you submit to an inferiority at sea, allow your men of war to rot in your harbours, and trust the existence of this country to the fate of a battle on shore ? " Notwithstanding the endeavours of such of the opposition as were present, at one o'clock that night the Bill was brought in and read a first and a second time. The House of Lords fortunately acted as a bulwark of the liberties of the subject, and though it was sent to the Upper House on the following day, the Bill did not receive the royal assent until the very end of the session. So much did the men who ruled England at this time consider of importance the maritime supremacy of England, that this measure was thus hurriedly brought in and attempted to be thus hurriedly passed, although, according to a speech made in the House of Commons about the same time, the number of our seamen was stated to be 81,000, notwithstanding that 18,000 of the sailors employed during the previous war had been lost to us through our not now having possession of America.

Parliament was prorogued on the 3rd July, but the warlike preparations of the country were not slackened. On the 9th a royal proclamation was issued, commanding all officers, civil or military, in the event of an invasion, to cause all horses, cattle, and provisions to be driven from the coasts. A boom was drawn across the entrance of Plymouth harbour, and the fortifications round Portsmouth were lined with troops and guns. Yet it does not appear that the country was sufficiently prepared against danger, at least if the statements of the opposition may be credited. It was said that at Plymouth there was no adequate supply of powder; that the diameter of the cannon balls was not adapted to the calibre of the guns; that there were no handspikes or sidearms, or small stores for the batteries; and that even flints for the muskets of the infantry were wanting. Most of these charges were hotly denied on the side of the government, and it is difficult to discover whether they were advanced with truth, or merely from party spirit. The Duke of Richmond declared in the Peers that he had in person examined Plymouth, and that he had found collected there nearly 5,000 soldiers, but not more than thirty-six invalids, as artillerymen, to handle 200 guns, which were mounted on the works. But the First Lord of the Admiralty asserted with equal vigour that at the time and place which the duke had named there were upwards of 500 seamen on shore well acquainted with gunnery, and quite ready to serve if required.

For some time a camp had been in existence on Coxheath, in front of Maidstone, at which were collected several regiments of militia drawn from various counties. A large force was arrayed on the opposite shores, and an invasion was every day expected. Yet the public credit was not diminished, and in the month of July, when the danger of invasion was at its height, the funds were never more than one per cent. below the point at which they stood in the preceding January. Both private individuals and public bodies, among whom the East India Company were perhaps the foremost, gave large subscriptions for raising troops, for giving bounties to seamen, and for equipping privateers. It was acknowledged, even by the opposition, that the militia then in arms did not fall far short of 50,000 men, and that there were within the kingdom almost as many regular troops, while the King himself had determined, if the French should land, to place himself at the head of his subjects in arms, and to animate them by his exertions and example.

On the other side of the Channel the preparations for invasion had been made upon a formidable scale. The finances of the French government, which lately had been on the verge of bankruptcy, had now been brought to a more flourishing, or, at least, more promising, condition, since M. Necker, a rich and able banker from Geneva, had been named Director-General of Finance.

A French army, amounting probably to close upon 50,000 men, had been directed on the various Channel ports from Havre to St. Malo, and had taken up their quarters in the maritime towns along the coast. The vanguard was under the command of the Comte de Rochambeau, while the Maréchal de Broglie commanded the main body. It was intended that a landing should be made on the shores of the south of England. The French fleet, having left the port of Brest without any interruption from the English, effected a junction with the Spanish, and the whole force, thus combined, amounted to no less than sixty-six sail of the line, with the proper complement of frigates and smaller craft. Never since the time of the Armada had so formidable a fleet appeared in the British Channel. Sir Charles Hardy, who commanded the English squadron, had with every exertion been unable to gather together more than thirty-eight men-of-war to dispute the passage with these sixty-six liners. He was powerless to prevent the enemy from insulting the coast of England, or from forcing him back, first near the Scilly Islands, and then compelling him to retire towards the narrow straits between Dover and Calais. The English admiral appears, however, to have acted with judgment and discretion. Only one ship, the *Ardent*, and that by mistaking the hostile fleet for the British, was captured. Hardy succeeded in drawing the enemy away from before Plymouth, and also in covering Spithead ; and, favoured by an easterly breeze, gained the greatest of all objects in defensive war, the power of temporising. Neither the Spanish nor the French ships were quite seaworthy. Both had been too hastily fitted out; and it was afterwards stated by Lord North in the House of Commons that had Sir Charles Hardy known then as well as he did afterwards the interior economy of the enemy's fleet, he would have wished and earnestly sought an engagement, notwithstanding their superiority of force.

Fortunately for England, the division of command—the offspring of divided opinions which is ever the danger of an allied undertaking—had arisen in the ranks of the enemy. The Spanish admiral desired to land the invading army without delay on the coast of England; the French commander, on the other hand, thought that it was necessary in the first place to attack and defeat the British fleet, and leave the passage of the Channel open. Sickness had broken out amongst the crews and the troops, and as the approach of the equinoctial gales was imminent, it was feared that the unseaworthiness of the allied ships would be prolific of grave disaster. Under these circumstances the Spaniard declared in a peremptory tone that it had become necessary for him to relinquish the present enterprise, and return to the harbours of his own country. The French commander, D'Orvilliers, had no choice but to follow his example. He sailed back, therefore, with his own fleet into Brest, where, mortified at his failure, he resigned the command, and afterwards, it is said, withdrew for the remainder of his life to a monastery.

The squabbles of two admirals thus for the time averted all danger of invasion from our country, and when the House of Commons again met, the Prime Minister of England described the proceedings of our enemies in the late campaign as follows:—" They had fitted out a formidable fleet, they appeared upon our coasts, they talked big, threatened a great deal, did nothing, and retired. Their immense armaments were produced to no purpose, and their millions spent in vain."

But though the combined fleets of France and Spain were unable to cover an invasion of the country by land forces some buccaneering transactions in the north bitterly mortified our national pride. Paul Jones, by birth a Scotchman, but by feeling a bitter foe to his native land, a bold and hardy seaman, though in his conduct a mere buccaneer, held at this time a commission in the American service. With three ships and one armed brigantine, off the Yorkshire coast, he attacked the English Baltic fleet, convoyed by Captain Pearson in the *Serapis*, and Captain Piercy in the *Scarborough*. After a desperate engagement, both the British vessels were taken, and though Jones's own best vessel, the *Bonhomme Richard*, which had been furnished to him by France, was so far damaged in the fight that it sank two days afterwards, he carried his prizes safely into the ports of Holland. Paul Jones with his remaining ships next appeared in the Firth of Forth. Sir Walter Scott, then still a boy, was at Edinburgh at this time, and has vividly described the humiliation felt that the capital of Scotland should be threatened by what seemed to be three trifling sloops, or brigs, scarcely fit to have sacked a fishing village.

But Edinburgh was not totally devoid of brave men to resist this insult. In the capital of Scotland there then happened to be Alexander Stewart, of Invernhale, one of the clan of the Stewarts of Appin; a veteran who, according to Scottish phrase, had been "out in the '45," and who now gloried in the prospect, as he himself said, of drawing the claymore once again before he died. He offered to the magistracy, if broadswords and dirks could be obtained, to find as many Highlanders among the lower classes as would be sufficient to defend the town. The magistrates deliberated, but came to no decision on his scheme. A steady and powerful west wind fortunately springing up settled the matter, by sweeping Paul Jones and his vessels out of the Firth of Forth.[1] It is stated that this west wind was the direct result of the prayers of a minister at Edinburgh.

The war continued in America. Attempts were made by the French and Spaniards on Gibraltar; and considerable popular ferment and excitement existed at home. It was well known that on any favourable opportunity an attempt at invasion might be made on our shores; and in 1782 a French descent seemed to be actually impending. By the demands of the American war, our country had been denuded of troops. From the absence of compulsory clauses, the Militia Act had remained a dead letter, and in the face of this danger the kingdom was found almost entirely defenceless. Official intelligence was received, though it was afterwards proved to be unfounded, that an attack was

[1] See the Historical Introduction to "Waverley."

meditated on the north of Ireland. At all events, the people of Belfast and Carrickfergus solicited the government to send some military force for their protection. The government of Dublin found at this time that they could not spare any greater force than sixty troopers. It was not unnatural, then, that the people of these towns, loyal as they were, notwithstanding some disaffection in Ireland, should endeavour to arm themselves for their own protection. They formed themselves into two or three companies. The spirit spread, and by degrees, through all parts of Ireland, but more especially in Ulster, there arose independent companies of volunteers. In May, 1779, this force was already computed to number upwards of 10,000. Many of the chief men in the country were in command, such as the Earl of Clanricarde in Connaught, and the Earl of Charlemont in Ulster. They chose their own officers, and though claiming arms as militia from the government stores, did not recognise any subjection to government control.

These irregular armaments caused great perplexity in the minds of the government. To defend their native country from invasion was a course not only excusable, but praiseworthy. But, on the other hand, it was clearly both unconstitutional and dangerous to assemble in arms without any orders from the crown. As soon as the immediate alarm of an invasion passed away, the Secretary of State, writing of the volunteer companies, directed the Lord-Lieutenant—" That they be discouraged by all proper and gentle means." But this order was more easily given than carried out. Delicate hints, implying disapprobation, though not boldly stating this opinion, fell unheeded on reluctant ears; and the volunteers continued to grow both in numbers and in repute. Before the end of 1779 they appear to have been not far short of 50,000 strong. By degrees they assumed a louder tone. No longer content with separate commanders, they combined to elect Lord Charlemont, a man deservedly esteemed on all sides, but far more accomplished than able, as their general-in-chief.

In 1783 definite treaties of peace were signed with France and Spain; the independence of the United States was recognised by the King of England, and a wretched civil conflict was brought to a conclusion. During this war, for three years, from 1779 to 1782, General Elliott held against famine and bombardment the rock fortress of Gibraltar.

From the hour of Chatham's death England entered on a conflict with enemies, whose circle gradually widened, till she stood single-handed against the world. A quarrel over the right of search banded Holland and the Courts of the North into an armed neutrality against her, and added the Dutch fleet and those of France, Spain, and America to the number of her assailants. Yet England held her own at sea, while her losses in the West were all but balanced by new triumphs in the East, where Hastings commenced the conscious and deliberate purpose of subjecting India to the British crown, and the progress of Hyder Ali was hurled back by the victory of Porto Novo. Now was laid the foundation of an Indian empire, which the genius of Hastings was bold enough to foresee.

But while our countrymen were triumphant in the East a terrible disaster fell upon our arms in America. Lord Cornwallis having failed in an attempt on North Carolina, fell back in 1781 on Virginia, and intrenched himself in the lines of Yorktown. Washington, by a sudden march, brought his army in front of the English troops, at a moment when the French fleet held the sea in their rear. The army of Cornwallis was driven by famine to a surrender as humiliating as that of Burgoyne at Saratoga. England seemed on the brink of ruin. Even Ireland turned against her. The Protestant volunteers who had been raised for the defence of the island made a demand which was in effect a claim for Irish independence. There were no means of resisting the demand, for England was destitute of any force which she could oppose to the Irish volunteers. The hopes of her enemies rose high. Spain refused peace at any other price than the cession of Gibraltar. France demanded that England should surrender all her Indian conquests save Bengal. At this moment the fleet of England restored the balance of the trembling scale.

Admiral Rodney, the greatest of English seamen save Nelson and Blake, saved our country from a dishonourable peace. He fell in with the Spanish fleet off Cape St. Vincent, and only four of its vessels escaped to Cadiz. The French admiral De Grasse had been triumphant in the West Indies, but Rodney, on the 12th of April, 1782, who had followed him to the

West, broke the French line by a manœuvre which he was the first to introduce, and drove the French vessels in confusion from the sea. The final repulse of the allied armament before Gibraltar, in September, 1782, concluded the war. In November the treaties of Paris and Versailles, while yielding nothing to France, and only Minorca and Florida to Spain, acknowledged without reserve the independence of America.

CHAPTER XVIII.

INVASIONS OF THE WARS OF THE FRENCH REVOLUTION.

AUTHORITIES.—Von Sybel's "History of the French Revolution;" Regimental Records of the British Army; Lord Cornwallis's Correspondence; Alison's "History of Europe;" Sir William Napier's "History of the Peninsular War;" Stanhope's "Life of Pitt;" Clode's "Military Forces of the Crown;" Clode's "Military and Martial Laws;" Walpole's "Memoirs of the Reign of George III."; Thiers's "Consulat et l'Empire" may be consulted, as well as the great bulk of the military works of French authors which refer to this period.

WHEN Europe was startled by the outbreak of the French Revolution, the state of England was very different from what it was at the time of the invasion of the Old Pretender. Men had expected that our country would be ruined by the loss of her American colonies, the independence of which was guaranteed by the peace of Paris. But these expectations were quickly disappointed. England rose from this struggle stronger and greater than ever. The ten years which succeeded the independence of America saw an increase of industrial activity within our country such as the world had never before witnessed. During the twenty years that again followed, our ancestors wrestled almost single-handed against the energy of the French Revolution, as well as against the colossal force of the empire of the First Napoleon, and emerged from the earlier struggle unconquered, from the later victorious.

In December, 1783, William Pitt occupied the post of First Lord of the Treasury, and at the general election of 1784 every great constituency returned supporters of his policy. The great strength of Pitt as a statesman lay in finance, and he was placed at the head of the administration of the country at a time when the growth of English wealth made a knowledge of finance essential to a minister. During the eighteenth century the population of our islands more than doubled, and the increase of wealth was even greater than that of the population. The war with America had added one hundred millions to the national debt, but the burden sat lightly on the country. The loss of America only increased our commerce with the independent colonies. Industry began that great career which was to make England the workshop of the world. During the first half of the eighteenth century the cotton trade, of which Manchester was the principal seat, had only risen from the value of 20,000*l.* to that of 40,000*l.*, and at the time that Charles Edward from Derby threatened the metropolis, the handlooms of Manchester still retained the primitive shape which is yet found in the handlooms up-country in India. Three successive inventions in ten years, in the latter part of the century, made Manchester the centre of a hive of industry which included the whole of Lancashire. The spinning machine invented by the barber Arkwright, in 1768, the spinning jenny by the weaver Hargreaves, in 1764, and the mule by the weaver Crompton, in 1776, together combined to effect that revolution. At the accession of George III. the whole linen trade of Scotland was of less value than the cloth trade of Yorkshire. On the retreat of Prince Charles Edward from Derby to Glasgow, a requisition to the amount of 10,000*l.* was all that it was considered could be borne by the citizens of that town; and so serious was this considered, that after the suppression of the rebellion Parliament made a special grant to compensate the city for its suffering. Before the close of the reign of the Third George Glasgow was already taking its rank as one of the great trading capitals of the world. The potteries which Wedgwood established in 1763 in Staffordshire soon eclipsed in fame those of France or Holland, and before the peace of Paris was signed more than 20,000 potters were employed in that county alone. This rapid growth of manufactures and increase of wealth brought about a corresponding improvement in the means of communication throughout the country. Up to the middle of the eighteenth century the roads throughout England had been of the rudest sort, and were for the most part so wretched, that all cheap or rapid transit was impossible. So much so that it was considered impossible to move a train of artillery which was intended for the Duke of Cumberland's army from London to Edinburgh by land, and it was necessary to forward it by the more precarious and uncertain method of a sea voyage. At the time of the outbreak of the rebellion caused by the landing of

Charles Edward, probably owing to Marshal Wade, roads were better in northern Scotland than in any other part of the United Kingdom. The cotton bales of Manchester were still at that time carried to Liverpool or Bristol on pack-horses. During the latter part of the eighteenth century one of the great works of which our country may be proud was carried out, and England was covered with a vast network of splendid highways. Nor were roads alone considered sufficient to supply the demands of the new commerce; in 1761 a canal which crossed the Irwell by a lofty aqueduct, constructed under the supervision of Brindley, was made to Manchester. This experiment was successful, and soon led to the general introduction of water carriage. The Trent was linked by a water way with the Mersey; the Thames with the Trent; the Forth with the Clyde. The economy of the new mode of transport, as well as the progress of engineering, developed English collieries to an extent that soon allowed coal a front place among our exports. Watt in 1765 discovered the value of coal in producing mechanical force through the steam-engine. During the same period, between the earlier and the later years of the eighteenth century, an agricultural change passed gradually over the face of the country. A fourth part of England was reclaimed from waste and brought under culture, while on the tilled land itself the production was more than doubled by the advance of the science of agriculture that began with the travels and treatises of Arthur Young, the introduction of the system of large farms by Mr. Coke of Norfolk, and the development of scientific tillage in the Lothians.

The steady progress of English industry was to be checked by a series of events with which England herself had no concern, save so far that she had given the model for constitutional privileges, the absence of which led to the French Revolution.

In 1783, before the conclusion of peace, the regular soldiers of Great Britain amounted to 54,678 men. The peace was signed, and in the succeeding year the estimates provided for only 17,483 men in Great Britain. This seems to have been the number for which barrack accommodation could be found. In the same year 17,247 men were voted for the plantations; and for the first time 6,336 regular troops for India. This strength was not changed till 1787, when a slight reduction was made, as there usually is in England shortly before a war. Till the year 1788 Parliament imposed no restrictions on the East India Company as to the number of its own army, but the company was commanded to maintain 12,200 Europeans beside part of the imperial troops in India. During the reign of George III. the Board of Control could order a force not exceeding 8,045 officers and men to be maintained in India out of the Indian revenue. This number was subsequently raised to 20,000 men. Such soldiery was on a different footing to the troops which now garrison Meerut, Agra, Delhi, or Peshwur. All the levies now sent to India are placed on the Indian establishment and paid by the Indian revenue, but are regular soldiers of the British crown, and there is no power to prevent the crown from recalling them to this country at any moment they may be required.

The Puritan opposition of the seventeenth century had succeeded in checking, as far as England was concerned, the general tendency of the time to religious and political despotism. Since the accession of William III. the people's right to govern itself through its parliamentary representatives and religious freedom of conscience had been practically established. From ages previous every man, from the highest to the lowest, was subject to and protected by the same laws. The aristocracy were possessed of few social privileges, and prevented from becoming a separate caste by the wholesome legal and social tradition which counted all save the single heir of a noble house as commoners. No insuperable boundary parted the nobility from the gentry, the gentry from the commercial classes, nor these from the working classes of the community, and public opinion was already one of the powerful elements of English government.

In the other great states of Europe, however, the religious wars of the seventeenth century had left but the name of freedom; governments tended to pure despotism, privilege was supreme in religion, in politics, and in society. Classes were rigidly divided one from the other, and the mass of the people were debarred from any equal rights of justice or protection for the fruits of their industry. In the eighteenth century such an arrangement of national life was rendered absurd through the wide diffusion of intelligence which was spread over Europe. In almost every country some far-sighted rulers endeavoured by well-timed reforms to satisfy to some extent the sense of wrong which they found amongst their peoples. Such were Frederick the Great in Prussia; Joseph II. in Austria and the Netherlands; while in France similar endeavours were made by such statesmen as Turgot. But in this last unhappy country the contrast between the actual state of society and the new ideas of individual rights were most keenly felt. In no other land in Europe had the victory of the crown been more complete. The aristocracy, though deprived of all share in the government of the country, enjoyed social privileges and exemption from taxation, without any of that sense of public duty which an influence on government would engender. Guilds and monopolies fettered the industry of the trader and the merchant, and parted these from the working classes, while the fictitious price set upon noble blood severed both from the nobility.

Yet in no country was public opinion more free, though powerless to influence the government, than in France. A literary class had sprung up which devoted itself with wonderful activity and wit to popularise the idea of social and political justice which had been learnt from English writers or from contact with English society. Throughout France the new force of intelligence found itself in direct antagonism with the existing state of affairs. The priesthood, who were predominant, were denounced by the philosophers, such as Voltaire and Montesquieu, as tyrants. The peasantry, feebly reflecting the opinions of the cities, grumbled at the absolute right of the lord to judge him in feudal courts and to exact feudal services from him. The merchant was chafed and annoyed by restrictions on trade and heavy taxation.

But none of these classes, philosophers, peasantry, merchants, nor even the country gentry, had much influence on the actions of the government. Yet it was by the force of public opinion that France was obliged to ally herself with America in its contest for independence. The public mind was however strangely excited by the conflict, and many French volunteers under Lafayette joined the army of Washington. The American war spread throughout the nation more widely the craving for equality of rights, while at the same time the exertions made by the government brought on the exchequer a financial embarrassment from which the rulers of the country could only free themselves by an appeal to the people. This necessity led Louis XVI. to summon the States-General, a body which had not met since the time of Richelieu, with a view of applying to the nobility to yield up their immunity from sharing the public burdens of the country. But the vision of popular representation stirred at once into vigour and energy the impulse and desire which had for years been seething in the minds of the masses. The States-General no sooner met at Versailles in May, 1789, than the whole fabric of despotism and privilege began to crumble. A riot in Paris destroyed the Bastile, and the fall of this fortress-prison was regarded as the inauguration of a new era of constitutional freedom for France.

In October of the same year the mob of Paris marched on Versailles, and forced both king and assembly to return to the capital, and a constitution, hurriedly drawn up, was accepted by the sovereign in lieu of despotic power.

Pitt, who was at the head of the administration in England, was little anxious to interfere with the internal arrangements for the new constitution or government of France. The natural conservative tendency of the English people against violent change was fanned by Burke into a detestation of the revolution, and a frenzied fear as to its consequences. Continental powers also would have been anxious at first not to have interfered with France. Russia had risen into greatness under Catherine II., and Catherine had resolved from the first on the annexation of Poland, the expulsion of the Turks from Europe, and the erection of a Russian throne at Constantinople. In her first aim she was baffled for the moment by the genius of the great Frederick. When Frederick, in union with the Emperor Joseph II., forced Russia to admit Germany to a share in the spoil of the partition of Poland, she had already made herself mistress of the whole of the kingdom; her armies occupied the entire country, and she had seated a nominee of her own on its throne. This Polish partition of 1773 brought the Russian frontier westward to the upper waters of the Dwina and the Dnieper, gave Galicia to Maria Theresa, Empress of Austria, and West Prussia to Frederick himself. When the death of Frederick removed Catherine's most watchful and dangerous foe in 1788, the Empress and Joseph joined hand in hand for a partition of the Turkish Empire. But Prussia, although deprived of the guiding mind of Frederick, was still wakeful; and England was no longer, as in 1773, fettered by troubles with irritated colonists. The wise friendship and alliance established by Chatham between England and Germany, which had been suspended temporarily by the feebleness of Bute, and all but destroyed during the northern league of the neutral powers, had been restored by the brilliant mind of Pitt, and its weight in Europe was now seen in the alliance of England with Prussia and Holland, in 1789, for the preservation of the Turkish Empire. It is to be hoped that both English and German statesmen may not hastily depart from the traditions hallowed by the genius of Chatham and adorned by the intellect of Frederick, which link our two countries closely together in alliance, as they are by nature and blood. A European war seemed at hand, but the treaty between England and Prussia swept away the danger of hostilities.

In 1791 the flight of Louis XVI. from Paris again for a moment brought Europe to the verge of war. But he was intercepted and brought back, and not only accepted the constitution prepared by his subjects, but earnestly begged the Emperor of Germany that no armed intervention should be made by foreign powers, as such a step would assuredly bring ruin to his crown. In August of the same year the Emperor and the King of Prussia met at Pilnitz, and contented themselves with a vague declaration, inviting the European powers to co-operate in restoring a sound form of government in France, but availed themselves of the neutrality which Pitt openly asserted England would maintain, as a reason for refusing all military aid to the French princes. The peace, however, that these sovereigns desired soon became impossible. The royalists in France availed themselves of the popular irritation caused by the declaration of Pilnitz to raise again the cry for a war, which, as they held, would give strength to the throne. The Jacobins, on the other hand, under the influence of the Girondists, or deputies from the south of France, aiming at a republic, saw in the prospect of a great struggle a means of overthrowing the monarchy. These determined, in spite of the opposition of Robespierre, on a contest with the Emperor. Both parties were at one in demanding the breaking up of an army which the French emigrant princes had formed on the Rhine; and though Leopold assented to this demand, France declared war against his successor, Francis, in April, 1792.

Pitt refused all aid to France in this war, but stipulated that Holland must remain untouched, although he promised the neutrality of our country, even though Belgium should for a time be occupied by a French army. In the King's speech at the opening of Parliament on the last day of January, the English cabinet had expressed a confident hope of the maintenance of peace, and as the best pledge of their belief, confidently recommended an immediate reduction in the naval and military establishments, and a proportionate relief of the people from the weight of taxation. On the conviction that peace could be preserved, Pitt himself bringing forward his budget, asked the House to vote only 16,000 seamen, being 2,000 less than the number voted in the preceding year. As to the land forces, he proposed not to renew the subsidiary treaty with Hesse

Cassel, which had been concluded in 1787, and by which, for 36,000*l*. per annum, England obtained the service of 12,000 Hessian troops to serve in the pay of Great Britain. So little was war anticipated at this moment in England, so high was then the public credit, that Pitt intended to propose a reduction of the 4 per cents to $3\frac{1}{2}$ per cents; but on further consideration he resolved to defer the measure until the next session, when he hoped to be able to reduce these funds to 3 per cent. Thus little did even the most prudent men in the country foresee what the next session would bring forth, and that not only many years, but tens of years, would pass ere any opportunity for reduction would again occur.

Peace grew hourly more impossible. The French revolutionists, eagerly anxious to find an ally in their war with Austria, strove by intrigues throughout England to rouse the same revolutionary spirit in our island as had been called forth in France. Burke, too, was working hard, on the other hand, in writings, whose extravagance of style was forgotten in their intensity of feeling, to spread alarm throughout Europe. At the threat of war against the Emperor the Courts of Austria and of Prussia had drawn together, and, reluctantly abandoning all hope of peace with France, concentrated 80,000 men under the Duke of Brunswick, who advanced slowly in August on the Meuse. France, though she had forced on the conflict, was in truth almost defenceless. Her army in Belgium broke on the first shock of arms into shameful rout; and the panic spreading from the soldiery to the nation at large, took violent and horrible forms. On the first news of the advance of Brunswick the mob of Paris broke into the Tuileries on the 10th August, and on its demand the king, who had taken refuge in the Assembly, was suspended from his office and imprisoned in the Temple. From this moment the progress of France towards political, social, and religious freedom was at an end. Licence was immediately substituted for liberty, and the populace of the capital, with the commune of Paris at its head, imposed its despotic will upon the Assembly and the nation. Liberty was crushed down by the horror which its extravagances hereafter evoked, and for years after, whether under the Commune or the Directory, or even the more enlightened rule of Napoleon, the government was a despotism.

The progress of Brunswick was stayed in the defiles of Argonne by the skill and adroit negotiations of Dumouriez. But while this general checked the advance of the invaders, bodies of paid murderers butchered in September the royalist prisoners who crowded the jails of Paris. The numbers of Brunswick's army delayed in the Argonne were so reduced by disease that the advance on Paris ultimately became impossible, and a brilliant victory gained by Dumouriez at Jemappes, laid the Netherlands at his feet. In November the New Convention decreed in Paris that France offered the aid of her soldiers to all nations who would strive for freedom. " All governments are our enemies; all peoples are our allies," said its president; and without any pretext for war, the French government resolved, encouraged by its victory at Jemappes, to attack Holland, and ordered its generals to enforce by arms the opening of the Scheldt.

To do this was to drive England into hostilities. Public opinion was urging daily more strongly upon Pitt the advisability of war. The horror aroused in England by the massacres of September, and the hideous despotism of the Paris mob, had powerfully estranged England from the revolution. Pitt alone of all men in our country held firm to the hopes of peace. At the opening of November he still urged upon Holland a studied neutrality. It was France, and not even popular opinion in England, which at last forced him reluctantly to draw the sword from the scabbard. The decree of the Convention and the attack on the Dutch left him no choice but war, for it was impossible for England to suffer a French fleet at Antwerp, or to desert allies like the United Provinces. Across the Channel the moderation of Pitt was only supposed to betoken fear, while in England the general mourning which was worn on the news of the execution of the French king showed the growing popular desire for a conflict. Both sides resolved upon hostilities, and on the 1st February, 1793, France issued her declaration of war against England and Holland ; and our shores again became exposed to the danger of an invasion. A similar declaration against Spain followed on the morning of the 7th March ; and thus the last hopes of peace departed, and trumpets once more sounded to battle.

At the same time England was little prepared for war. A charge indeed has been made against Pitt, that under his administration the English army was the laughing-stock of Europe. No doubt during the administration of this .statesman there were many miscarriages by land to set against our victories at sea ; but the same fate attended all the armies which at that period were formed in line against France. It was no easy matter to prevail over a nation at all times most brave and warlike, and then inflamed to a preternatural strength by its revolutionary ardour. When, therefore, the English army is declared at that period to have been the laughing-stock of Europe, we may ask what other European army at the same time enjoyed better fortune,. or was more justly entitled to smile at ours ?

It must also be borne in mind that the military failures laid to the charge of Pitt continued long after Pitt had ceased to live. With the greatest failure of all which stains our military administration at the commencement of this century, the expedition to Walcheren, Pitt was not at all, except in kindred, connected. The truth is that at the time of the outbreak of the revolutionary wars our generals for the most part were anything but men of genius. Those who had served in the campaigns in America had not gained lessons of much avail in European warfare ; nor, indeed, had the army acquired such honour in the American war as would tempt men of talent and vigour to enter its ranks. While the navy, on the other hand, was certainly at that time in England the popular service. Lord Granville, writing to his brother, in strict confidence, on the 28th of January, 1799, even some time after war had broken out, "What defence have we to oppose to our domestic and external enemies? Some old woman in a red ribbon!" The truth is that these miscarriages in our military enterprises, far from being confined simply to the time of the administration of Pitt, continued, with few exceptions, in regular and mortifying series, till, happily for England and for Europe, there arose a man as great in the field as was Pitt in the cabinet; and till the valour which never had failed our troops even in their worst of battles was led to victory by the surpassing genius of Wellington.

The campaign commenced early on the side of Flanders. Scarce a fortnight after the declaration of war, Dumouriez crossed the frontier and invaded Holland; but was called to the Meuse by the advance of the Prince of Saxe-Coburg at the head of some Austrian troops, and defeated at the battle of Nerwinde, by which the Austrians recovered the whole of Belgium almost as rapidly as they had lost it. From the lower Rhine the French were driven back to Alsace, and the city of Mayence was besieged, and after an obstinate resistance taken by the Prussians. Dumouriez was so chagrined at this reverse of fortune that he entered into secret communications with the enemy, and passed over into the hostile lines, but refused to take any part in carrying on war against the French arms, and finally settled in London.

In England there were about 10,000 troops ready for

the defence of Holland when invaded by Dumouriez; being freed from that duty by the retreat of the French, they were designed to take part in the campaign of Flanders, and accordingly were landed at Ostend. Their commander was Frederick, Duke of York, who from early youth had applied himself with zeal to the study of military science.

All seemed now to go ill for France; she was girt in by a ring of enemies; the Emperor, Prussia, Saxony, Sardinia, Spain, were leagued in arms against her, and their efforts were seconded by civil war. The peasantry of Poitou and Brittany rose in revolt against the revolutionary government. Marseilles and Lyons were driven into insurrection, and the enemies of the government in a great naval port, that of Toulon, not only hoisted the royalist flag, but admitted an English garrison within its walls to hold its works. This garrison, which was thrown in by Lord Hood, consisted of only 1,500 men for the defence of the place, but received some succours from the Sardinian and Neapolitan armies. Quickly were they surrounded by republican besiegers, and although the great importance of holding Toulon was felt and acted on by the English government, its fate was decided before reinforcements could arrive. The attacks made upon the works were frequent and formidable, and the artillery directed against them was handled by a young Corsican officer, whose name then first rose to distinction, but ere long resounded through the world. The lieutenant of artillery was Napoleon Bonaparte. By the middle of December the besiegers obtained possession of the fort which commanded the inner harbour, and the allied troops found themselves compelled without delay to relinquish the town and re-embark.

But the chance of crushing the revolution was lost by the greed and rapacity of the allied powers. Russia, as Pitt had foreseen, was now free to carry out her schemes of aggrandizement in the East ; and Austria and Prussia turned from the vigorous prosecution of the French war to the final partition of Poland. The Duke of York, in conjunction with the Prince of Coburg, found themselves opposed to Dampierre, the successor of Dumouriez, and, under the advice of General Mack, an excellent officer as far as paper was concerned, but with little of the dash necessary to the successful prosecution of a campaign in the field, frittered away their forces, which should have been pushed into the heart of France, in a succession of profitless sieges. The garrisons which capitulated were left free, although engaged not to serve against the Emperor or his allies, to crush down with no sparing hand the civil revolts which, if encouraged in France, might have aided the allied cause. At the same time the Austrian chiefs appear to have contemplated the curtailment of French territory, if not the partition of France. Whatever were the crimes and violence of the Jacobin leaders at this time, the whole body of Frenchmen felt the value of the revolution, and rallied enthusiastically to its support. New levies flocked in great numbers to the tricolor standard, and filled the ranks of the revolutionary armies. Fired with no common ardour, without even for a moment belying the martial spirit of their race, they seemed careless alike of danger, privation, and fatigue.

The fruits of this new spirit soon appeared. The Duke of York was compelled by Hoche and Houchard, without the walls of Dunkirk, to raise the siege of that place. The chiefs of the Convention displayed terrible energy against the insurgents within the limits of France. Lyons was retaken, and laid waste with fire and sword; its buildings were ordered to be rased to the ground; its very name was decreed to be obliterated, and changed to Commune Affranchie. Marseilles, in like manner, was forced to yield to the regular troops; while at Le Mans the Vendéans were utterly routed, and great numbers of them butchered.

Throughout this winter the most strenuous exertions had been made in France for the prosecution of the war. The Committee of Public Safety, with Robespierre for its leader, seemed to imprint its savage energy on all around it. Above a million of Frenchmen, as was computed, or guessed at, took up arms. Every frontier of the new Republic was lined with numerous and daring levies. The army of the north, as it was termed, that is in front of Flanders, mustered, including the garrisons, 250,000 men. Its command was entrusted to Pichegru, while Jourdan was at the head of the army of the Moselle. On the side of the allies a combined march to Paris was intended, and great hopes were founded on the arrival of the Emperor of Austria at Brussels. It was thought that his presence might serve to restore the loyalty of his ill-affected subjects in the Low Countries, and compose the dissensions of his jarring generals. In April he came to the Belgian capital, and reviewed an army of no less than 140,000 men, with which the siege of Landrecies was shortly afterwards undertaken. During this operation the Duke of York, with one division, covered the right flank of the main army in the direction of Cambray, and repulsed an attack of the French against his lines, capturing thirty-five pieces of cannon. But the French were far from dispirited; they quickly resumed the offensive, and crossed the Sambre, and the battle of Fleurus, in June, allowed Pichegru and Jourdan, advancing in consort, to enter Brussels and to recover all the recent conquests of the allies.

In the Mediterranean an insurrection in Corsica allowed the British to throw a force into that island under a convention with General Paoli, who had been elected General-in-chief by the popular deputies; and while our General Sir David Dundas lay idle at San Fiorenze, not giving one of the five regiments he had there to assist in the operations, Captain Nelson, of the *Agamemnon*, who afterwards became so famous, and Lord Hood, seized the town of Bastia, where 4,500 men laid down their arms to less than 1,000 British marines, and ensured the full possession of the island. Corsica was afterwards annexed to the throne of England, as another kingdom, and with a free constitution of its own.

In the Channel a formidable French armament was cruising, which threatened this country with an invasion, as, should it be able to defeat the English fleet, the passage would have lain open for any number of the hastily raised levies of the Republic to be poured on to our southern shores. The French vessels in the month of May left the harbour of Brest, in pursuance of orders from Paris, for the purpose of protecting a large convoy, laden chiefly with flour, which was expected from America. It consisted of twenty-six sail of the line, equipped with great care, and having for its chief admiral Villaret Joyeuse; but his authority was often overruled by a commissioner from the terrible Convention, Jean Bon St. André, who, though totally ignorant of seamanship, and trained in his youth as a Calvinist divine, had come on board and assumed the tone of a great naval authority. Nor was the French admiral adequately supported by his captains or his crews. The revolution had been the means of driving the best naval officers from the French service; for under the influence of the new ideas every attempt at maintaining discipline in a ship of war was denounced by the Jacobins at the seaports as savouring of aristocracy, and as an inroad on the rights of the people. Lord Stanhope, in his Life of Pitt, states that even before the close of 1791 it had been calculated that three-fourths of the officers of the royal marine had either retired or been dismissed. Their places had been supplied from the merchant service, with a very searching test as to politics, but with a very slight test as to naval knowledge or skill.

The commander of the British Channel fleet was at this time Earl Howe. He had reached the verge of three score years and ten, but he possessed the mind of forty years of age, and had not a thought separated from honour and glory. Under him sailed several gallant admirals, as another Hood, afterwards Lord Bridport, and Admirals Graves and Gardiner, both subsequently raised to the peerage. In the action of the 1st of June, which derives its name from no local connection, but from its date, the French were superior to the English by one line-of-battle ship, and by a considerable weight of ordnance.

When after daybreak the English ships bore down together for close action, the attack was commenced by the English admiral. His object was to break the enemy's line. On the French side a heavy fire was opened against the English as soon as they came within range; but Howe, in his own ship, the *Queen Charlotte*, 100 guns, ordered his men to return none of the broadsides poured in upon them until his master could place him alongside of the French admiral's ship, the *Montagne*, 120 guns, the largest vessel at that time in the whole French navy. Thus breaking the French line of battle, and closely followed by five vessels of his own fleet, he closed upon the *Montagne*. So unpleasant on board the enemy's flagship appeared the sight of the advancing Englishman, that M. Jean Bon St. André, with a total want of the polemical courage which might have been expected from his early education, abandoned the deck, and retired into the cockpit below water mark. The battle raged furiously, but after a harassing conflict the French admiral gave way, and, followed by all his ships, still in sufficient order, made sail away. One of his seventy-fours, the *Le Vengeur*, went down during the action, with many hundred men on board, as also did some nearly disabled ships, that might otherwise have been secured; still five were left as prizes and brought home in triumph by Howe. This victory was most seasonable in its influence on England. It proved the continued supremacy of our navy on its own element, as we love to call it, the sea. It revived the spirits that were drooping from the adverse results of the continental campaigns. It secured also for the time our southern shores from the danger of invasion.

The battle of the 1st June, though it secured England from an invasion, had no effect in facilitating the offensive movements against Paris on the part of the allies, which, if successful, would have been the best means of obtaining peace, and of guarding our country for some considerable time from danger. On the contrary, a serious and unexpected blow was dealt in the winter against the allied armies. These had withdrawn to winter quarters. It was thought that the campaign had concluded; but, as it chanced, the winter in the Low Countries set in with extreme severity, such as had not been experienced for many years. The great rivers that form the barriers of Holland to the south were frozen over, and their condition seemed to invite rather than guard against invasion. General Pichegru, who was ill at Brussels, hastened back to his troops. The French soldiery, displaying their usual alacrity for action, came forth with tattered clothing and worn-out shoes, but without a murmur, from their winter-quarters. The ice was strong enough to carry them, and they crossed with the greatest ease both the Meuse and the Waal. General Walmoden, with the English and Hanoverians, fell back to Deventer to effect their retreat to Hanover by way of Westphalia. The Prince of Orange, with the Dutch, retired on Utrecht and Amsterdam. He asked for a suspension of hostilities, and offered terms of peace, but both were disdainfully rejected. Thus no other resource was left to him. The French troops pressed forward in overwhelming numbers, and the French party, which had been crushed down in 1787, again raised its head. The prince relinquished the contest and embarked for England, while Pichegru entered Amsterdam in triumph on the 20th March.

Yet this was not all. The greater portion of the Dutch fleet lay ice-bound in the Zuyder Zee. Some regiments of cavalry and horse artillery were at once despatched against it by Pichegru; and for the first time perhaps in the annals of war did ships surrender to horsemen. Only a small proportion of armed vessels that lay in the outer ports could get away to England and remain of use to the House of Orange.

During the spring and summer of 1795 there was for the most part a lull in the military operations. The French rulers seemed satisfied with the rapid conquest of Holland and the formal annexation of the Belgic provinces. But in this year many of the allies who formed the coalition against France fell away from the common cause. The Grand Duke of Tuscany made peace with the Republic on the 9th February. On the 5th April there followed the signature at Bâle of a treaty with Paris, by which the Court of Berlin consented that the French should remain in full possession of their conquests to the left of the Rhine, and in July the King of Spain concluded peace with the French. England, anxious for peace, was unable to obtain terms which could be accepted. The French attacked our country by raising an insurrection of the Maroons in Jamaica. England retaliated by the reduction of the ancient colonies of Holland, which now were under French subjection. The Malaccas and others surrendered without a blow. A small expedition was sent to the Cape of Good Hope, which, although no more than 1,600 men could be landed, overpowered the resistance of the much larger Dutch forces and gained this important colony.

But England at this time, under the wise administration of Pitt, fully perceived the danger of trusting its defence to a mere inactive, defensive policy. A descent was projected on the western shores of France, where it was believed that an insurrection against the Republican government would break out as soon as a British fleet with a body of land forces appeared in sight. A descent was accordingly made at the bay of Quiberon by a considerable body of French emigrants in English pay, protected by an English fleet under Lord Bridport. These were within three days joined by 10,000 men, but General Hoche, who was then commanding for the Republic in Brittany, assailed the position taken up by the invaders at Quiberon, put them to rout, and drove them in utter confusion into a narrow space on that peninsula. Great numbers were slain; the rest, though protected by a sharp fire from the English gun-boats, were driven back to the extreme end of the tongue of land, where those who were not shot down by the musketry of Hoche, or drowned in their endeavours to get through the raging waves to the English boats, capitulated.

The subjugation of Holland by the French arms, and the capture of the Dutch fleet, added much to the danger of invasion to England, as it placed the Dutch flotilla at the disposal of the Republican government.

At the time when the head of Louis XVI. fell beneath the guillotine it was certainly not foreseen that the chief of the still reigning Bourbon princes would be the first to conclude a treaty of alliance with the regicidal Republic. Such however, was now the case with Spain. Its feeble sovereign, Charles IV., was wholly governed by his queen, Elizabeth of Parma, and she in her turn by a favourite, Don Emanuel Godoy, created Prince of the Peace. Partly through dread of the French armies, and partly by means still more unworthy, a treaty of alliance with France was signed at San Ildefonso on the 19th of August. In pursuance of the measures then concerted, war was declared against England by Spain on the 5th October, 1796.

In September of the same year Mr. Pitt travelled to Weymouth, the main object of his journey being to lay before the king a project of negotiation with France. George III. assented to the proposition, and Lord Malmesbury, as ambassador, arrived at Paris in the latter part of October, having been furnished with the requisite passports from the Directory, which now formed the executive government of the Republic.

But while the directors thus openly expressed a willingness to treat, they were actively in secret pursuing a project for the invasion of our shores. Ireland was the chief objective point. A large fleet had been equipped at Brest, to which was now expected the accession of some Spanish vessels that had been ranged in the fleets antagonistic to England by the treaty of San Ildefonso. Considerable land forces were collected near Brest, and General Hoche was appointed to the chief command. Theobald Wolfe Tone, a man of no common aptitude and ardour, received the rank of Adjutant-General in the French service. To the expedition also was attached General Clarke, who was described by Tone then as a handsome, smooth-faced young man. He had come from America to take part in the expected enterprise, and was known well in after years, under the title of Duc de Feltre, as minister of war both to Napoleon and Louis XVIII. Born of Irish parents, and having once travelled for a few weeks in Ireland, he claimed an intimate knowledge of Irish affairs. Yet, according to the account of Tone, this knowledge must have been rather superficial, for he expected that in the event of a French invasion the Lord Chancellor would aid the invaders.

The king's speech at the opening of the new parliament alluded to this project of invasion, and the ministry lost no time in bringing forward measures for defence. "Our navy," said Pitt, "is the national defence of this kingdom in case of invasion. In this department, however, little remains to be done ; our fleet at this moment being more formidable than at any former period of our history. .... But I would propose in the first place a levy of 15,000 men from the different parishes for the sea service and for recruiting the regiments of the line. Of all the modes to obtain any further force there is none so expeditious, so effectual, and attended with so little expense, as that of raising a supplementary body of militia, to be grafted on the present establishment. I would propose that this supplementary body should consist of 60,000 men, not to be immediately called out, but to be enrolled, officered, and gradually trained so as to be fit for service at a time of danger. ..... Another measure which I would suggest to the committee is, to provide a considerable force of irregular cavalry, with the view of repelling an invasion. The more this species of force is extended, the greater advantage is likely to accrue from it, as an invading enemy, who must be destitute of horses, can have no means to meet it upon equal terms. . . . By the produce of the recent tax we find that the number of horses kept for pleasure in England, Scotland, and Wales is about 200,000."[1]

"It certainly would not be a very severe regulation, when compared with the object to be accomplished, to require one-tenth of those horses for the public service. Thus might we raise a cavalry force of 20,000. .....

[1] As far as can be ascertained from the returns of the Board of Trade, it would appear that the number now in the same countries is over three millions.

There is still another resource which ought not to be neglected. The licences to shoot game taken out by gamekeepers are no fewer than 7,000. Upon the supposition of an invasion, it would be of no small importance to form bodies of men, who, from their dexterity in using fire-arms, might be highly useful in harassing the operations of the enemy."[1]

These measures were opposed by the Opposition even at a time of great public danger, and when the very existence of our country might be at stake. Both Sheridan and Fox inveighed with great warmth, but with little success, against the propositions of the minister. Another member, the celebrated Mr. Wilberforce, had another grievance. In one of the new bills it was provided that the supplementary corps of militia should be trained on Sunday afternoons. Against this clause he strongly protested, and finally prevailed; and the country, even at this crisis of peril, refused to allow its volunteers to be exercised on Sunday.

At this point it may not be uninteresting to review generally the position of the British army at this time, and also of that body, the national militia, to which Mr. Pitt alluded in the above speech. At this very time Mr. Pitt and Mr. Dundas caused the archives of the state to be ransacked for all information relative to the defensive measures adopted against invasion at the time of Elizabeth, when England was threatened by the Armada. And a most interesting report was then drawn up for the government, both as regards the

[1] Speech in the House of Commons, October 18th, 1796.

defensive and offensive measures that have been adopted by England when threatened with attack. The militia, to march which out of its several counties the elder Pitt took Parliamentary powers, was a force of long standing in the British Islands. The conquest of England by William the Conqueror did not alter the original military constitution of the kingdom so much as is generally supposed. Most histories tell vaguely of the feudal system, feudal arms, and knights' service. Those, however, who will take the time and trouble to seek deeply into the old records will find that from the time of the Conqueror to the present day the principal of the natural force for the defence of the realm has remained much the same. The general levy of free men which was recognised by the laws of the Conqueror for the defence of the realm is still represented, though in a considerably altered form, by the militia. This force, however it may have been named in different periods, has always been the defensive army of England. In the Early-English days it is seen as the assembly of the trythings and hundreds; under the Plantagenets and Tudors as the *posse comitatus;* and under the House of Hanover as the militia. It little matters whether it was officered and commanded by trything-men, hundreders, sheriffs, or lord-lieutenants; it has always existed in England, and till quite modern times service in the militia has been a compulsory duty of every English freeman. Legally it is so still, though the laws of the ballot have been allowed to fall into abeyance.

In the early days of English history, after the Norman

conquest, the militia, or natural force of the country, although it was never legally abandoned, was not at all an important part of the forces at the disposal of the crown. It was natural that this should be so; the militia has in every age been an eminently national force, and till within almost the eighteenth century was composed of the masses of the people. After the Conquest the masses of the people were, however, strongly opposed to the foreign invaders and the buccaneers from Normandy, who had conquered England and divided among themselves the lands and property of the island. At that time, except among the clergy, land was almost the sole species of property, and the men of England who had formerly been rich landowners were by the results of the battle of Hastings reduced to penury and misery, and sometimes to serfdom. With the rich landowners their relations and dependents suffered. To all these classes with want came naturally discontent, and to such a discontented and depressed people the Norman Conqueror could not look for the safe defence of his newly-acquired possessions either from external or internal enemies.

It was not so much by design as by force of circumstances that the feudal system was accordingly introduced into England. The same would be the case in all conquered countries, and the result has been similar in the lands of Europe that were subjected by military power to Turkish domination. The Norman expedition to England was not an invasion by one irritated nation into the dominions of another to seek revenge or satisfaction. It was pre-eminently a filibustering expedition; in it the chieftains, and indeed the people of Normandy, took but an insignificant part. The soldiery that followed the Conqueror from the valley of the Seine across the Channel were widely recruited from desperadoes and soldiers of fortune from Flanders, Germany, and France. Their object was plunder, their aim the forcible exchange of penury for plenty. The skill of their leader, the courage of the men themselves, and the internal jealousies of Englishmen gave them the victory of Hastings, and, with one pitched battle won, England fell without another stalwart blow into their hands. Thus vainly do those argue who maintain that the spirit of Englishmen is indomitable, and that, contrary to all military and political expectation, England would form an exception to the general rule of human nature, and would maintain an undying and perpetual conquest against an army of invaders, however powerful or however successful.

When England had been occupied and its lands divided after the battle of Hastings, it was requisite not only to seize the property that had been acquired, but to preserve it. The Norman adventurers, though largely recruited from beyond the Channel, after fortune had once declared in their favour, were but an insignificant minority in the face of the whole English people. The latter were disarmed, but the laws which rendered them liable for a defence of their country were not repealed, and although the national militia was suspended, it was not abolished. Yet the national militia could obviously not be trusted to defend the conquests of its conquerors, either from other adventurers who might be tempted by the success of the former expedition to attempt another descent on the island, or from insurrections on the part of their own countrymen. It was necessary to establish a guard and a garrison for the conquered possession against either foreign or native assailants.

This led to the introduction of what is termed the feudal system into the country about the year 1086. A considerable change was then made in the military establishment of the nation, but was adopted not by the sovereign alone, but with the consent of the great council of the realm assembled at Sarum, where all the principal landholders subjected their possessions to military services, became the king's vassals, and did homage and swore fealty to his person for the lands held of him as over-lord.

By this system all the lands in the country were divided into certain portions, each producing an annual revenue, called a knight's fee. By the feudal laws every tenant holding immediately from the king the quantity of land amounting to a knight's fee was bound to hold himself in readiness with horse and arms to serve the king in his wars, either at home or abroad, at his own expense, for a stated time, generally forty days in a year, which were reckoned from the time of joining the army. Persons holding more or less were bound to do duty in proportion to their tenures.

Sometimes the king compounded with his tenants for particular services, accepting in lieu thereof pecuniary payments, with which he hired stipendiary troops. This arrangement was soon found to be more convenient for both sides: the king naturally could rely little on a force which was likely to break up at the end of forty days. It would be impossible with such an army to venture on a distant expedition, or to enter upon any campaign that might be of any long duration. Gradually fines to the crown in lieu of personal service became the custom, and subsequently were levied by assessments at so much per every knight's fee, under the name of scutages. These appeared to be raised for the first time in the fifth year of Henry II., on account of his expedition to Toulouse, and were apparently mere arbitrary compositions, as the king and the subjects could agree.

But side by side with the feudal force, the constitutional force of the militia, such as had existed in the Early-English days, was continued, and in internal struggles the local militia, under the name of *posse comitatus*, was occasionally called out. This *posse comitatus*, or power of the county, included every free man between fifteen and sixty, and was only liable to enrolment in case of internal trouble or actual invasion. But though not legally abolished, we find no trace of the *posse comitatus* being employed till 115 years after the landing of the French, and when time had allowed the English and invaders to become fused together. Then a law was enacted to provide for the armament of the national force. In the time of Edward I. effective measures were taken for the efficiency and armament of the militia in the celebrated statute of

Winchester. By that law every one possessed of lands to the yearly value of 15l. and 50 marks of goods, was forced to keep a habergeon, an iron headpiece, a sword, knife, and horse. Those with property under this amount had to keep the arms, but were excused from the horse. This statute was repealed in the first year of Philip and Mary, and another enacted, wherein armour and weapons of a more modern date were inserted.

The invention of gunpowder in the thirteenth century laid the foundation of great changes and new systems of military organisation. Under the altered conditions of war new arms were required, and the equipment became more costly and difficult. It was generally found advisable to train up bodies of men for the sole purpose of war, and to separate them as much as possible from those other employments in which formerly all soldiers were occasionally engaged.

Thus standing armies arose in England. Soon after the invention of gunpowder the Tudors established their standing guards, the earliest symptom of our present standing army, in the two bodies which still exist as the gentlemen-at-arms and the yeomen of the guard. The custom of employing mercenary troops was also henceforth much developed, and the practice was finally established in the latter part of the fourteenth century.

As the regular troops were always available and better disciplined, it naturally followed that the old militia fell into disrepute, especially on the Continent.

But in England the militia was never entirely superseded by the standing army, nor was it utterly neglected, as in most other European nations. In the time of Philip and Mary an Act was passed for the general armament of the kingdom. By this statute it was enacted that all persons having an estate of a thousand pounds and upwards should from May 1st, 1558, keep six horses or geldings, and for maintaining demi-lances, three of them at least to have sufficient harness, saddles, with bows covered with steel, and weapons for the said demi-lances. Other requirements were also made, and it was further enacted that any person whose wife wore any kind of silk, French hood, or burnet of velvet, or any chain of gold about her neck, except the sons and heirs-apparent of dukes, marquises, earls, viscounts, barons, and others having hereditaments of the yearly value of 600 marks or above, during the life of their fathers, should keep and maintain a gelding, able and meet for a light horseman, with sufficient harness and weapons for the same. Thus the maintenance of horses and armaments for war was made a land and income-tax.

The apprehension of the Spanish invasion during the reign of Elizabeth caused attention to be seriously bestowed on the militia. A commission was issued in 1572, by which all men over sixteen, and not physically incapable, were obliged to be mustered and reviewed. Such as were liable to provide horses and arms by the statute of Philip and Mary were obliged to furnish them within a limited time. From the whole population thus mustered as many men were taken as could be kept furnished at the expense of each shire, and these were formed into bands and properly drilled, and each band of 100 was made to contain forty arquebusiers and twenty archers. In these we now find the musket and the bow arrayed side by side. Those who were over sixteen, and not enrolled in these bands, were not released from service. They were exercised in the use of their arms, and held liable to be called up if required by the necessities of war. The muster in consequence of this commission amounted in England and Wales to a total of 132,689 men.

In the reign of James I. many old statutes were repealed that related to the armament of the people, and that were now found to be unsuited to the spirit of the times. Such were the statutes of Winchester and the statutes of Philip and Mary. The repeal of these laws was a strong proof of the altered circumstances of the country. It is true that there were no more borderers since England and Scotland were united under one crown. The necessity for armies was lessened, but the increased use of gunpowder had shown that untrained bodies were not trustworthy for regular war, and therefore it was useless to maintain a general armament of the whole population. In this reign it was found that the militia had fallen into great decay, since nothing had stirred the national blood since the time of the Spanish Armada, and some measures were taken to restore its efficiency. Lord-lieutenants had been instituted as military authorities of counties instead of sheriffs, who previously held that position. As early as the reign of

Edward VI. there were ordered to make a general muster of the trained forces and foot in their counties, and see to the efficiency of men, horses, and arms. As a rule the arms of the militia were placed in magazines, but the City of London retained its train-bands and artillery company.

The great struggle between Charles I. and the Parliament broke out on the question of the control of the militia. The King and Parliament both called out the militia, and lord-lieutenants of counties obeyed the side which they favoured. Under the Protectorate the militia of each military district was organised apart under the general of the district, and was kept distinct from the standing army, which was maintained on permanent pay.

Although a standing army was maintained by Charles II. and his successors, the only army then recognised by law was the militia. Two Acts of Parliament were passed shortly after the Restoration which remodelled that force. By these every man who possessed 500*l*. a year derived from land, or 6,000*l*. of personal estate, was bound to provide, equip, and pay at his own expense one horseman. Every man who had 50*l*. a year the product of land, or 600*l*. of personal estate, was similarly charged with one pikeman or musketeer. Small proprietors were united in a kind of confederation, and each county, according to its means, was forced to furnish a horseman or a foot-soldier. The whole force thus maintained was popularly estimated at 130,000 fighting men. This number appears very small after the 132,000 which could be raised in the time of Elizabeth. It would seem as if the result of the civil war was equivalent to an entire stagnation of population.

The king was by the ancient constitutional law, and by the recent acknowledgment of both Houses of Parliament, the sole captain-general of this armed force. The lord-lieutenants and their deputies held commissions from him, and appointed assemblies for drills and inspections. The time occupied by such assemblies was not allowed to exceed fourteen days in each year. For breaches of discipline every justice of the peace was authorised to inflict certain penalties. The ordinary cost of the militia was paid by the county, but when the trained bands were called out against the enemy their subsistence became a charge on the general revenue of the state, and they were subject to the articles of war. There was no legal sanction issued for the government of the standing army. Men who had been on the Continent and seen the warlike resources of continental powers looked afterwards with apprehension on the English militia. Those who knew the bastions and the ravelins of Vauban, who had seen the armies poured out by Germany to drive the Ottoman from Vienna, or the gorgeous processions of the *maison du roi* at Versailles, saw with a shudder the way in which the peasants of Lancashire and Sussex marched and wheeled, trailed pikes or carried muskets, and reflected with horror when they thought of the battalions which a westerly wind might bring to the shores of Hants or Dorset. Yet the militia was dear to the Tory party. These rural levies were almost entirely commanded by country gentlemen and noblemen, and any disparagement of the citizen soldiers was considered as a direct insult to themselves.

The Revolution, which changed the relative position of the King and the Parliament, and placed the Crown and the Commons at unity, exposed England also to the threat of an invasion. In a few weeks a host of veterans, inured to conflict and conducted by able and gallant officers, might have been landed on our coasts. Before such a force the militia would be scattered like chaff, and a regular army was accordingly developed, and a Mutiny Bill passed. When the Militia Acts were passed in the reign of Charles II., as all the men who were to be arrayed in arms were to be placed under the control of the crown, a direct prohibition was laid down against the continuance of train-bands after 1663. The train-bands of the City of London, however, and their auxiliaries, were excepted and continued.

The Acts passed in the reign of Charles II. continued in force till the middle of the following century. These placed the militia of each county under a lieutenant, to be appointed by the crown. This lieutenant had the power of appointment of deputies and officers. The pay of the soldier and the ammunition used in his training were paid for by the provider, while the county was charged with a fund to furnish necessaries. All offences were punished by the civil magistrate, the power to make articles of war being advisedly left out of the Act. It is noteworthy that this organisation of the militia was arranged directly after the Restoration, and was not affected by the revolution which placed William III. on the throne of England. Mr. Clode says that the militia force, though strictly local, could be led to any county for the suppression and defeat of insurrection, rebellion, or invasion. This, however, appears to be an error, as if such had been the case there would have been no necessity for the elder Pitt in 1758 to take powers to remove regiments of militia beyond their own counties. Mr. Hallam says that on this point at the time of the rebellion the royal prerogative was plainly deficient; and that it still remained so in the middle of the eighteenth century was clearly the view of Lord Chatham. Yet we find in the rebellion of 1745 that the Argyleshire militia was certainly moved from its own county, as well as that of Glasgow and Paisley, and the former took part in the battle of Culloden. But the militia of Argyle was rather the clan Campbell, raised by their chieftain, than a government force, and the other militia were but train-bands levied for a particular occasion. The point appears doubtful, and I have endeavoured in vain to clear it up.

The militia force, as established by the Acts of Charles II., was to consist of horse and foot-soldiers, provided by or at the expense of the owners of all property, not of land exclusively. Its numbers, as dependent on the wealth of the inhabitants, were undefined; nor does it appear from the Commons' journals that any exact estimate of the probable number that would be available under these statutes was ever laid before Parliament, though in the debate on the 15th March, 1688-9, the number of the militia is spoken of as 150,000 men. The county was charged with making provisions for a fund, afterwards known as trophy-money, which was to be appropriated to munitions of war and other necessaries, and afterwards, as the lieutenant should see fit, to the inferior officers employed in the force for their pains and encouragement. This trophy-money is still levied in the City of London. Although in the time of Charles II. considerable doubts were entertained as to the loyalty of many of the men who might be enrolled under arms, it was considered absolutely necessary that all men trained and arrayed in the use of weapons should be organised under lawful authority proceeding directly from the crown, and a direct prohibition was laid down against the continuance of train-bands. The City of London was, however, too powerful to be treated in this manner, and the train-bands of the city and their auxiliaries were continued, and are still represented in the Honourable Artillery Company. These train-bands sprang out of a voluntary association, called the Artillery Company, formed in the reign of Henry VIII. for the encouragement of archery, and which acquired a more respectable and marked character at the time of the Spanish Armada.

Such was the footing on which the militia force was placed by the legislature in the reign of Charles II. for the security of the people from foreign enemies on the one side, and from military oppression on the other. During the reigns of that sovereign and his successor,

Parliament reposed its confidence in the militia, and frequently mistrust of the standing army was manifest, as the regular army was at the time maintained exclusively by the crown, and was regarded, not unjustly, as a constant threat against the liberties of the people. The officers of the militia were under the immediate influence of the English aristocracy; the officers of the regular army were courtiers, and owed their allegiance entirely to the king. The militia was beyond the control of the crown so far that its numbers could not be reduced by the sovereign; nor could the influence of the crown be exercised on its ranks except through the lieutenants or deputy-lieutenants. With regard to the army the case was the converse. Its existence was wholly dependent on the crown; the promotion of the officers and men depended entirely on the favour of the king. The army was as dependent upon the crown as the crown was upon the army; and the militia became a standing counterpoise to the standing army and a national security, and consequently enormously popular with the people. To the present day even, when the regular army of England is as constitutional a force as can be found in the whole world, as it is voted by Parliament, and its numbers determined by the House of Commons, it is still the custom amongst old-fashioned people to talk of the militia in contradistinction to the regular army as "our constitutional force."

After the Revolution it was proposed that the militia should be reformed and made a substitute for standing armies, but no measure was passed for the purpose, and the militia had attracted little attention until the middle of the succeeding century, when the war with France directed the genius of the elder Pitt to the formation of defensive forces for our country.

During the years from 1757 to 1763 the militia law, and the principle of raising the militia by ballot, which was now for the first time introduced with parliamentary sanction to recruit the defensive forces of the kingdom, engaged the serious attention of Parliament. In 1756, to supply the regular troops with recruits, a Conscription Act had been passed, applicable to men not following " any lawful calling or employment." A similar Act to supply the regular forces with recruits had been passed during the reign of Anne. In the following year it was proposed to raise a militia force of 32,600 men by ballot, the principle of voluntary service being ignored. As the Conscription Act, which ignored voluntary service for the regular forces, applied only to the pauper classes, not unnaturally the common people objected to this Act relating to the militia. The gentlemen in many counties stood aloof, and the officers' commissions remained for some months unfilled. Opposition to the Act sprang up in various districts, amounting, in Yorkshire, to high treason, where four persons were found guilty of that crime for obstructing the Militia Act, and one underwent the punishment of death.

Invasion was still threatening, and in 1759 the Commons petitioned the Throne that direction might be given to the lord-lieutenants to use their utmost diligence, and to put the militia law into execution. Yet at this time some result had already been obtained, as by July, 1759, 17,436 men had been raised, and 6,280 were then upon embodied service. The plan upon which the militia was now organised differed greatly from the organisations which had existed under the Acts of Charles II. The crown had more direct authority given to it over the appointment of officers, as the names of deputy-lieutenants were in future to be approved, and those of the officers to be submitted before appointment. From this time, too, the crown had the appointment of adjutants and sergeants. All the officers, except the king's adjutant, were to have a property qualification. The men were to be raised from each county in specified proportions, to serve for three years. Any balloted man might pay a forfeit of 10*l*., to be applied in providing a substitute. The pay was to be the same as that of the army, and the clothes were to become the property of the men after one year's embodied or three years' disembodied service. Every fourth year one-third of the officers, save the king's adjutant, were to be discharged for others willing to accept commissions. The militia when out for training, or embodied was henceforth to be under the Mutiny Act and Articles of War. The crown gained also the power of calling out the militia in case of war, and placing it under the general officers of the army. An Annual Pay and Clothing Act was required to be passed to provide for the pay and clothing of the men. This Act is still continued. The most important provision contained in the Acts passed under George II. was that which enabled the crown, under the condition of previously apprising parliament thereof if sitting, or of calling parliament together if not sitting, to draw out and embody the militia in case of actual invasion, or upon imminent danger thereof, or in case of rebellion, and to place it under the general officers of the regular army, to serve in any part of the kingdom for the suppression of such invasion or rebellion. No express limits were imposed by Parliament upon the duration or period of the embodied service. It appears that whenever actual danger of invasion threatens, it is seen that it becomes more and more necessary that every defensive force, such as the militia, should be more closely allied to the regular army, and placed more under the direct control of the officers appointed by the crown for the government and conduct of the regular troops. The relative ranks of the officers in the militia was laid down then as equal in degree but junior in service to those of the regular forces. In 1760 an attempt was made to introduce the system of militia then adopted in England into Scotland, but the Bill was lost by a considerable majority.

The militia system instituted by the elder Pitt endured a quarter of a century, after which the militia laws were consolidated, in the year 1786, in one Act, containing as its preamble the words, that "a respectable militia force, under the command of officers possessing landed property within Great Britain, is essential to the constitution of this realm; and the militia now by law established has been found capable of fulfilling the purposes of its institution."

At the outbreak of the French revolutionary wars the statutory quota of militia for England and Wales was 30,740 men, to be raised by ballot, or by parish officers obtaining volunteers, to be paid by a bounty from the rates. In 1794 the militia was augmented by permitting persons to raise companies of militia, and so to obtain rank; and in 1795 men were allowed to volunteer from the militia into the artillery or navy. In 1796 Parliament sanctioned the raising of a supplementary militia of 59,441 men for England and 4,437 for Wales. In the same year a provisional cavalry force was to be raised by ballot in the proportion of a horse and man for every ten horses kept.

In 1797 the militia system was first applied by law to Scotland. Although we find that in the rebellion of 1745 militia regiments were employed, it would appear that these were much more volunteers and train-bands than actual militia, such as we should consider to be militia in the present day. Scotland at the end of the last century had to raise 6,000 militiamen, who were embodied in 1798; and in 1802 its quota was fixed at 7,950 men. At the present time 10,000 men can be raised in Scotland in ordinary times, and an addition of 5,000 in case of war.

In Ireland the militia establishment dates from 1715, when an Act of the Irish Parliament was passed, on account of the rebellion, authorising the governors of counties to array all persons between the ages of sixteen and sixty. In 1809 the militia laws of Ireland were consolidated by the Parliament of the United Kingdom. The number of Irish militia is now 30,000, with power to raise an additional 15,000 in time of war. In 1802 the militia ceased to be exclusively Protestant; in that year it numbered 46,963 men. Since those times the area for the service of the militia has been much widened. Though the militia of each kingdom exists as a separate force, by statute, the whole militia force of the three kingdoms can be used interchangeably, or consolidated in one kingdom, if desired. The crown has now also the power to accept voluntary offers from the militia to serve in the Channel Islands and the Isle of Man.

The militia since 1757 has rendered embodied service for the country on several occasions. During the Seven Years' War it was embodied against invasion. In 1778, during the American war, it was again embodied, and the force remained embodied till March, 1783. Again for the suppression of insurrection and rebellion, succeeded by the threat of invasion, the proclamation for embodiment was issued in December, 1792, and it was disembodied in April, 1803. After the rupture of the peace of Amiens, on the apprehensions of the descent of Napoleon on the coast, the militia was again embodied. The policy of the Act of 1802 was to prohibit the men of the militia from entering the regular army; but in the time of the Peninsular war the difficulty of finding recruits for the army caused the government to make an alteration. Thus the militia was invited to change its character from a defensive to an offensive force, and to join the army in Portugal. Again in the Crimean war, the same reason led to volunteers being freely accepted from the militia to join the regular ranks as recruits. By the laws at present in force service in the militia is obligatory on all men balloted between eighteen and sixty, but the ballot is not practically put in force.

The first symptom of the formation of a standing army in England is to be found in the shape of the body-guards raised by the Tudors, which still endure as the gentlemen-at-arms and the yeomen of the guard. These were of small numbers. But each successive improvement in fire-arms made the government depend more and more on mercenary troops, till after the Restoration it was necessary to form a regular standing army. In the time of Henry VII. the only foreign war was a military expedition to Boulogne; and in that of Henry VIII. the battles of the Spurs and Flodden took place; but these were conducted by regular mercenary troops. In the reign of James I. it was proposed to send an army from England of 25,000 infantry, 5,000 horse, and twenty pieces of artillery to aid in the recovery of the Palatinate; but this force was far too large to suit the parsimonious tastes of the king, and ultimately only one regiment was sent. This body consisted only of 2,200 men, and was composed chiefly of noblemen and gentlemen. Later in the reign of James, on account of the war with Spain, an army of 6,000 men was sent over to the United Provinces. And in the first year of Charles I. an army of 10,000 men "raised by the press," as the Commons refused to grant supplies, was sent against Cadiz. This army, without encountering the enemy, succumbed in the wine cellars of the town, and became so insubordinate that it had to be re-embarked and brought home. In 1627 the expedition which was so unfortunate was sent against the Isle De Ré. It consisted of 7,000 men; those who were saved from annihilation were billeted on their return in various parts of England, and the conduct of this soldiery had much to do with the framing of the Petition of Right, which was founded on the four grievances—exaction of money under the name of loans, suspension of the Habeas Corpus, billeting of soldiers on private persons, and the exercise of martial law.

The civil war was fought out chiefly by volunteers, train-bands, and militia. The king was supported by most of the nobility and gentry, by the Church of England and the Catholics. On the other hand, the City of London, most of the corporations, and the commercial portion of the community upheld the Commons. Both sides levied troops of a volunteer description, as far as they possibly could, and the custom then was introduced, which has lasted to the present day, of designating regiments by distinctive appellations. We hear of the King's Life Guards Foot, dressed in red, the Royal Horse Guards, the Prince of Wales's regiment of horse, and others. The Parliamentary regiments were usually dressed in the liveries of their colonels, and designated according to their colours. Thus we find Sir William

Constable's Blue Coats, Lord Robart's Red Coats, Colonel Meyrick's Grey Coats, &c. But none of these regiments have any connection with those who at the present day are designated Life Guards, Blues, or Buffs. The best troops on the Parliamentary side were the celebrated Ironsides raised by Cromwell.

Under the Protectorate Cromwell kept up the army. It was well organised and regularly paid, and at one time consisted of 80,000 men.

During the reign of the Stuarts, after the Restoration, the Commons were strongly opposed to a standing army within the country, having been sickened by the military despotism of the Protectorate. But the necessity of keeping garrisons in the various fortified places, such as the Tower of London, Portsmouth, and Pendennis Castle, was admitted. A guard to the sovereign was also a necessity in the days when police were unknown, and for this purpose a small standing army was allowed.

On the restoration of the monarchy in 1660, the army which was at that time in existence, consisting of fifteen regiments of horse and twenty-one regiments of foot, was disbanded by the Convention Parliament. The Act of Disbandment, however, sanctioned the continuance of guards and garrisons. The garrisons were to be re-established and placed in the same condition as they were in the year 1637, and out of the residue of soldiers, including some regiments that were on the Scottish establishment, the king was at liberty to retain as a guard such of them as his majesty should think fit to provide for at his own expense.

The Act gave an authority to the king which was easily abused, for it did not specify the points on which all parliaments since the Revolution have laid such stress, namely, the number of men to be retained in pay as soldiers. During the reign of Charles II. the retention of these troops in the employ, and nominally in the pay, of the crown, was a grievance to the people, as they were often left at free quarters.

From the Restoration date the title-deeds of the present standing army of England, the army which has carried with honour and glory the colours of our country in Germany, the Low Countries, the Peninsula, India, and Africa.

Of the Parliamentary army which had existed before the Restoration, after the accession of Charles II., General Monk's regiment, which had been raised at Coldstream, was retained, and is still known in the Army List as the Coldstream Guards. This regiment was placed on the English establishment as the second regiment of Guards. Two troops of Life Guards, now the 1st and 2nd regiments of Household Cavalry, were formed from gentlemen who had been in exile with Charles. In the autumn of 1660 a regiment of horse commanded by the Earl of Oxford was raised; it was then known as the Oxford Blues, now as the Royal Horse Guards Blue. In 1661 the first regiment of Guards, now known as the Grenadier Guards, was formed. In the same year Douglas's regiment, which had been serving on the Continent, was brought to England. This regiment is now the 1st Royal Scots. At the same time the present 2nd Queen's, which had been raised for the garrison of Tangier, and which still bears the Paschal Lamb, that had been assumed as a device when fighting against the Moors, as well as the 3rd Buffs, were placed on the English establishment. On the Scottish establishment, which existed separate from the English till the Union, there was a troop of Life Guards and a regiment of Scotch Guards, now known as the Royal Scots Fusilier Guards, which at the time of the Union were transferred to the English list. There were also some dragoons in Scotland as well as the infantry regiment now known as the 21st North British Fusiliers. These troops may be regarded as the nucleus of the present standing army. During the reign of Charles II. there was also the Admiral's regiment, which then ranked as the third of the line. This regiment, after being on various occasions disbanded and restored, has been gradually converted into the Royal Marines. With the exception of the Admiral's regiment, which was employed on particular service, and the fixed garrisons of the fortified places, the remainder of the army was chiefly used as armed police. It was employed in enforcing the laws against Dissenters. One of the few statutes which have ever expressly sanctioned the employment of the military in the discharge of civil duties was that passed in the time of Charles II. for the suppression of conventicles. On this account orthodoxy appears at this time to have been considered a most rigorous necessity in the soldiery. So much was the army subject to ecclesiastical domination, that in the old articles of war of the time of James II., it is declared that any soldier who blasphemes shall have his tongue burnt through with a red-hot iron. This punishment is now obsolete, and therefore we may presume that anathemas are now unknown in the British army, and that there is no necessity for their suppression.

The military forces were also employed in other police duties : to apprehend highwaymen and thieves, to put down riots, to arrest runaway seamen from ships, to pluck up and destroy all tobacco planted, to patrol the roads round the metropolis against footpads, and to furnish escorts for specie being sent to Portsmouth for the use of the fleet.

At this time the army claimed immunity from the civil law and to be responsible solely to the crown. It was held that no magistrate could imprison an officer or soldier except for high treason, or for killing or robbing any person not being a soldier. There was no Mutiny Act, and the army was governed solely by articles of war arbitrarily issued by the crown.

At this time there were no barracks, and the soldiers were billeted in taverns and public-houses, and often to the great grievance of the people, in private houses. The men were supposed to find their own food out of their pay, but the pay depended entirely on the civil list, and was often not provided for, or much in arrear; so that practically the troops generally lived at free quarter, and the people on whom they were billeted were glad to pay each man 5d. or 6d. a day to find himself in food. Notwithstanding that there was an article of war which condemned every man who abused or beat his host to be put in irons, or who exacted free quarter without leave of his chief officer to be punished by court-martial, this billeting of soldiers was a great grievance to the people; but it continued in England through full a century even in time of peace. When Englishmen complain of the expenses of their army they should bear in mind that one of the serious items of army expenditure consists in the cost of the barrack establishment, which provides for the retention of the soldiers in special barracks, and the freedom of the householder from their entertainment. This and the freedom from conscription are two great luxuries which the Englishman enjoys in comparison with the foreigner.

Under the Stuarts the distribution of the army rested solely with the crown. A regiment might be ordered to any place that convenience might suggest. When a town was selected, the Secretary of State intimated to the local authorities that they must find the necessary accommodation for officers and men. In Westminster special parts of the town were told off for each contingent of the Life Guards and Household Infantry, who crowded every alehouse and brandy shop round Whitehall, from the country end of Piccadilly to the city gate of the Strand. The standing army in the early days of Charles II. consisted of about 5,000 men; but when the Dutch ravaged the coasts 12,000 men were raised for the land service. The Commons looked with great jealousy upon this increase, and passed a Bill to humbly request his majesty that, when a peace was concluded, the new force was to be disbanded. In the next year the Commons voted the standing army a grievance, and on the announcement of peace the king declared that the army in England should be reduced to a less number than in 1663.

At this time the crown had the power to keep an army of any strength abroad. It was attempted, indeed, to raise a force of 20,000 foot and 2,000 horse in Scotland ; and it would have been possible for the king to maintain a large English army in the pay of France, which the crown could bring over when required to subvert the liberties of England. In 1677 and 1678 these dangers were cancelled by the introduction of a Subsidy Act, with a sort of estimate and appropriation clause.

In the reign of Charles II. the purchase of commissions by officers was established. A warrant was issued for the regulation of prices to be paid, and the royal assent gave the system legality. These prices were with some modifications retained till our own day, when the purchase system was abolished, and compensation given to the officers interested, in 1871. For poor soldiers, before this time, who were worn out in the service, there were no pensions. Such were thrown on the poor-rates, and looked on as a nuisance by the guardians. This increased the unpopularity of the army among the people. Chelsea Hospital was then founded as a hospital for aged and infirm soldiers upon an estate vested in the crown. The cost of its erection and maintenance was defrayed by a poundage levied on the pay of every soldier ; and this system was only abolished in

1847. Thus Chelsea Hospital has not been supported by the state or by the people, and belongs to the British army; this point should be borne in mind in any scheme that may be brought forward for the reorganisation of this establishment.

The ordnance department had existed before the time of Charles II., but in 1660 a royal warrant was issued, by which the department was re-organised on a civil footing and entrusted with the supply of stores to the army and navy. Transport was at that time provided by the impressment of carriages or ships, when required by the ordnance or navy. The present condition of the royal artillery, which sprang from this small beginning, is due in great measure to two of the invasions of which this work treats. It was to the rebellion of 1715, and through the experience gained in that contest, that the origin of the royal regiment of artillery was due, and it was through the invasion of 1745 that the corps of military drivers were added to field artillery, and that it acquired its mobility.

Before the close of the reign of Charles II. the fortress of Tangier, which had formed a portion of the dowry of the queen, was given up. The garrison which, consisted of one regiment of horse and two of foot, was brought to England and placed on the English establishment. This regiment of horse was formed into the corps which is now designated as the first regiment of dragoons. The second regiment of foot which returned from the war was formed into the corps which now rank as the second and fourth of the line.

In the time of Charles II., on the separate Scotch and Irish military establishments, there were only sufficient troops to keep down the Puritan malcontents in the former country and the Popish malcontents in the latter. The king had, however, an important military resource. In the pay of the United Provinces there were six fine regiments; of these three had been raised in Scotland and three in England. The King of England had the power to recall these if he had occasion to require their services; meantime they were maintained free of charge to the British crown, and kept under excellent discipline.

James II. had a great desire to raise a large standing army; not perhaps so much for the sake of the security of the realm as for the coercion of his own subjects. He took advantage of the rebellion of Monmouth to increase his forces. The regiments now known as the first six regiments of dragoon guards were raised as regiments of horse in consequence of that rebellion. Of these regiments of horse, the King's Horse, Queen's Horse, and Wade's Horse were, after the rebellion of 1745, reduced to dragoons on account of economy, and called the 1st, 2nd, and 3rd Dragoon Guards. The remaining regiments of these horse, and a regiment which was subsequently raised, were reduced to dragoon guards only in 1788. The regiments which are now known as the 4th, 5th, 6th, and 7th Dragoon Guards, were at the time of the rebellion in 1745 on the Irish establishment, and were known as the Blue Horse, Green Horse, Carabineers, and Black Horse, from the colour of their facings. At the time of the rebellion of Monmouth there were also raised the 3rd and 4th regiments of dragoons; the corps which is now known as the 2nd regiment of Dragoons being already in existence on the Scottish establishment as the Scots Greys. The nine regiments of infantry which now rank as the 7th, 8th, 9th, 10th, 11th, 12th, 13th, 14th, and 15th of the line, were also raised at this time. The result of these augmentations and the recall of the garrison of Tangier was that the standing army was increased from the numbers of the previous reign to nearly 20,000 men.

When James was threatened with the invasion of the Prince of Orange, his regular army was the largest that any king of England had ever commanded. It was rapidly augmented; new companies were added to the existing regiments, and fresh commissions were issued for raising more regiments. Four thousand men were added to the English establishment; 3,000 were sent for with all speed from Ireland; as many more were ordered to move southward from Scotland; and it was estimated that the king could meet the invaders at the head of 40,000 men besides the militia. But the army was not to be trusted in the cause. It was, like the people, anxious for a liberal prince; and though the soldiery did not desert their sovereign, the officers did in large numbers; and it was impossible to oppose the enemy in more than one skirmish near Reading. Lord Faversham, on hearing of James's flight, ordered his army to disband; but the Protestants were re-assembled by William, and the Irish soldiers sent home.

Two regiments which had been in the service of the United Provinces were brought to England in William's reign at the time of the war in Ireland. These are now known as the 5th and 6th of the line. At the time of Dundee's rebellion in Scotland, from among the western Scotch, who were of strong Puritan principles, the Cameronian regiment was raised, and is now the 26th of the line. This regiment had a very peculiar character; the soldiers were all strict Puritans; one of their first acts was to petition parliament that all drunkenness, licentiousness, and profaneness should be rigorously punished. It was intended to establish a Puritan organisation in the regiment; each company was to provide an elder, and these, with the chaplain, were to form a court for the suppression of immorality and heresy. The elders were not however appointed, and from the regimental records it does not appear that this peculiar regimental court has been established, even up to the present day.

In the year 1693, on account of the war, the army was increased by four new regiments of dragoons, six of horse and fifteen of infantry. By the time of the peace of Ryswick the army consisted of 87,000 excellent soldiers, which in three years were reduced after the peace to 7,000 men. It must be borne in mind, however, that a large number of the former were foreigners in English pay.

After the peace of Ryswick a serious question arose

as to what was to be done with the army. A strong party wished the regular troops disbanded altogether, and the safety of the country entrusted solely to the militia. The court wished to maintain an army of 30,000 men. The Commons, however, passed a resolution which reduced the army to the same strength as that at which it had been after the peace of Nimeguen. This, according to Macaulay, was about 10,000 men. The resolutions passed by the Commons were: first, that all the land forces of England in English pay, exceeding 7,000 men, commissioned and non-commissioned, officers included, be forthwith disbanded; secondly, that all the forces in Ireland exceeding 12,000 men, including officers, be forthwith disbanded, and that such forces as should be kept in Ireland should be kept by the kingdom of Ireland. Thus a standing army in Ireland was established by a permanent statute. It was increased to 15,234 men in the reign of William III. by a statute which remained in force till the time of the union.

Notwithstanding these reductions, we find, however, that there were on the English establishment 14,834 men; and on that for the Plantations and abroad 1,258; and the Irish establishment had 15,488 men. The reason of the surplus of troops can be accounted for. The Commons did not then fix the amount of the force to be maintained by the crown; they merely voted the money to support the army, and if the crown could make the money suffice for a larger number it seems to have been permitted to do so. The army vote at this time amounted to 350,000*l*. As usual with our

English system of military administration, before Lord Cardwell assumed the reins of the War Office, an unsparing reduction caused a most expensive and lavish increase. The war that soon followed obliged Great Britain again to engage a large force. This consisted of foreign rather than of native troops. In 1711 the soldiery mustered in the pay of England amounted to 201,000 men. The peace of Utrecht was afterwards made, and the Secretary for War laid his first estimate before the Commons for his Majesty's forces in the Plantations, Minorca, Gibraltar, and Dunkirk, showing 11,125 men to be in pay there. He was the following day ordered by the House to bring forward an estimate of 8,000 men; this second estimate was adopted. A Mutiny Act was passed which limited the force to 8,000 men with regard to his Majesty's person and the safety of his kingdom. This economy led to a rebellion and the raising of an army of 15,000 men—such is generally the result of the sudden reduction of military establishments.

In the reign of George I. the conspiracy against the king's life was the avowed reason for the augmentation of the army. Its duration was to be for one year; but the last estimate submitted in the reign of George I. was for 18,226 men, besides an increase of 8,286 men to the guards and garrisons of Great Britain. During the reign of George II. there were several augmentations to the army, and some new services provided. The Admiral's regiment, which had been raised as a marine force in the reign of Charles II., was disbanded at the revolution; and the Buffs, or Holland regiment, then took the rank of 3rd of the line. In the year 1694 two regiments of marines were raised by order of council; they were placed under the direction of the Admiralty, and under the command of the naval officers when on board ship. In 1702 the 30th, 31st, and 32nd regiments of the line were formed, and served as marine regiments. On the peace of Utrecht they were disbanded, but in the year 1739 the marine force was again established. In 1746 it was restored, and at the peace of Aix-la-Chapelle in 1748 again totally disbanded. The marine force as at present established under the Admiralty dates from the year 1755. The marines, when serving in the army, rank between the 49th and 50th regiments of the line.

In 1735 Walpole considered that there should never be less than 18,000 regular troops in this country; and in 1763 there were 18,000 men voted for England, 10,000 for America, and the usual number of a little over 12,000 for Ireland. In 1739 the Highland regiment now known as the 42nd Highlanders, or the Black Watch, was regimented, being formed of the independent companies of Highlanders then in English pay for the protection of the northern portion of the island against robbers. After the suppression of the rebellion in 1745, two troops of Life Guards were disbanded and the Life Guards were reduced to two troops. At the time of the peace of Aix-la-Chapelle in 1748 the estimates showed for the army in Great Britain 49,939 men; and 15,627 for the Plantations and abroad. As soon however as the war was brought to a close, as usual, the estimates show a reduction of the forces to 18,857 men for Great Britain, and 9,542 for the Plantations.

No sooner almost were these reductions made, without any care as to future necessity, or without any organization of reserves, while no power of recalling men into the ranks had been provided, than an augmentation was necessary. In 1755 this was gradually increased, till in 1762 the aggregate of men voted was 67,766 for Great Britain and Germany, and 37,347 for the Plantations. Yet so difficult was it to house troops on account of the want of a barrack establishment, that immediately on peace being made, for this reason, as well as on account of economical considerations, the estimates were reduced to 17,536 men for Great Britain, and 28,406 for the Plantations and abroad.

In 1770 there was an apprehension of war with Spain, and 5,000 additional men were voted for one year. With this exception, no important increase was made to the army till 1778, when the numbers were increased to 20,057 men. The recognition of the independence of America by France led to war with the latter country, and in 1779 the estimates showed 30,346 men for Great Britain; 47,038 in the Plantations, besides 5,360 of the Irish establishment; 14,440 men in augmentation; 24,039 foreigners, besides 786 foreign artillerymen serving under treaties in the pay of Great Britain. In 1783 the soldiers in Great Britain were augmented to 54,678 men. The peace followed, and in the succeeding year the estimates provide, with an extraordinary decrease, for only 17,483 men in Great Britain. This number, which now for fifty years seems to have been the number allotted to Great Britain in peace, appears to have been the amount for which barrack accommodation could be found. In this year, for the first time, 6,336 men were voted for India. The strength voted in 1784 was not changed till 1787, when a slight reduction was made, as there usually is in England just before a war.

In 1787 the crown subsidised Hesse Cassel, and for 36,000*l.* per annum obtained the services of 12,000 Hessian troops to serve in the pay of Great Britain. That subsidy did not pass without debate in the House of Commons, but being supported by Burke, was eventually agreed to without a division.

Now comes the period of the wars of the French Revolution. It was necessary to increase the army in 1794, and no reduction could effectively be made till after the Waterloo campaign of 1815, as Mr. Pitt was too prescient to allow the reduction which would probably otherwise have been made directly after the peace of Amiens, and pressed upon Mr. Addington, the Prime Minister, the necessity of careful and vigorous military preparations in view of another outbreak of hostilities. No serious reduction was accordingly made till after the fall of Napoleon I. From that time the army has never been reduced in peace to the low state in which it was previously held. Barracks have been provided, which relieve the people of the onus of billeting, while a wider diffusion of education, and more liberal views, have convinced even those most wedded to sole reliance upon the militia, that under the happy constitution of this country a standing army is not a menace, but a strength and a defence to the liberties of our nation.

Besides the measures taken for the increase of the army, the ministry did not neglect financial arrangements. The National Debt had now risen to upwards of 400,000,000*l.*, and the strain upon the public resources was indicated by that sure barometer, a steady decline in the price of stocks. In January of this year the lowest point to which the Three per Cents had fallen had been 67; in the September following they fell at one time to 53. A new loan of 18,000,000*l.* was announced at 5 per cent., to be taken at 112*l.* 10*s.* for every hundred of stock; and with an option to the proprietors to be paid off at par within two years after a treaty of peace. But these terms, which at the present time would appear exorbitant, under the threat of an invasion were considered but scanty, and the subscription list for the loan could never have been filled had not Pitt, in proposing it, addressed himself to higher motives than the love of gain. He urged it to be taken up, not as a profitable speculation, but as a patriotic duty, and hence it was called the Loyalty Loan. This surely ought to be an example to the people of England to be careful in maintaining their defences against invasion in a state of preparation, when we see that on the mere threat of an invasion the funds fell to 53; and it was only through patriotic spirit, and not through any sense of profitable investment, that a loan for eighteen millions at 5 per cent. could be obtained in the rich city of London and throughout the country.

The negotiations begun by Lord Malmesbury at Paris went badly. The English government insisted that the Low Countries should not remain a part of France. It became clear that the French government were wholly adverse to such a sacrifice; and on the 19th December, 1796, M. Delacroix, as Minister for Foreign Affairs, wrote to Lord Malmesbury, requiring him and his suite to quit Paris within forty-eight hours, and to lose no time in departing from the territory of the French Republic.

During the whole of the summer and autumn of 1796 General Hoche in Brittany had been indefatigable in his exertions to prepare for the invasion of Ireland. For a long time he was thwarted by the incapacity, perhaps even the ill-will, of the naval commanders employed. But at the beginning of December he held at Brest, ready to embark, 15,000 regular troops, with transports to convey them, escorted by about twenty frigates and seventeen sail of the line. Under him were serving Colonel Shee and other good officers of the Irish brigade raised in the French service. Some of these, however, were to him the less useful, as having in great part forgotten their native language Wolfe Tone, whose journal of this expedition is one of the best authorities to consult in its study, was also there, full of his old hatred against the British government. He had drafted addresses and proclamations to the peasantry of Ireland,

and spoke confidently of a popular rising as soon as the army of invasion landed.

The preparations made at Brest for this invasion have in them nothing at all repugnant to the rules and usages of ordinary war, calculated as they were to cause civil strife and bloodshed. But another scheme proposed by the French government at this time can hardly be classed in the same category. The Directory had equipped a large number of felons and galley-slaves. It was their intention to cast these loose on the shores of England, not with any purpose of conquest, of victory, or even of an organised scheme of requisitions, but merely with the view of havoc and destruction to the lives and honour of the defenceless country people. These scoundrels were not admitted into the regular French service, but were organised into a special body, distinguished by a black uniform, and called La Légion Noire. They were under the command of Colonel Tate, an American officer, who volunteered his services for this special unsavoury duty. Wolfe Tone in his journal of 10th November writes:— " I saw the Légion Noire reviewed, about 1,800 men. They are the banditti intended for England, and sad blackguards they are ; they put me in mind of the Green-boys of Dublin." Again on the 26th of the same month he says :—" To-day by the general's orders I have made a fair copy of General Tate's instructions, with some alterations, particularly with regard to their first destination, which is now fixed to be Bristol. If he arrives safe it will be very possible to carry it by a *coup-de-main*, in which case he is to burn it to the ground. I cannot but observe here that I transcribed with the greatest *sang-froid* the order to reduce to ashes the third city of the British dominions, in which there is perhaps property to the amount of 5,000,000*l*. . . . ." And yet once again. "A conflagration of the city of Bristol is no slight affair. Thousands and thousands of families, if the attempt succeeds, will be reduced to beggary. I cannot help it; if it must be so, it must; and I will never blame the French for any degree of misery which they inflict on the people of England. For the truth is I hate the very name of England; I hated her before my exile, I have hated her since, and I hate her always." To such dangers as the burning of an important centre of commercial industry such as Bristol does the absence of security against invasion expose us.

The Directory had sent their final orders to General Hoche to attempt the invasion, while the negotiation with Lord Malmesbury was still in progress in Paris, and the armament sailed from Brest on the 15th December, four days before the injunction to quit Paris was transmitted to the English ambassador. "We are all in high spirits," writes Wolfe Tone, "and the troops are as gay as if they were going to a ball."

Bantry Bay was assigned as the place of general concentration. The French vessels succeeded in avoiding the English fleet, which was cruising off the coast of Brittany to stay their passage, and from which they were hidden by a thick fog. But the same fog that was favourable to their passing round the English fleet was a great obstacle to their keeping safely together and making the proper course; while heavy gales which also sprang up tended to disperse the convoys. Only a part of the armament reached Bantry Bay and anchored there. General Hoche, who was on board one of the frigates with his whole staff, found himself driven to a different point of the Irish coast. Thus on the shores of Ireland at this time there was an invading general without troops and a force of invading troops without a general. The officers who were in command had at one time determined to land without Hoche, and push forward into the country; but they found that they could not get together half of the original force; and such as was in Bantry Bay was almost without artillery, stores, or supplies. In the absence of the general the admiral refused his sanction to placing the men on shore, weighed anchor, made sail, and steered back to France. The convoy reached Brest in safety, but not without some loss of ships, and Hoche with his staff came back to La Rochelle. The idea of invasion was now relinquished, because Hoche was appointed to the command of the army of the Sambre and Meuse.

The French government seems to have abandoned this invasion without any valid cause, and to have given it up on the very slightest symptom of failure. It is of course difficult to calculate what would have been the results had the army landed in Ireland. Wolfe Tone considered that their success would have been great; but in this it is not unlikely that he deceived himself with that impetuosity which usually characterises exiles hoping to return to their own country.

Meanwhile the government had taken vigorous measures for defence, and several friends of Tone, on whose assistance he calculated, had already been arrested for high treason. We find that the Lord-Lieutenant reports to the Secretary of State that the volunteers seemed to vie with the regular troops in loyal ardour, and he adds, " About the time the army was ordered to march the utmost attention was paid them by the inhabitants of the towns and villages through which they passed ; so that in many places the meat provided by the commissioners was not consumed. Some of the poor people even shared their potatoes with them, and divided their meal without demanding payment. The roads, which had been in parts rendered impassable by the snow, were cleared by the peasantry. At Carlow a considerable subscription was made for the troops as they passed through. A useful impression was no doubt made on the minds of the lower Catholics by an address of the titular Bishop of Cork." Much reliance, however, cannot be placed on the conduct of the peasantry to an army marching through the country. It is well known that the peasantry in any country will always work for the officers of an army who pay them for their labour ; while the individual soldiers are usually on good terms with the people in whose houses they are billeted, unless they are stirred up by their officers to plunder and ferocity.

The banditti expedition to England was not, however, given up when the expedition from Brest was abandoned. In hopes of more favourable weather than had befallen the armament of Hoche, it did not set out till the month of February. Then two French frigates, a corvette, and a lugger, sailed from Brest, and entered the Bristol Channel with Colonel Tate, and about 1,200 of his blackguards on board. They anchored at Ilfracombe on the 22nd of February, and scuttled several merchant ships, but, notwithstanding their instructions, attempted no further progress in that quarter. Hearing that some troops were out against them, they steered to the opposite coast of Pembrokeshire, and anchored in Fishguard Bay the same evening. Here they landed and began to plunder; but here again the volunteers and militia were instantly in front of them, commanded by Lord Cawdor. These were only a few hundred strong, but they were joined by great numbers of the country people, armed with implements of husbandry, or with the first weapons they could lay hands on. Another incident of a humorous kind is said to have done great service. A large crowd of old Welsh women had gathered on the beach, dressed in the scarlet cloaks which then, and for some years afterwards, were in common use among the female peasantry of England. These being seen from the ships afar off, led to the idea that they were regular troops. Colonel Tate, impressed with the scarlet cloaks, and being deprived of any means of retreat by his ships having sailed away, sent a flag of truce with an offer of capitulation. Lord Cawdor answered by requiring the invaders to surrender themselves as prisoners of war. They complied, and next day accordingly laid down their arms without a blow. Both the frigates which had brought them were taken by English men-of-war on their return to France, and thus ingloriously ended this unwarrantable enterprise.

Till this invasion it had been usually understood that a descent could not be effected without transports. In the present instance the French government appears to have considered that the best transport vessels which could be used for the conveyance of troops were those which carried guns; and the soldiers were embarked on the men-of-war which under ordinary circumstances would have been required to act as the fighting convoy of the transport fleet.

The design of Hoche and the buccaneering expedition of Tate were, however, only designed as the forerunner of a more important expedition against our shores. To invade England upon a larger scale was now a favourite scheme with the French Directory and the French people. With the object of obtaining a large naval force with which they might gain the command of the Channel and cover the convoy of troop-ships, they had recourse to their new allies at Madrid and at the Hague. It was intended that the great body of the Spanish fleet and also of the Dutch fleet should sail out of the harbours of Spain and Holland and unite with the French armament at Brest. It was calculated that by this union of perhaps full seventy ships of the line the French government would have naval strength sufficient to command the British Channel and to render easy a descent upon the south coast of England.

The main Spanish fleet, commanded by Don Joseph

de Cordova, was lying at this time in Carthagena Bay. It sailed on the 1st February, with Cadiz as its first destination, but it was driven from its course by contrary winds off Cape St. Vincent. There on the 14th Sir John Jervis, with the British squadron from the Tagus, fell in with it. Cordova had with him twenty-five sail of the line ; one of these, built at the Havana in 1769, named the *Santissima Trinidad*, had four decks and carried 130 guns, and was the largest ship which at that time existed in the world. The Spanish crews were, however, for the most part untrained and ill-affected to the service, having been recently raised by a forced conscription of landsmen.

At this moment Sir John Jervis had been most seasonably joined by Admiral Parker from England and Commodore Nelson from Elba ; yet notwithstanding this accession of strength, Jervis could only place fifteen ships of the line in action. By a splendid manœuvre, however, at the beginning of the contest, his fleet passed through the hostile ships, cutting off from the latter a division of six vessels. The main brunt of the battle that ensued was sustained by Commodore Nelson and Captain Collingwood. Nelson most gallantly boarded one of the Spanish eighty-gun ships, the *St. Joseph*, crying, " Victory, or Westminster Abbey," as he rushed forward, fighting, from deck to deck, and, supported by Collingwood, he finally prevailed. In a private letter Collingwood thus describes the scene : " The Commodore on the quarter-deck of a Spanish first-rate, receives the submission of the swords of the officers of the two vessels ; one of his sailors, William Fearney by name, bundled up the swords with as much composure as he would have made faggots, though twenty-two sail of their line was still within gun shot."

At the close of the action there had struck their flags, besides the *St. Joseph*, three Spanish ships of the line, while several others, and among them the *Santissima Trinidad*, were almost entirely disabled. The Spaniards showed no inclination to renew the fight, but retired during the night to the refuge of Cadiz Bay. This victory, though not comparable either as to the fierceness of the struggle or the magnitude of the results, to some others at sea that followed it, was, as far as England was concerned, of the utmost moment. By the action off Cape St. Vincent the Spanish fleet was prevented from joining the armament at Brest, and thus Jervis defeated one of the divisions of the enemy's squadron in detail, and prevented the concentration, which would have been full of peril to our country.

It was intended that the Dutch fleet should have been ready at the same time to assist the Spanish fleet to gain the French armament at Brest, but with signal good fortune to England the equipment of the Dutch was delayed until the celebrated mutinies of the fleet at Portsmouth and Sheerness, which broke out about this time, had passed away. It was not till near the close of June that the preparations in the ports of Holland were completed. Then Wolfe Tone was summoned to the Hague ; here General Hoche had already arrived just before him, and cried, in welcoming Tone, " Good news for you; the two Dutch chiefs, the Governor-General Daendels and the Admiral de Winter, desire to do something striking that shall rescue their country from decline. By the most indefatigable pains they have got together at the Texel sixteen sail of the line and eight or ten frigates, all ready for sea, and in the best condition ; the object they have in view is the invasion of Ireland. For this object they will embark the whole of their national troops, amounting to 15,000 men, besides 3,000 stand of arms and eighty pieces of artillery."

But there was an obstacle. The French government demanded that of the invading force 5,000 men at least should be French, and that General Hoche should have the supreme command of the whole. On the other hand, the Dutch government, who had met the entire expense, wished to have the whole glory of the expedition. General Hoche ultimately, in a generous spirit, waived his pretensions, and went back to Paris, and from thence to his army on the Sambre and Meuse. The French Directors, not a little annoyed, ordered another armament of their own to be prepared at Brest, for the command of which, when ready, they again designed Hoche.

The Dutch fleet was now ready to set sail, and at this time had a fair chance of success. The British admiral, Duncan, off the Texel, had only eleven sail of the line ; but as it chanced the Dutch ships were kept in port the entire summer by adverse winds. If ever a fair breeze sprung up, it either changed or died away again in the course of a few hours. During this time the favourable season passed by, and the English fleet was reinforced. The journal of Tone at this period abounds with dismal entries :—"*July* 19.—Wind still foul. Horrible, horrible! Admiral de Winter and I endeavour to pass away the time playing the flute, which he does very well; we have some good duets. *July* 26.— I am to-day eighteen days aboard, and we have not had eighteen minutes' fair wind. Well,

" ' It's but in vain
For soldiers to complain.' "

At length, towards the middle of August, the admiral summoned Tone to a private conference. He pointed out that the fleet of Duncan had now increased to seventeen sail of the line, so that the British vessels at Texel were superior in force to the Dutch. Moreover, that the Dutch land troops, so long pent up on shipboard, had at this time consumed nearly all the provisions supplied for the expedition, and that even a victory over Duncan in such circumstances would not allow the expedition to go forward. In this case he considered that it would be wiser to relinquish the expedition to Ireland, although a descent on a much smaller scale upon some point of the English coast might perhaps still be attempted. Tone, though most bitterly annoyed, had little to advance against such arguments. Soon afterwards he quitted the fleet, and went to join the head-quarters of General Hoche at

Wetzlar, where another mortification not less keen
awaited him, as Hoche, whom he found in declining
health, died a fortnight afterwards. With General Hoche
died the master-mind that planned the expeditions
for the invasion of Ireland. Henceforth the preparations of the armament at Brest were only slowly and
languidly carried on; but the French government hoped
to strike a blow against Duncan: they brought pressure
to bear on the government of Holland, and caused
Admiral de Winter to be ordered to sail out and engage
the English fleet. The Dutch admiral accordingly
sallied forth with the first favourable wind. Admiral
Duncan, on the other hand, having sustained some
damage in the recent gales, had crossed over to repair
in Yarmouth Roads; but he had left behind him some
armed sloops to watch the Dutch fleet, and no sooner
did he learn its advance than he returned with all the
sail he could carry. He found the Dutch ships not yet
out of the sight of that part of the coast of Holland
which lies between Camperdown and Egmont. Without
any hesitation he forced his own vessels between the
Dutch and the land, so as to drive them to an action
even if they had desired to avoid it. The two fleets
were nearly equal in their number of ships, since the
British had sixteen sail of the line and two frigates, and
the Dutch fifteen sail of the line and four frigates; but
the English were superior both in the number of men
and the weight of metal. Shortly after noon on
the 11th October, the English fleet bearing down in
two lines, the battle began. Admiral Onslow, in the

Monarch, led the van. As he went on his captain drew his notice to the fact that the enemy's ships lay close, and that he could find no passage through them. "The *Monarch* will make a passage," answered Onslow, and still held on his course. Then the Dutch ship opposite gave way, and he passed through, engaging without delay the officer of corresponding rank, the Dutch vice-admiral.

An action commenced with such a spirit augured victory. Duncan himself, on board the *Venerable*, and at the head of the second line, brought his own vessel alongside the *Vryheid*, the flag-ship of De Winter. The two ships, each of them carrying seventy-four guns, sustained a well-matched conflict within pistol-range for the space of three hours. So heavy was the firing that at last De Winter was, it is said, the only man on his quarter-deck who was not either killed or wounded. Not in the *Vryheid* alone, but throughout the fleet, the Dutch fought with a courage and perseverance worthy of their ancient renown. But fortune declared against them. By four o'clock De Winter's ship had struck to Duncan, and the Dutch vice-admiral to Onslow. The action ceased, and the English found themselves captors of nine Dutch ships of the line besides two of the Dutch frigates. The scanty relics of De Winter's fleet sought refuge along the coast or in the Texel, while Duncan through a heavy gale carried his prizes to the Nore. The loss in both fleets had been most severe in the well-sustained fight. Of killed and wounded there had been upwards of 1,100 on the Dutch and upwards of 1,000 on the English side.

Duncan himself in his official report declared the carnage on board the two ships that bore the admirals' flags had been beyond all description.

The battle of Camperdown, which name it has borne since, was hailed by England with applause. And worthily so, as Duncan in that battle broke up another division of the fleet which might, united with the French at Brest, have been used to sweep the Channel and cover the passage of an invading force.

In the autumn of this year England found herself almost the sole antagonist of France, and with scarcely an ally except the small kingdom of Portugal, as a definitive treaty of peace between the Empire of Germany and the French Republic, consequent upon the great victories gained by General Bonaparte in Italy, was signed at Campo Formio on the 17th October. By this Venice was granted to the Court of Vienna in return for the cession of Belgium and Lombardy to France.

INVASION OF THE IRISH REBELLION.

On the very day after the proclamation in Paris of the treaty of Campo Formio an order was issued by the Directory decreeing the formation of an army on the coast, to be called L'Armée d'Angleterre. To the command of this force General Napoleon Bonaparte was appointed. Wolfe Tone writes of this:—"Bravo, this looks as if they were in earnest!"

At first Bonaparte displayed his characteristic energy. He paid a visit of inspection to the northern ports, and directed active preparations; but by degrees his mind and the minds of the Directors appear to have been diverted from the invasion of our country to the superior importance of striking a deadly blow against England on the more vulnerable point of her communications with the East. The expedition which had been ostensibly prepared against our own shores was designed to be diverted towards Egypt. With the greatest secrecy plans were formed that it should start in the spring of 1798. From the Irish exiles this change of plan was most studiously concealed. These continued to be flattered with a hope that the full force of France was to be employed in the aid of the rising in Ireland against the English rule.

At the outbreak of the French Revolution, the Irish were already sufficiently disposed to ally themselves with an army which promised to liberate them from the odious yoke of the Saxons. The dreams of liberty and equality which the French spread wherever they went, and that turned so many of the strongest heads in Europe, proved altogether intoxicating to their ardent and enthusiastic spirits. From the beginning of the Revolution its progress was watched with intense anxiety in Ireland. The horrors of the Reign of Terror had no effect in opening the eyes of Irishmen to the tendency of revolutionary principles. The greater and more energetic portion of the Catholic inhabitants, who constituted above three-fourths of the whole population, soon became leagued together for the establishment of a republic in alliance with France, the severance of the connection with England, the restoration of the Catholic religion, and the resumption of the forfeited lands.

Judicial proceedings were instituted against those who formed themselves into associations with the object of raising an insurrection against the government. With these judicial proceedings were combined military measures. In March, 1797, a proclamation was issued by General Lake, requiring all persons in his military district, namely, in the five northern counties, to surrender their arms. To assist in recovering the weapons that might remain concealed, the proclamations invited the aid of all informers, promising inviolable secrecy and a reward of the full value of the arms that might be seized.

In the following May this proclamation was extended to the whole kingdom, in the form of a proclamation from the Lord-Lieutenant.

Thus at the beginning of 1798 all in Ireland was dark and lowering, and foreshadowed a coming storm. The revolutionary association formed in the island under the name of United Irishmen, at the beginning of that year, pressed for succour for their rising against the English government on the Directory of France. Since Hoche had first formed his armament at Brest in 1796, the leaders of the French Republic had watched attentively the course of events in Ireland, and had perceived that the opportunity to inflct a blow against the United Kingdom existed in the difficulty of the management of the sister island, and that a force landed in Ireland would at least provoke a considerable diversion, and tend to lessen resistance to an invasion of the southern shores of England.

In the months of May and June the long-smouldering insurrection burst forth. Some districts in Leinster were the first to rise. The mail-coaches in various directions near Dublin were stopped and plundered. Kildare, Naas, Hacket's Town, and other places, became scenes of conflict, and at Prosperous the rebels achieved a slight success by surprising the small town in the middle of the night and putting to the sword almost to a man the few soldiers by whom it was garrisoned.

The real conflict was however in Wexford county, where a large body of peasants had assembled under the command of Father John Murphy, curate of Bonvalogue. He, with a force of 4,000 men, occupied the hill of Oulart. On the morning of Whit-Sunday, 27th May, Lieutenant Foote, with only 110 men of the North Cork militia, rashly advanced against the insurgents. As might have been expected, the militiamen were defeated and slaughtered, only the commanding officer himself and four privates being spared.

This easy victory added very considerable numbers to the insurgent ranks, and the principal insurrectionary army gradually swelled to a force of 15,000 strong. This body turned to Enniscorthy, a town of no inconsiderable commerce on the river Slaney, which was carried in the face of 300 regular soldiers. From Enniscorthy they advanced upon Wexford, whence the royal troops retired on their appearance.

The estimates and preparations of Great Britain for

the year 1798 were on a reduced scale, as on account of the loss of allies no foreign subsidies were required. The approach of a serious struggle for existence on our own shores was however apprehended. A message from the king on the 20th April announced :—" Considerable and increasing activity in the ports of France, Flanders, and Holland, with the avowed design of attempting the invasion of his Majesty's dominions;" and had called for "such further measures as may enable his Majesty to defeat the wicked machinations of disaffected persons." A Bill was introduced by the government at once for the suspension of the Habeas Corpus Act, and another Bill as to aliens. The regular army was fixed at 109,000 men, besides 63,000 militia. One hundred and four ships of the line and 300 frigates and small vessels were put in commission, manned by 100,000 seamen.

At this time a great change was made in the military policy of our country, which was fraught with the most important results both upon the public mind and the final issue of the war. This was the introduction of the volunteer system and the general armament of the people at large. During the uncertainty which prevailed as to the destination of the great armaments that were being prepared by France, both in the harbours of the Channel and of the Mediterranean, the British government naturally felt the greatest anxiety as to the means of providing for the national defence, without incurring a ruinous expense by the augmentation of the regular army. The discipline of the regular troops was, as at present, admirable, and their courage, as it has always been, unquestionable; yet the numbers of the regular soldiers were limited, and it appeared desirable to provide some subsidiary body which might furnish supplies of men from a class that could not, except in times of considerable national emergency, afford to abandon labour and serve continually in the ranks. For this purpose the militia was insufficient. Under the pressure of the danger of the invasion which was anticipated, the government, with the approval of the king, ventured on the bold, but as it turned out wise, step of allowing regiments of volunteers to be raised in every part of the kingdom. On the 11th April of this year, 1798, the cabinet determined to take this step, and soon afterwards a Bill was brought into Parliament by the Secretary for War, Mr. Dundas, to permit the regular militia to volunteer to go to Ireland, and to provide for the raising of volunteer corps in every part of the kingdom to replace the militia as a garrison army at home.

The statesman who brought in this Bill made no attempt to conceal the danger which menaced the country. "The truth," said he, "is undeniable that the crisis which is approaching must determine whether we are any longer to be ranked as an independent nation. We must take the steps which are best calculated to meet it. Let us provide for the safety of the infirm, the aged, the women, the children, and put arms into the hands of the people. We must fortify the menaced points, accumulate forces round the capital, affix on the church doors the names of those who have come forward as volunteers, and authorise members of Parliament to hold commissions in the army without vacating their seats."

The danger to national independence from foreign invasion was obvious. The Bill passed the House without opposition, and in a few weeks 150,000 volunteers were in arms in Great Britain. Another Bill, which at the same time passed through Parliament, authorised the crown in the event of an invasion to call out a levy *en masse* of the population, and conferred extraordinary powers upon lord-lieutenants and generals in command for the seizure, in case of an invasion, of horses and carriages, and provided for the indemnification at the public expense of such persons as might suffer in their properties in consequence of these measures.

And there was grave reason that England should arm. In Ireland insurrection was more than smouldering. An extraordinary degree of activity prevailed in all the harbours, not only of France and Holland, but of Spain and Italy. The fleets at Cadiz and Toulon were in a condition to put to sea. That at Brest only awaited their junction to sally forth and form a preponderating force in the Channel, where the utmost exertions were being made to construct and equip flat-bottomed boats for the conveyance of land troops. Men of-war were already collected in the harbours on the south side of the Channel for the transport of 60,000 men. A great part of the armies of the Rhine was brought down to the maritime districts, and lined the shores of France and Holland from Brest to the Texel. Nearly 150,000 men lay on these coasts, forming, the Armée d'Angleterre. This immense force would have occasioned even greater anxiety to the British government, had it been supported by a powerful navy; but the battles of St. Vincent and Camperdown had relieved our island of considerable apprehension. Immense preparations were made at the same time in Italy and the south of France. The whole naval resources of the Mediterranean were put in requisition. The flower of the army of Italy was marched to Toulon, Genoa, and Civita Vecchia.

However, it is doubtful whether the embarkation of an invading force was seriously intended by the French government. The Directory, secretly alarmed at the reputation achieved by the conqueror of Italy, were more anxious to see Napoleon engulfed in the sands of Lybia than a conqueror on the banks of the Thames; while he himself, whose whole thoughts and passions at this time centred in the East, the theatre of ancient glory, dreamt more of emulating the career of Alexander towards India than the descent of Cæsar in Britain.

In the middle of February of this year General Bonaparte visited the coasts, accompanied by Lannes and Bourrienne. In less than ten days he inspected Boulogne, Calais, Dunkirk, Antwerp, and Flushing. Till midnight he sat up at every town, interrogating sailors, fishermen, and smugglers; and it is said that to that period is to be assigned the origin of the great conceptions concerning Antwerp which, after he became emperor, he executed with such vigour. Having acquired all the information which could be obtained, he turned away from an expedition which was distasteful to him, and said, "It is too doubtful a chance; I will not risk it; I will not hazard on such a cast the fate of France."

It may be supposed that from this observation the great military genius of Napoleon considered an invasion of our shores extremely hazardous, if not impracticable. Such does not, however, appear to have been the case. It must be remembered that at this tme Napoleon was eager to rival the glories of Alexander in the East, and dreamt of there extending an empire greater than that of ancient Greece. It is confessed that it was not the difficulty of transporting 60,000 or 80,000 men to our shores that deterred General Bonaparte, even at a time when the transport of such a force was much more difficult than it would be at the present day. He considered the great difficulty would be the power of supporting and sustaining his army after once having effected their landing, as the naval force of Britain was superior to that of France, and it could only be rationally expected that the French army in England would be severed from all supplies of stores from its own country. At the present time such arguments would be little considered by the leader of an invading force. The richness of the southern counties of England is such that an army could live upon the country, and would be dependent upon its base of communications for no supplies except those of ammunition. A sufficiency of ammunition could be brought over with an invading force to last it for any time which the war might be expected to continue.

To return to Ireland. The capture of the important town of Wexford gave the insurgents possession of a considerable train of artillery which was stored there, and also opened a port for communication with France. The Bill permitting the militia of England to volunteer for service in Ireland was of effect. On the 16th June Mr. Secretary Dundas brought down to the House of Commons a message from the king, announcing that several regiments had freely tendered the extension of their services to Ireland. Several militia regiments accordingly went over. By the middle of June the commanders of the troops of the government had collected about 15,000 men in the county of Wexford. On the 20th June one body of the insurgents was routed by General Moore at Goff's Bridge, and on the following day General Lake attacked their principal encampment at Vinegar Hill. He had with him about 13,000 men in four columns, with which it was intended to attack the position simultaneously at four different points. But the accidental delay of one of these left the insurgents a loophole for escape; for this reason probably only a faint resistance was made. The whole loss of the royal army was only one man killed and four wounded. On the same day General Moore reoccupied the town of Wexford, and although some thousands of fugitives from Vinegar Hill, armed with pikes, sought shelter in the Wicklow mountains, the main strength of the insurrection was now stamped down, and the favourable opportunity for the French invasion of Ireland had for the time passed away.

A month before the action at Vinegar Hill General Bonaparte sailed from Toulon on the 19th May, with the greater portion of the army which had been intended for the invasion of England, for Egypt. He reduced the island of Malta on the way, and began to disembark his troops on the coast of Egypt on the 1st July, having eluded the British fleet which, under Admiral Nelson, was watching in the Mediterranean to prevent the expedition. But while the main body of the force destined for the invasion of England was diverted to Egypt, the Directory did not totally neglect the assistance of the insurrection in Ireland. Their armaments for this purpose were, however, so small and so tardy that practically they only injured the cause which they were designed to serve. One small division intended to assist the Irish rebellion, consisting of three frigates and some transports, sailed from La Rochelle under the command of General Humbert, who had with him about 1,100 men. This force was evidently only to be auxiliary to the force of native Irishmen who were expected to rise on its landing, as the expedition carried with it a considerable number of spare muskets and some Irish exiles, among whom was the celebrated Tone. The force had with it a considerable quantity of officers and engineers, and was intended to be rather the skeleton of a force than an active army itself. Humbert sailed from La Rochelle about the beginning of August, and eluding the British cruisers, though seventeen days at sea, appeared off the Irish coast on the 22nd. He landed in Killala Bay, in the county of Mayo, and took up his quarters in the bishop's palace at that place. He then called upon the peasants to join his standard.

At Killala there was almost no garrison, but an officer and twenty men of the Prince of Wales's Fencibles, who occupied the place, were taken prisoners, as well as the Bishop of Killala and his two daughters, and were kept as hostages.

Lord Cornwallis, who at that time had lately been appointed Lord-Lieutenant and Commander-in-Chief in Ireland, on hearing of the landing of the French at Killala, immediately sent General Lake across the Shannon, intending himself to follow in a few days. General Lake accordingly took the command of several regiments of the Irish militia, that were quartered at Castlebar. The French under General Humbert, though inferior in numbers to this body of militia, pushed forward from the sea-coast and boldly attacked them at Castlebar on the morning of the 27th. The Irish regiments behaved with considerably more caution than valour, as the greater portion of them bolted without firing a shot, leaving behind them seven pieces of cannon and six hundred prisoners. An officer who was present, the secretary of General Lake, declared that he never saw so shameful a rout. Two of the colonels—Lord Ormonde and Lord Granard—exerted themselves with great spirit to hold and rally their men, but in vain; though it is probable, as Lord Stanhope says, that many of the militiamen may have run through disaffection quite as much as through panic, since immediately afterwards several hundreds of them joined the French.

But the triumph of General Humbert did not long endure. Lord Cornwallis came up with some regular forces and considerably superior numbers. On the 31st August General Humbert issued a proclamation, being a model of a provisional government for the county of Connaught, whereof John Moore was appointed president. But the latter did not long enjoy the dignity, as he was soon afterwards taken and hanged.

Lord Cornwallis made the necessary dispositions either for supporting a general attack or intercepting the march of the enemy. On the 8th September General Humbert, who had pushed forward to Ballinamuck was attacked by considerably superior forces, and forced to surrender. Of the insurgents who had joined him about 400 were killed in action, and about 180 suffered by sentence of court-martial.

About the same time a single French brig from Dunkirk, the *Anacreon*, appeared off the coast of Donegal with the notorious Napper Tandy on board. He published a vehement proclamation, calling upon his fellow-countrymen to take up arms against the government, and exhorting them to refuse to grant any concession to the English. He had boasted that, land where he pleased, he would be joined by 30,000 men. But when the *Anacreon* appeared on the coast, there was not the slightest sign of any rising. And the conduct of the intended leader was far from keeping pace with his vehement protestations. No sooner did he hear of the reverse sustained by the French troops who had landed under Humbert in Killala Bay, than he re-embarked with great precipitation and sailed off to Norway. These two descents appear to have been part of three intended expeditions which were formed at Brest and Dunkirk. The *Anacreon* was the only vessel of the whole armament from Dunkirk which could escape from the English blockade and reach the coast of Ireland by going north about.

But the most formidable force in appearance and actual strength was yet to make its attempt. It had been for some time past prepared at Brest, and consisted of the *Hoche* of seventy-four guns, eight frigates, and a schooner, containing 3,600 men, with great quantities of arms and stores of every kind. The vessels were commanded by Admiral Bompast, and the troops by General Hardi. Only four Irish exiles accompanied this expedition, but among them was the ablest of them all, Wolfe Tone, who now bore the commission of a French officer under the name of Smith. On the 11th October this armament entered the Bay of Killala, but it was pursued by a superior squadron under Commodore Sir John Borlase Warren. It appears that the French vessels hardly dropped anchor in Killala Bay, for on the following day—the 12th—this squadron was engaged off Tory Island, the north-westermost point of Ireland, by Warren, who had with him the *Canada*, the *Robust*, the *Foudroyant*, the *Magnanime*, the *Ethlion*, the *Naelampus*, and the *Amelia*. After a severe engagement the *Hoche* was taken, as well as four of the French frigates. Three of those that escaped anchored on the following morning in Donegal Bay, and sent a boat with sixty men on shore. But these were repulsed in their attempt to land by the Mount Charles Yeomanry, commanded by Captain Montgomery. Wolfe Tone, who was taken prisoner in the sea-fight, in which he had shown great bravery, was tried by court-martial, but anticipated the sentence by suicide.

Although the French government did not lose sight of the advantage that might accrue from an invasion of England, their thoughts were diverted from our shores by the victory gained by Nelson on the 1st August, 1798, over the French fleet in Aboukir Bay, by which the army of Bonaparte in Egypt was cut off from communication with France, and in the following year by the ill-success of the French arms in Italy. In the same year (1799) the British government, with a true appreciation of the importance of offensive action, despatched an expeditionary force to Holland, and by subsidies encouraged its allies on the Continent to push forward against French territory. In 1799 the campaign in Italy was eminently successful for the allies, but the return of Napoleon from Egypt and the battle of Marengo again laid Italy at the feet of France in 1800. In that year Mr. Pitt, anxious to settle the Irish question, and to soothe the disaffection in Ireland, proposed and carried the union of Ireland with England. On the completion of this measure the regiments which had hitherto been borne on the Irish military establishments were transferred to the imperial establishment.

No further serious attempt was made at an invasion until after the rupture of the peace of Amiens. Military preparations in England were continued on a considerable scale. In the first year of this century the land forces of Great Britain amounted to 168,000 men, exclusive of 80,000 militia; and for the service of the fleet 120,000 seamen and marines were voted. In this same year the ships in commission were no less than 510, including 124 of the line. From a return made to parliament at this time it appeared that the whole troops, exclusive of militia, which had been raised for the service of the state during the eight years from 1792 to 1800, had been only 208,000, a force not greater than might have been easily levied in a single year out of a population then amounting to nearly sixteen millions in the three kingdoms, and which, if ably conducted and thrown into the scale of continental warfare when the balance of the contest hung almost suspended between France and Austria, would unquestionably have terminated the war in the late campaigns. So shortsighted is it to dally with war. True policy must ever be to strike with all available force at the very commencement of a campaign and drive the conflict home with all rapidity into the vitals of an enemy.

CHAPTER XIX.

ATTEMPTED INVASION BY NAPOLEON.

AUTHORITIES.—Von Sybel's "History of the French Revolution;" Regimental Records of the British Army; Lord Cornwallis's Correspondence; Alison's "History of Europe;" Sir William Napier's "History of the Peninsular War;" Stanhope's "Life of Pitt;" Clode's "Military Forces of the Crown;" Clode's "Military and Martial Law;" Walpole's "Memoirs of the Reign of George III.;" the "Consulat" of M. Thiers now becomes of considerable interest, as well as "Le Précis des Affaires Militaires," by Dumas.

So early as the autumn of 1802 it was foreseen that the peace of Amiens, which had been ratified only in the October of the previous year, would not be of long duration; and on the 11th October of the later year Mr. Pitt himself underlines the words in his letter to the Prime Minister, Mr. Addington, "Content ourselves with the state of *very increased and constant preparation*, both naval and military." For Mr. Pitt himself now was no longer Prime Minister, having resigned on account of his views on Catholic Emancipation being in opposition to the wishes of the king. At the same time Colonel Sebastiani had been sent by Bonaparte, who was now the First Consul of France, to Egypt and Syria to prepare an elaborate military report, which proved that the idea of conquest on the banks of the Nile had not been abandoned by the French government. The conduct of France with regard to Italy and Switzerland also demonstrated some ambition for foreign annexation, while England was resolved not to yield up the possession of Malta. Influenced by these circumstances, the British government sent orders to delay the evacuation of Malta, Alexandria, and the Cape of Good Hope, which had before been resolved upon and in part commenced, and openly declared its resolution to retain these important stations till some satisfactory explanation was obtained of the French movements. This resolution gave rise to an angry diplomatic correspondence between Paris and London, and there could be little doubt that the anger of diplomatists would soon lead to the clash of arms.

The result was that the English cabinet gave orders for the collection of forces. On the 8th March, a message from the king to both Houses of Parliament announced that "As very considerable military preparations are carrying on in the ports of France and Holland, his Majesty has judged it expedient to adopt additional measures of precaution for the security of his dominions. The preparations to which his Majesty refers are avowedly directed to colonial service, yet as discussions of great importance are now subsisting between his Majesty and the French government, this communication has been deemed necessary." On the 10th there was another message from the king, with a view to call out the militia. On the 11th a vote was carried in the Commons for 10,000 additional men for the sea service. A few days afterwards the militia was called out, and preparations were made in the principal harbours in the kingdom for the most vigorous hostilities. Thus it will be seen that no energy was spared and no time was lost. These measures were immediately met by corresponding preparations on the part of the French.

Lord Nelson was entrusted with the command of the Mediterranean fleet; Lord Keith set out for Plymouth; Sir Sidney Smith received orders to put to sea with a squadron of observation. A hot press for seamen was immediately made in the Thames, sixteen ships of the line were put in commission, and, as Alison says, "England resumed her arms with a degree of enthusiasm exceeding even that with which she had laid them aside." So fickle is the English people.

The First Consul was as active with diplomatic measures and endeavouring to contract alliances on seeing that a conflict was approaching, as he was in military energy and forwarding warlike preparations. Ambassadors were sent to Berlin and St. Petersburg to endeavour to rouse the northern powers to reassert the principles of the armed neutrality and join the league against Great Britain. The army of France was put on a war footing. An immediate levy of 120,000 men was ordered; the troops both in Holland and Italy were reinforced; Flushing and Antwerp were placed in a state of siege; the great arsenal which was afterwards constructed in the Scheldt was commenced at this time. The naval preparations of the country were pressed on with the most incredible activity, and already numerous corps began to be directed to the shores of the Channel, which under the name of the army of England so seriously were to menace the independence of Great Britain. Patriotic feeling was roused to the highest pitch in France as well as in England, and never was war commenced with more cordial approbation on the part of the people of both countries.

An ultimatum presented by England was rejected by the French government. No hope of peace remained. On the 12th May Lord Whitworth, the British ambassador, left Paris; on the 16th, General Andréossy, the French envoy, departed from London. On this latter day also a message from the king was brought down to both Houses, by which his Majesty announced that the negotiation with France was over, and that he appealed with confidence to the public spirit of his brave and loyal subjects. Letters of marque were issued by the British government on the 16th, the same day as the French ambassador embarked at Dover. While the French embassy was still in England, agents had been sent in the train of the ambassador with instructions to take soundings in English ports and obtain information as to the military situation in all the provinces of the kingdom; and when the government of England appealed to the French ambassador to have these removed, the First Consul avowed a determination to introduce authorised emissaries, under the name of commercial agents, to prepare in the midst of peace the most effectual means for our annoyance and destruction in time of war.

It would appear that the English government, although they have been blamed for hurrying on this war, acted only wisely. Napoleon himself in his works has said that he had no wish to go to war in 1803, or expose his infant navy to the risk of being swept from the ocean or blockaded in its harbours. He had resolved upon a strictly defensive plan till the affairs of the Continent were finally settled, and his naval resources had accumulated to such a degree as to enable him to strike a decisive blow. He ordered the construction of canals in Brittany, by the aid of which, in spite of the English navy, he could maintain an internal communication between Rochefort, Nantes, Holland, Antwerp, Cherbourg, and Brest. He proposed to have at Flushing or its vicinity, docks which were to be capable of receiving the whole fleet of Holland fully armed, from whence it could put to sea in twenty-four hours. He projected in Boulogne a dock similar to that of Cherbourg, and between Cherbourg and Brest a roadstead like that of L'Isle de Bois. Sailors were to be formed by exercising young conscripts in the roads, and performing gun practice and other operations in the harbours. He intended to construct twenty or twenty-five ships of the line every year; at the end of six years he would have had 170 ships of the line, at the end of ten as many as 300. The affairs of the Continent being finished, he would have entered heart and soul into the operations against England. He would have assembled the greater part of his forces on the coast from Corunna to the mouth of the Elbe, having the bulk on the shores of the Channel. All the resources of the two nations would thus have been called forth, and he conceived that he would either have subjected England by his moral ascendency or have crushed it by his physical force. He believed that the English, alarmed, would have assembled for the defence of Plymouth, Portsmouth, and the Thames; the three French corps from Brest, Cherbourg, and Antwerp would have fallen on their central masses, while the wings turned the garrisons of Scotland and Ireland. Everything then would have depended on a decisive action. And as Napoleon himself says, " I was establishing my ground, so as to bring the two nations as it were body to body; the ultimate issue could not be doubtful, for we had forty millions of French against fifteen millions of English. I would have terminated by a battle of Actium." All this was justly prevented by the initiative taken by the English government.

The renewal of the war was immediately followed by hostile preparations of unparalleled magnitude on both sides of the Channel. Ten days after the French ambassador embarked at Dover, the French army in Holland advanced against Hanover and overran the electorate, which was then ruled by the same king as England. On the 23rd June the First Consul formally commenced that contest which he so bitterly and so long maintained against English commerce. He published a decree that no colonial produce, and no merchandise coming directly from England, should be received in the ports of France, and that all such produce or merchandise should be confiscated; and that any vessel coming from or which had touched at a harbour of Great Britain was declared liable to seizure.

The most extraordinary efforts were also made for a descent on the shores of Great Britain. The official journals openly announced the intention of the First Consul of putting himself at the head of the expedition, and called on all the departments to second the attempt. The public spirit of France and the hereditary rivalry with which its inhabitants were animated against England produced the most strenuous efforts to aid the government. The tapestry of Bayeux, on which was embroidered the incidents of the landing of William the Conqueror, was passed from town to town, and hung up in the theatres to encourage the people in hopes of another conquest of the island. All the arsenals on the coast were in activity from the Texel to Bayonne. Forts and batteries, thrown up on every hillside and accessible points of the French shores, secured the coast from insult, and gave protection for the small craft proceeding from the places of manufacture to the general places of rendezvous. The departments vied with each other in gifts and offerings for the patriotic cause. That of the Upper Rhine contributed 300,000 francs for the construction of a vessel to bear its own name, and that of Côte d'Or furnished at its own expense 100 pieces of ordnance to arm the flotilla.

The object of all these preparations was the assembly at a single point of a flotilla capable of transporting an army of 150,000 men, with its field and siege equipments, ammunition, stores, and horses. At the same time a sufficient naval force was to be provided to cover the passage of the flotilla across the Channel and to secure the safe disembarkation of the land troops, notwithstanding every resistance that could be opposed by the enemy.

The harbour of Boulogne was adopted as a central point for the assembly of the vessels destined for the conveyance of the troops. The natural harbour was not of sufficient size to contain the flotilla, but a new basin of large dimensions was dug out of the sand by the labour of soldiers, protected by an enormous tower, and armed with heavy cannon, ranging for a couple of miles. Similar excavations were made at the neighbouring ports of Etaples, Ambleteuse, and Vimereux. In every harbour, from Brest to the Texel, gunboats of different dimensions were built in the dockyards. The shipwrights were working day and night. As fast as vessels were finished they were sent round under the protection of the numerous batteries with which the coast was studded, to Cherbourg, Boulogne, Calais, and Dunkirk. The British cruisers in the Channel rendered this a work of danger and difficulty ; but the First Consul impressed the energy of his own character on those who worked under him, and at length made great progress in the assembly of naval forces within sight of the shores of ritain. No sooner were the English cruisers driven from their stations by heavy winds, than semaphores announced the favourable opportunity to the different harbours, and numerous vessels were quickly seen speeding round the headlands and closely creeping along the shore, while gunners with lighted matches in their hands and shotted guns stood in the batteries along the coast to shield their passage. The small draught of water of the gunboats enabled the greater part of them to reach Boulogne scatheless, though a considerable number were intercepted and destroyed by the British seamen.

The small vessels collected at Boulogne consisted of four different sorts. The praams carried each six 24-pounders, and were intended rather as a convoy for the smaller vessels, which were to carry the troops, than to be actually employed as transports themselves. The next class bore four 24-pound guns and one howitzer; they were intended each to carry from 150 to 200 men, and were constructed with flat bottoms, in order that they might draw as near as possible to the shore. The third kind were armed, each with two 24-pounders, and were capable of conveying eighty men each; while the smallest description had a 4-pounder at the prow and a howitzer at the stern, and bore from forty to fifty men each. It was intended that the artillery should be embarked in the larger vessels, the cavalry in those of a medium size, and the foot soldiers in the smallest. So good was the organisation with which the descent was planned, that every man knew the vessel on board of which he was to embark, and his place in that vessel. It was proved by trial that a hundred thousand men could be in their places in the boats in less than half-an-hour.

In the course of the year 1803 more than 1,300 vessels of this nature were collected at Boulogne and the neighbouring harbours. But it was not on them alone that the First Consul relied for the execution of his project. Numbers of transports were at the same time assembled, which although armed were intended as the receptacles of the stores and ammunition of the army. Napoleon himself went to the coast to hasten by his presence the preparations which were going forward, and to judge with his own eyes of the measures which should be adopted. He stayed in the camp at Boulogne and occupied a tent on the summit of the cliff which looks over towards England, where the site occupied by his quarters is still marked by a monument. All the material points in the maritime districts were visited. He inspected at Flushing the new docks and fortifications which had been commenced and quickly decided upon Antwerp as a central point for the chief arsenal where the naval subjugation of England should be prepared. By a decree of the 1st of July it was enacted that a dock should be there constructed capable of holding twenty-five ships of the line and a proportionate number of frigates and smaller vessels. Those immense works were immediately commenced, which in a few years rendered this the greatest naval station on the Continent.

But the naval forces of France constituted but a portion of those destined to be employed in the conquest of our country. The whole fleets of Holland and Spain were to be engaged in this great enterprise. The design of Napoleon, which he himself has pronounced to have been the most profoundly conceived and nicely calculated that he ever formed, was to assemble the fleet intended to compose the covering naval force at Martinique. By a junction of all the squadrons in all the harbours of Spain and the Mediterranean and the West Indies, this combined armament was to have been brought rapidly back to the Channel, while the British blockading squadron was traversing the Atlantic in search of the enemy. It was then to raise the blockade of Rochefort and Brest, and enter the British Channel with the whole of its force, amounting to seventy sail of the line. Under cover of this irresistible armada, Napoleon calculated that he should cross over to England at the head of 150,000 men, with whom he could reach London in five days.

The English government were really little aware of the danger which threatened them. For the successful issue of this attempt a large military as well as naval force was necessary. The First Consul turned his attention to the need of restoring the strength of the army, which the expedition to San Domingo and detachments into Italy and Hanover, had much diminished. The soldiery of France, long accustomed to the plunder and excitement of war, had become weary of the monotony of a garrison life. Discipline was considerably relaxed, and desertion, especially among the old soldiers, had increased to an alarming extent. Energetic measures were rapidly taken to arrest this evil. New regulations were issued to insure a rigid enforcement of the conscription. The height required for recruits was reduced to five feet two inches, a proof that the expenditure of human life in the preceding wars had already begun to exhaust the stronger portion of the population. The conscription laws were now enforced with such punctuality that escape became hopeless, and the price of a substitute, which rose soon to 500$l.$, made it almost impossible for the middle class to avoid personal service. At this period not much over 200,000 men in the French empire annually reached the age of twenty, the period when liability to personal service commenced. The conscription required from 120,000 to 200,000, thus nearly all of every class except the aged and infirm were thrown into military life. In the meantime foreign aid was also invited to assist in the descent on our shores. Ney, who had been in command in Switzerland, concluded a capitulation by which 16,000 troops in the service of the government of Berne were placed at the disposal of the First Consul, and soon afterwards formed near Amiens the reserve of the army of England. To Compiègne, an Italian division under General Pirio, came across the Alps to form part of the same expedition, while a corps was formed at Bayonne under Augereau to force the Courts of Madrid and Lisbon into the conclusion of treaties on the footing of the desires of the Tuileries, while the province of Louisiana was sold to the United States of America, and the English navy was thus deprived of one of the points where a blow might have been inflicted on the French government.

By an order addressed to the minister at war on the 14th of June, 1803, the organisation of the expeditionary army was established. The whole army was divided into six corps, each of which was to occupy a separate camp. Among the names of the leaders were Ney, Soult, Davoust, and Victor. The cantonments of the expeditionary force spread along the whole coast from the Texel to the Pyrenees. The first camp lay in Holland, the second at Ghent, the third at St. Omer, the fourth, as reserve, at Compiègne, the fifth at St. Malo, the sixth at Bayonne. The total force of troops concentrated at these various points over against England was to exceed 150,000 men. The camp of Holland was to consist of 30,000 men; 18,000 of these were to be French troops, and 12,000 Dutch; those of St. Omer and Compiègne, each 15,000. As yet the strength and composition of the camps of St. Malo and Bayonne had not been determined. All the corps united in these camps had orders to be ready to furnish at the end of the summer their two first battalions completed to a strength of a thousand men each. The command of the forces so assembled was to be entrusted to the most famous generals of the French army.

Such was the first basis of organisation of the grand army which the Continental powers saw without uneasiness being assembled on the shore of the ocean. Yet the wide dispersion of the troops along the coast might have led to the supposition that only a portion was intended really for the invasion of our country, and that this invasion was perhaps not seriously contemplated by the First Consul, but that, under the cloak of an attack upon our island, steps were secretly taken which allowed military operations to be arranged and military organisation to be completed, with a view to the subjugation of Continental states.

The French troops assembled at all points consisted of 341,000 infantry, 26,000 artillery, over 46,000 cavalry, and between 14,000 and 15,000 invalides, thus amounting to the aggregate of nearly 430,000 men, independent of the national guards and coastguards, who numbered alone more than 200,000. Besides these there were arrayed in line or in reserve the forces of Holland, Switzerland, and the Italian States.

On the other side of the Channel the government and people of England were equally determined on war, and equally eager in preparation. The militia, 73,000 strong, were called out on the 25th of March. On the 6th June the army estimates came before the House, and Pitt himself stated. that the number of militia should not bear too large a proportion to the whole of our force. He considered that a war that should be solely defensive would be in his opinion both dishonourable and ruinous. He urged an expedition, and proffered himself as ready to assist with others in sharing the obloquy of harsh measures of defence and finance at such a crisis. On the 10th of June a vote for 40,000 additional seamen was passed without opposition, and almost without remark; and on the 20th of June Mr. Charles York, as secretary at war, submitted his plan relative to the defence of the country. The House of Commons agreed to the unusual step of raising 50,000 men as an army of reserve by ballot, to serve four years, in the proportion of 34,000 for England, 10,000 for Ireland, and 6,000 for Scotland. This, it was calculated, would raise the regular troops in Great Britain to 112,000 men, exclusive of the troops in the colonies.

On the 18th July another measure for the public defence was brought before the House of Commons. It was named the Military Service Bill, and was introduced by Mr. York. The object was to bring into form and shape the great national movement now in progress— the volunteers. With this view the Bill gave powers for the enrolment and embodying of all men between the ages of seventeen and fifty-five capable of serving, and for their being exercised and drilled. These were to be divided into regiments according to their several ages and professions. All persons, however, were to be exempt from this conscription who were members of a volunteer corps approved by his Majesty. Such was the general zeal and enthusiasm of the country that in a few weeks 300,000 men were enrolled, armed, and disciplined in the different parts of the kingdom, and the compulsory conscriptions fell to the ground.

Nor with regard to the land forces only were preparations made on a gigantic scale. Fifty thousand seamen, including 12,000 marines, had been voted in the first instance for the service of the year, then 10,000 additional were granted when it became probable that war would ensue, and when war actually broke out 40,000 more were added. Immense activity was shown in the fitting out of adequate fleets for all the important naval stations, although the dilapidated state of the navy in consequence of the economy which was instituted after the peace of Amiens rendered it a matter of considerable difficulty. Seventy-five ships of the line and 270 frigates and smaller vessels were put in commission. The harbours of France and Holland were closely blockaded. Nelson rode with a squadron in the Mediterranean, and except where the small craft were stealing round the headlands of the coast of France towards Boulogne, the tricolor flag disappeared from the ocean.

Colonel Crawford brought forward in the House of Commons on a subsequent day a motion for a more extensive measure of national defence, and Mr. Pitt spoke in approbation of the idea. Colonel Crawford dwelt strongly on the great danger of the capital and the principal depots for naval and military sources being wholly unfortified, and mentioned with truth and justice that, under these circumstances, the loss of a single battle might draw after it the surrender of the metropolis and chief arsenals of the kingdom, the effect of which both in a political and military point of view would be most disastrous. Mr. Pitt supported Crawford, and declared himself as clearly in favour of defensive works for London. He said, " We are told that we ought not to fortify London because our ancestors did not fortify it. Why, sir, that is no argument, unless we can show you that our ancestors were in the same situation as we are. We might as well be told that because our ancestors fought with arrows and lances we ought to use them now, and that we ought to consider shields and corselets as affording a secure defence against musketry and artillery. If the fortification of the capital can add to the security of the country, I think it ought to be done. If by the erection of works such as I am recommending you can delay the progress of the enemy for three days, these may make the difference between the safety and the destruction of the capital. It will not, I admit, make a difference between the conquest and independence of the country, for that will not depend upon one nor upon ten battles; but it may make the difference between the loss of thousands of lives, with misery, havoc, and desolation, spread over the country, on one hand, or on the other of frustrating the efforts, of confounding the exertions, and of chastising the insolence of the enemy."

On the close of the session Mr. Pitt himself did not disdain to take command of the Cinque Porte volunteers. By great activity and energy he had very soon on foot an excellent regiment, divided into three battalions, and numbering 3,000 men. He was constantly seen on horseback, and in full volunteer uniform as the colonel-in-chief, exercising and reviewing his men. He also obtained an offer from the people of Deal of fifty gunboats, which he immediately communicated to the government, and it was accepted. Convinced of the great utility of such a defence, he obtained from some other places an offer of fifty more; and before he was regularly authorised to communicate this to the administration he received a private letter from Lord Hobart, requesting him to get more boats if he could. He wrote to the Admiralty to beg that the second set might be fitted, to which he obtained an answer that other measures were being taken for obtaining gunboats, to be equipped, as well as found, by the ports which furnished them, and that the Admiralty had no carronades to spare. So powerless are even the greatest against bureaucracy.

The arguments advanced in support of the fortification of London produced little practical result; but there can be no doubt that they were well founded, and all must have had bitter cause to regret their neglect if Napoleon with 100,000 men had landed on the southern coast. Central fortifications round a metropolis are of unquestionable importance in order to gain time for the disciplined strength of the kingdom to assemble when it is suddenly assailed. Such was proved in 1870 and 1871, when two great armies advanced upon Paris; and fortifications might have saved France in 1814, when the allies then concluded the war by the occupation of the French metropolis. The only result of the arguments in favour of the fortification of London seems to have been that some block-houses were erected to guard the entrance to the Thames. The construction of these works and the stupidity of the ministry with regard to further fortifications called forth the following lines, which are ascribed to Canning—

> "If blocks can from danger deliver,
>   Two places are safe from the French;
> The one is the mouth of the river,
>   The other the Treasury Bench."

The spirit of the volunteers was animated by a grand review on the 24th October, in Hyde Park, where there passed before the king sixty battalions of volunteers, amounting to 27,000 men, besides 1,500 cavalry, all equipped at their own expense, and in a remarkable state of efficiency. The total number of volunteers in the metropolis amounted to 46,000, and a second review, comprising other regiments from the same districts, was held on the 26th. It has been declared by a spectator that this was the finest sight he had ever seen. The king himself was in high health and excellent spirits. When the Temple companies marched past, his Majesty inquired of Erskine, who commanded them as their colonel, of what the corps was composed. "They are all lawyers, sir," said Erskine. "What, what?" exclaimed the king, "all lawyers, all lawyers! Call them the 'Devil's Own.'" And the "Devil's Own" they were called accordingly. Even at the present day this appellation has not wholly died away from the volunteers of the Inns of Court.

On the 7th of December, 1803, the army estimates were brought forward for 1804. Mr. Wyndham began by a most ingenious and amusing speech in disparagement of the volunteers. While admitting their zeal, he said that the country could not rely on their exertions, and must place entire dependence on regular troops. Mr. Pitt spoke in the debate, and said that the country should not trust alone to the regular army, even aided by the militia. He said, "It appears to me extremely desirable that the discipline of the volunteers should be improved; that every battalion of volunteers should in addition to its own officers have the assistance of two officers of the service, one a field officer, and one an adjutant, to assist in the drill and discipline of the troops. These officers should be considered as belonging to the army, and should in every respect enjoy their rank, pay, and other advantages as if they were serving in the army." The regular military and naval forces kept on foot for this year were more considerable than that of the previous years. The land troops amounted, including 22,000 in India, to about 300,000 men, exclusive of 340,000 volunteers. The naval forces also were very considerably augmented, there being no less than 100,000, including 22,000 marines, voted for the services of the year, and 83 ships of the line, 390 frigates, and smaller vessels were in commission.[1]

Yet notwithstanding the regular forces at their command it was evident that the government was not competent for administration, and small successes or advantages were gained during the first year of the war. Popular dissatisfaction increased; the maladministration of the navy excited great discontent. The majority of the government in the Commons continually declined. On the 25th of April, on a question of the army of reserve, it was only thirty seven, and on the 30th of April Mr. Pitt was recalled to the direction of affairs.

[1] The force was distributed as follows :—In the British Isles, 129,039; colonies, 38,630; India, 22,897; recruiting, 533; militia in Great Britain, 109,947 : total, regular and militia, 301,046. Volunteers in Great Britain, 347,000; total, 648,046; Irish volunteers, 70,000; military total, 718,046; navy, 100,000 : total in arms, 818,046.

Till the early summer of 1804, in the contest with France, England had stood single-handed. But besides the return of Mr. Pitt to power other events which had recently occurred were at that time tending to a renewal of concert and alliance with the great European powers. Foremost amongst these events was the melancholy tragedy of the death of the Duc d'Enghien, who was executed on the 21st of March at Vincennes, having been seized on neutral territory. Another circumstance of a different kind was the re-establishment of monarchy in France. On the 18th of May the First Consul was solemnly proclaimed sovereign of the French by the title of the Emperor Napoleon. This would appear to have added little interest to the war, as it was a matter that seemed at first solely of concern to the French themselves. But it was not so. The fact of Napoleon being crowned emperor excited the jealousy and hostility of other sovereigns, and notably of Russia.

Immediately on the return of Pitt to office he anxiously applied himself to prepare and produce a measure for the public defence, the Additional Force Bill, as it was called. He gave notice of it for the 1st of June, but desiring still more time to mature its details, it was deferred till the 5th. On that day it was unfolded to the House of Commons. Pitt desired above all things to remove the difficulties which stood in the way of recruiting for the regular army, by putting an end to the competition which prevailed between those who recruited for a limited time and those who recruited for general service. Out of this competition a system of enormous bounties had arisen. Yet he would not be satisfied merely to do away with these obstacles. He desired to create a new additional force that should be a permanent foundation for a regular increase of the army. There was at present, he said, a deficiency of nearly 9,000 men in the number appointed to be raised under the Army of Reserve Bill. It would be his first object to complete that number; his next would be to reduce the militia, which had grown to 74,000, to its ancient establishment of 40,000 for England, and 8,000 for Scotland. The remainder, and what was then deficient of the number voted, he wished to be transferred to the additional force. This, he conceived, would lay the foundation for a permanent establishment, which would yield 12,000 recruits annually to the regular army. The disadvantage of the army of reserve at present was that its severe penalties caused such high bounties to be given for substitutes. He therefore wished to make the ballot less burdensome on individuals, and to encourage and in some cases oblige the parishes to find the number of men that was assigned as their portion. If the parishes failed, he wished to impose on them a certain and moderate fine, to go into the recruiting fund. The new force he would propose to be raised for five years, to be joined to the regular army in the way of second battalions, and not to be liable to be called out for foreign service, but to act both as an auxiliary force to the army at home, and as a stock from which the army could be recruited. The plan, it was considered, would have the further effect of rendering the regular army far more capable of becoming a disposable force for any distant enterprise. These measures were carried with finally only a majority of twenty-eight, and it was expected by the opposition that Pitt would in consequence be obliged to vacate office.

It shows from these measures, which Mr. Pitt was obliged to bring in in 1804, that the popular enthusiasm evoked by the threat of invasion in 1803 was already melting away, as it is now evident that it was necessary to have recourse to the ballot to supply not only the army of reserve, but the regular forces.

During the autumn there was no relaxation for the prime minister. Under his master guidance active measures of defence were everywhere in progress. Martello towers, so called, according to Mr. Wyndham, from the place of that name in Corsica, rose at intervals along the southern coast. A defensive canal and dyke of great strength were thrown across from Hythe to Rye, cutting off Romney Marsh from the interior of the country. This canal is still known as the Royal Military Canal. The chief direction of such measures was nominally vested in Lord Chatham, but in truth devolved upon Mr. Pitt himself. The Prime Minister was constantly riding from Downing Street to Wimbledon, and from Wimbledon to Cox's Heath, to inspect military carriages, camps, and reviews. Nor was it out of place that he should do so, for although some statesmen, who should have been well informed, thought it ridiculous to expect the coming of Napoleon at that period, it was the very period at which Napoleon had absolutely determined to come. This fact is placed beyond question by the French archives. As M. Thiers says : " It has sometimes been doubted, but can be doubted no longer by any one who sees, as I have seen, several thousand letters which all combine to the same point." It may be added that several of the secret letters from Napoleon to Decres, minister of marine, and from Decres to Napoleon, are interspersed by M. Thiers in the course of his own most valuable narrative, and tend materially to the elucidation of this point.

Napoleon had then fully decided upon his plan; though, understanding thoroughly that secrecy must be one of the main conditions of success, it was imparted to as few persons as possible.

On the 20th July, soon after the ceremony of the inauguration of the Legion of Honour, the emperor repaired to the headquarters of the grand army at Boulogne, and took on himself the chief command. He intended to attempt the invasion of Kent some day in the month of August, but he did not rely solely on the great army, or the vast flotilla there assembled, to support and assist the enterprise. He had found another project well worthy of his genius. It was of the greatest importance that when his troops began to cross the Channel they should be protected by a large French fleet, if possible superior to the British. At Brest there lay eighteen ships of the line under Admiral Ganteaume, but these were held blockaded by the English. Five ships of the line were at Rochefort under Admiral Villeneuve, but these also were blockaded by an English squadron.

Toulon, from its greater distance, was less suspected, and from its geographical situation could be less easily watched. Here there were eight, and if necessary, would be ten ships of the line. It was intended that these, under the command of a skilful and intrepid seaman, Latouche Treville, to whom the high task was assigned by Napoleon, should sail out in the direction of Egypt, and spread abroad reports that the re-conquest of that country was to be attempted. As soon as the fleet were out of sight of land, however, it was to turn suddenly through the Straits of Gibraltar, appear first before Rochefort, then before Brest, give an opportunity to the squadron of Villeneuve and the flotilla of Ganteaume to come out by raising the blockade, and with all the vessels combined to sail straight to Boulogne. It seemed assured that for two or three days at least the British navy would not be able to oppose to these combined squadrons an equal force, and during those two or three days the descent might be thoroughly carried out. "Let us be masters of the Channel for six hours, and we are masters of the world," so wrote Napoleon himself in a secret letter to Latouche Treville on the 2nd July. Thus was the whole of this able plan decided and matured. On arrival at Boulogne, Napoleon saw no cause to alter the principal arrangements, but decided, on a view of the works, that a little further time was desirable for their completion, and postponed the date of the undertaking from August to September, and he anticipated that he should be able to return in triumph from England by November, when the Pope was to be in Paris to crown him emperor in the cathedral of Notre Dame.[1] Napoleon also directed M. Dénon, then the chief of the French mint, to strike a medal in commemoration of his expected conquest. The die was accordingly made ready to be used in London, but owing to the course of events was subsequently broken.

All preparations being thus complete, even to the medal which was to commemorate the result, orders were sent by Napoleon to Admiral Latouche Treville to put to sea; but Treville suddenly fell sick, and on the 20th August died. There was no second officer of the fleet in the secret of the intended expedition. No longer at Toulon was there either the head to plan or the hand to execute. After some hesitation Admiral Villeneuve was sent to the vacant post. But the favourable moment had passed. No sufficient time remained that summer to allow the new chief to master the details of his fleet or the minutiæ of the difficult operations which he was required to undertake.

Before the death of Treville at Toulon, on the 16th of August, the anniversary of the *fête* of the titular saint of the empire, a grand and imposing spectacle took place. Marshal Soult had received orders to assemble the whole of the troops in the camps of Boulogne and Montreuil. A force of nearly 80,000 men were massed on the slopes of a vast natural amphitheatre situated on

---

[1] Does not this recall—
"Go, and return in glory,
To Clusium's royal dome,
And hang o'er Nurcia's altars
The golden shields of Rome"?

the western face of the hill on which stands the tower of Cæsar, lying immediately to the eastward of the harbour of Boulogne. In the centre was raised a throne mounted on a platform of earth, on the summit of which a flight of steps led up to the seat. The serried masses of soldiery were arranged in the manner of rays of a circle, the centre of which was the throne. The cavalry and artillery stationed beyond the infantry formed the exterior ring of the glittering host, while beyond the troops an innumerable multitude of spectators crowded the slope, in a dense mass of black, up to the very summit of the hill. On the right and left of the central mound were ranged the music of all the regiments of the army. Punctually at mid-day the emperor ascended the throne amidst· the thunder of a salute from all the batteries of the army and the trumpet calls of all the trumpets. In front of him was the buckler of Francis I. and the helmet of the Chevalier Bayard, containing the crosses and ribbons which he was about to distribute. Round about him were grouped his brothers and the chief officers of state, the marshals of the empire, the staff of the army, and all the generals and field officers of the troops. Above the heads of the soldiers waved in the bright sunlight the standards of the regiments, some of them new and yet unstained by war, others torn by shot and shell, and blackened with smoke and battle. In the ranks there were a few of the conquerors of Hohenlinden, though the greater majority of the troops which had served under Moreau had been drafted to St. Domingo, for fear of being inclined to support the republican proclivities of their leaders. But the heroes of Marengo, the coming heroes of Austerlitz, were there, with many who had shared the Italian campaign, and already carried the standards that they so proudly reverenced, into the heart of Austria. The ceremony of taking the oath of the Legion of Honour concluded with a general review of the army, which marched past in front of the throne.

But Napoleon was doomed to be disappointed even at the hour of this magnificence. It had been arranged as a part of the spectacle that a naval display should take place at the same time. When the troops had defiled the eyes of the Emperor and minister of marine anxiously gazed towards the headlands round which the vanguard of the flotilla was intended to appear. About four o'clock the leading vessels came in view, but at the same moment a violent tempest arose; the wind blew with terrible force, and several of the vessels, in the hands of unskilled seamen, were stranded on the shore. This unfortunate accident, though of little importance to the operations of the war, was excessively mortifying to Napoleon, the more so as it occurred not only beneath the eyes of his own army, but also of the crews of the English cruisers, who were hovering in front of Boulogne, and were much amused by the catastrophe.

While the French army was being massed on the shores of the Channel these cruisers had not been inactive. In May Sir Sidney Smith made a dash before Ostend, with the object of preventing the juncture of a small part of the hostile flotilla from Flushing. In July Captain Owen, of the *Immortalité* frigate, attacked some of the boats in front of Boulogne ; and in August at Havre, Captain Oliver of the *Melpomene,* made a similar attempt, but these officers, in the face of the bristling batteries which guarded vessels of light draught, were able to effect but little damage to the enemy.

On the 16th of August the brilliant pageant was enacted at Boulogne. On the 20th Latouche Treville died at Toulon. The expedition had to be deferred for the present, but the emperor was not idle. Starting from his camp opposite the British shores, he traversed the coast of the Channel as far as Ostend, everywhere reviewing the troops, inspecting the harbours, stimulating the preparations, and communicating to all classes the energy and vigour of his own indefatigable spirit. From the shores of the Channel he proceeded to Aix-la-Chapelle, where he endeavoured by all means to revive the recollections of the empire of Charlemagne, and thence to Mayence, where he matured the design that he had already contemplated for a confederation of the Rhine under the protection of France, which would extend the power of the empire into the heart of Germany. Here also he conceived the plan of the great combination to elude the British fleets by concentrating an overwhelming force in the Channel, which so nearly proved successful in the following year, and placed England and its sovereign in greater danger than the country had incurred since the expedition of 1744 was blown back to Dunkirk, or William the Conqueror had landed at Pevensey.

After the emperor had departed from Boulogne, an

enterprise from which much was expected was attempted against the French flotilla. At that port the British Admiralty had formed a high opinion of the effect which would be produced with some vessels filled with combustibles and explosives, which were named catamarans. It was intended that these should be towed close under the enemy's gunboats, and there exploded in a certain time, according to the length of the match left burning in them. The experiment was considered of so great moment that Lord Keith with his whole squadron appeared off the coast of France to arrange its execution and witness its success. On the 2nd October the attempt was made. About 150 of the French flotilla were lying outside the harbour of Boulogne. The catamarans were directed against them. Twelve in succession were sent forward. They slowly drifted down towards the enemy, and amidst the breathless expectation of the British fleet, exploded. Not the slightest mischief resulted to either the ships or batteries of the French, except the loss, which was afterwards acknowledged, of twenty-five men killed and wounded. This was the sole result of an experiment on which the government and public in England had been taught to build, and had built, the most exorbitant hopes.

A few days after this abortive attempt had been made to blow up the flotilla that threatened England with invasion, another incident occurred on the sea which added to the enemy's force another fleet to aid in the invasion of our country. During the autumn of this year Charles IV. King of Spain and the Indies, or perhaps, more properly, Godoy, Prince of the Peace, who ruled in his name, became from a secret and unavowed an open and declared enemy. For more than a year the Spanish government had been wholly subservient to the ruler of the French, and by a convention in October, 1803, the extra force which Spain by the treaty of San Ildefonso, that had been concluded in 1796, was bound to furnish to the French government, was commuted into a subsidy to the amount of 2,880,000*l.* yearly. The large amount of this subsidy and the hostile nature of this treaty was a matter of considerable jealousy to the British government, since it evidently furnished money, the sinews of war, to France. The money also was directly applied to the equipment of the armaments and the gunboats intended for the invasion. But it was well known in England that the Spanish Cabinet in paying this tribute were truly constrained by necessity, and England abstained from any measure of retaliation. Still in February, 1804, Mr. Frere, the British minister at Madrid, according to his instructions, delivered a note, stating that so long as the Spaniards continued in a position of merely nominal neutrality, any naval armament in their ports must be considered as immediately terminating the forbearance of England.

Thus matters endured for more than six months, but in the following September Admiral Cochrane, who was posted with his cruisers off the coast of Gallicia, reported home that orders had been given by the Cabinet of Madrid to fit out immediately at Ferrol four ships of the line and two smaller vessels. His despatch also stated that similar orders had been received at Carthagena and at Cadiz. At this time a French naval force of four ships of the line was lying at Ferrol, and several detachments of French troops, amounting in all to about 1,500 men, had marched from Bayonne to Ferrol, apparently to be embarked upon them. Information also came that all the vessels which were thus to be fitted out were to be assembled at Ferrol, and that the concentration would be effected within a month; that though the ships were said to be bound for America, they were victualled for three months only, and that the Spanish government was merely awaiting the arrival of the treasure frigates from the western hemisphere to abandon further concealment and openly avow hostile intentions against England. The English Minister of Foreign Affairs had directed the ambassador at Madrid to use the strongest language to the Spanish Minister of Foreign Affairs. "You will state to M. de Cevallos that it is impossible to consider this proceeding, unaccompanied as it has been by any previous explanation whatever, in any other light than as a menace directly hostile. It imposes upon his Majesty the duty of taking without delay every measure of precaution, and particularly of giving orders to his admiral off the port of Ferrol to prevent any of the Spanish ships of war from sailing from that port, or any additional ships of war from entering into it. . . . His Majesty cannot allow Spain to enjoy all the advantages of neutrality and at the same time to carry on against him unavowed war by assisting his enemies with pecuniary succour, to which no limit is assigned, and by obliging him at the same time to divert a part of his naval force from acting against those enemies in order to watch the armaments carried on in ports professing to be neutral."[1]

The answers returned by the Spanish Minister of Foreign Affairs were, as was expected, thoroughly unsatisfactory. Mr. Frere demanded his passports, which were forwarded to him on the 7th of November, but the English government had in the meantime considered itself justified in acting on the warning which had already been given to the Court of Madrid by Mr. Frere in the preceding February. Orders were sent to the British cruisers to stop the treasure-ships laden with dollars from the Rio de la Plata, which were then on their way from America to Spain. Under these instructions four English frigates, on the 5th of October, closed with as many of the Spaniards laden with treasure. The officer in command of the English vessels, Captain Moore, informed the Spanish commander that he had orders to detain his vessels, and earnestly intreated that this might be done without bloodshed. The Spanish officer, not unnaturally, declined to submit in this way. An engagement took place, and in less than ten minutes one of the Spanish ships blew up with a terrible explosion. The result, as might be expected, was, in the course of December, a declaration of war against England by the Court of Spain.

On the 2nd December Napoleon Bonaparte was crowned in solemn state by the Pope at Notre Dame as Emperor of the French. On the news of the Pope's

[1] Despatch from Lord Harrowby to Mr. Frere, September 29th, 1804.

journey to Paris it was clear to everybody that the French descent was for a time no longer imminent. The expectation of battles by land or sea passed away, popular enthusiasm became evanescent, laxity of discipline and of energy became manifest amongst the volunteers, and the nation began to sink into that state of lassitude and indifference which is so characteristic of our countrymen with regard to military preparation, except at the very moment when a terror of an imminent danger forces them to devote to defence some of the energy and vigour which is a marked trait of our race in all other circumstances of life.

At the beginning of 1805 there came a letter from the Emperor Napoleon to King George III. This communication expressed, though in very general terms, a strong desire for peace. But details and particulars were so much needed that Mr. Pitt and his colleagues in the cabinet considered that the overture was designed to conciliate popular opinion much more than to lead to practical negotiations. An answer was drawn up and forwarded, not from the king to the emperor, but from the English Minister of Foreign Affairs to M. De Talleyrand, who filled the similar post in Paris. It stated that the king had most sincerely the object of peace at heart, but that he must, in concluding it, act in concert with certain powers on the Continent, and especially with the Emperor of Russia. On the 15th January, 1805, the session of the British Parliament was opened by the king in person. The royal speech announced the war with Spain, and promised some explanatory papers.

It also communicated the recent advance made by the French government, and the nature of the answer which had been returned. While calling for measures to prosecute the war with vigour, the king congratulated his parliament on the many proofs of the internal wealth and prosperity of the country. It also stated that the Emperor of Russia had given the strongest proof of the wise and dignified sentiments with which he was animated, and the warm interest which he took in the safety and independence of Europe.

It was not without reason that this allusion was made to Russia. Mr. Pitt, wisely seeing that the only chance which England had of ultimately beating back all danger of the French invasion, and of securing a peace which should guarantee the safety of our shores, was in an offensive attack against the territories of the enemy, had throughout the whole course of this winter and spring been busily engaged in diplomatic negotiations. It was apparent to him that England at the present time, unprovided with a large military force, could not alone invade France with any prospect of a successful termination of a campaign by the capture of Paris; nor that she would be able to inflict such serious damage on French territory as to force the energetic emperor to conclude, worsted, a treaty of peace. It was Pitt's object to look round for allies, united with whom an advance might be made against the enemy, which would divert his intention from the English shores, and cause him to withdraw the forces united for offensive action to cover his own country defensively. The object of the minister was, that England should no longer stand alone as she had during the last few years. The differences which in the course of the past year had arisen between the Courts of Paris and St. Petersburg were highly favourable to his plans. The Emperor Alexander, irritated with the Emperor Napoleon, began to appreciate the English character, and seek concert with the English arms. A treaty between Russia and England was concluded in April, 1805, for offensive and defensive measures. The objects of the alliance were that Russia and England should endeavour to form a general coalition of the powers of Europe, and to collect upon the Continent a force of 500,000 effective men for operations against France. The objects of these operations should be the evacuation of the Hanoverian territory and all northern Germany by French troops, the independence of Holland and Switzerland, the re-establishment of the King of Sardinia in Piedmont, with an increase of territory, the complete evacuation of Italy and of the Island of Elba, and the formation of an order of things in Europe which should present a solid barrier against future French annexations. To this compact the accession of Austria was afterwards obtained, and it was through the operation of this treaty that the force that was threatening England on the cliffs of Boulogne was drawn away to the valley of the Danube.

In the early part of the year 1805 Napoleon went to Italy, and was crowned with the Iron Crown of Charlemagne, in the Cathedral of Milan, as King of Italy. The assumption of this title gave great offence and alarm to

Austria. It seemed to involve a claim to the Venetian Provinces, which she had only lately acquired by the treaty of Campo Formio. But greater jealousy and greater alarm soon sprang from other acts of Napoleon at nearly the same time. The one was the annexation of the Republic of Genoa to France; the other was the grant of Lucca as a fief to one of his sisters, the Princess Eliza Baciocchi. The Emperor Francis of Germany signified his accession to the treaty between Russia and Austria on the 9th August. In the same month also Sweden acceded to and concluded a similar convention with the English government. Thus was formed, under the guidance of Mr. Pitt, a coalition against France, to cover, indirectly, England from French invasion.

In the meantime Napoleon, having accomplished his objects beyond the Alps with his usual energy, flew back from Italy. He left Turin on the evening of the 8th July, reached Fontainebleau on the morning of the 11th, and on the 3rd August was once more at his camp at Boulogne, surveying the preparations for the descent, and intent on the accomplishment of the enterprise. The day after his arrival he wrote to Decrés in nearly the same language as he had employed the year before. "The English do not know what is hanging over their heads; if we can be but masters of the passage for twelve hours *l'Angleterre a vécu—England will have ceased to be.*" The most minute movements of the navies of France, Spain, and Holland, which were all to co-operate in the expedition, as well as of the vast army destined for his immediate command, were regulated by his personal activity. Napoleon was well aware that if England was destroyed the Continental coalition would fall to pieces, as it was only sustained by English subsidies, and that a blow struck on the banks of the Thames would much more effectually break up the league against him than the most brilliant success in the valley of the Danube, or even on the frontiers of Russia.

The army which the Emperor of the French had now assembled for the invasion was one of the most formidable in point of numerical strength, and the most perfect in point of organisation, that had ever been brought together. The combatants mustered 114,000 men, accompanied by 432 pieces of ordnance and 14,654 horses. They were massed in the camps of St. Omer, Bruges, Montreuil, and Boulogne; besides a detachment of 12,000 at the Texel and Helvoetsluyes, and a similar force at Brest, ready to embark in the vessels of Admiral Ganteaume. Thus England was threatened at this moment with an invasion by nearly 150,000 men in the highest state of discipline and equipment. The composition of the armament at Boulogne and the amount of stores which were collected to accompany it are given by Dumas as follows :—

Infantry	76,798
Cavalry	11,640
Artillerymen	3,780
Waggoners	3,780
Non-combatants	17,476
Total	113,474
Gunboats	1,339

Transport vessels	954
Which would carry	161,215 men.
And horses	6,059
Guns mounted on armed vessels	3,500
Horses	7,394
Spare muskets	32,837
Cartridges	3,000,000
Flints	1,268,400
Biscuits (rations)	1,434,800
Bottles of brandy	236,230
Intrenching tools	30,375
Saddles	10,560
Field-pieces	432
Rounds of ammunition	86,400
Loads of hay	70,370
Loads of oats	70,370
Sheep	4,924

It is curious to notice by the above table what views the emperor must have had as to his landing in England. The amount of spare muskets would seem to imply that he expected to raise in the country a certain small force of adherents, while the quantity of saddles, to which probably would be attached suits of harness, may lead us to suppose that he intended to seize many horses of the country for transport purposes; while the loads of hay and of oats are calculated for about two days' rations for the horses which could be carried across in the boats in one journey. It is probable that the intention was to effect a landing on the shores of England, fortify the position with entrenchments as the base of operations, send back the boats for more troops, and push forward with the great bulk of the army immediately on London. At Boulogne provisions for the whole army for three months were collected.

During its encampment on the shores of the Channel the organisation of the army of the emperor had been placed on a footing different from that which had as yet been employed in modern European warfare. At the commencement of the revolutionary wars the French army was formed in divisions, which generally mustered 15,000 or 18,000 combatants; and these, on the outbreak of hostilities, were hurried under the first general officer who could be attached to them into the field. It was found by experience that few generals were capable of directing with skill the strategical movements of such large bodies of troops; while on the other hand, if the divisions were curtailed, there was a want of that unity in tactics which is requisite on the battle-field to ensure success.

Napoleon adopted a system by which the advantages of both methods were embraced in his organisation. His army was divided in the first instance into corps composed of from 20,000 to 30,000 men each, and the direction of each was entrusted to a Marshal of the Empire. To each of these corps was allotted, in proportion to its numerical strength, a suitable complement of field and heavy artillery, and two or three regiments of light cavalry, in order to perform the outpost duties of the corps. The heavy cavalry and dragoons were, however, not embodied with the infantry divisions, but were retained in separate divisions, and frequently were united in one corps and placed under the command of one general. This same organisation, slightly modified, has existed for some years in the

German army, and has been productive of the victories which have led to the resurrection of the German Empire under the head of the House of Hohenzollern, and the affiliation of the provinces of Alsace and Lorraine to the Empire. In each corps there were four or five divisions, various in strength, commanded by generals of division, who received their orders from the general of the corps. The troops in these divisions were always under the same officers. In this way the generals came to know their officers, and the officers their soldiers; while a spirit of *esprit de corps* grew up, not only among the members of the same regiment, as in our service, but among those of the same division and corps.

The camps in which the soldiers were lodged during their long stay on the shores of the Channel were admirably organised, though Napoleon was far too careful of the mobility of his army to allow his troops to be encumbered with camp equipment. They were laid out in squares intersected by roads, and composed of huts constructed with the materials which were furnished from the neighbouring country. At Ostend the huts were formed of light wood and straw; at Boulogne and Vimireux, of sharp stakes cut in the forest of Guenis, supported by masonry. The beds of the soldiers, raised two feet above the ground, were formed of straw, on which the camp blankets were laid. The utmost care was taken to provide for cleanliness in every particular. These field barracks were found to be extremely healthy even during the winter, on the cold and bleak shores of the British Channel. But constant employment was the true secret, both of the good health and of the improved discipline of the soldiery. Neither officers nor soldiers were ever allowed to remain idle. When not actually engaged in drill or parade they were constantly employed in raising or strengthening the field-works on the different points of the coast, levelling embankments, draining marshes, or filling up hollows to form pleasant esplanades or parade grounds in front of their camps. There was much emulation between the different corps and divisions in the performance of these works of utility. Labours of pure ornament were also undertaken, gardens were formed, flowers were cultivated, and in the vicinity of a stirring military life the aspect of nature was successfully improved.

Frequently the camps were amused and entertained by the spectacles of the assaults of the English cruisers on French vessels. While from the system of divisions and corps discipline was much more easily maintained, the habit of acting together in large masses was roused, and a high degree of precision in the performance of manœuvres on a great scale, and the result was a facility of movement which had never been before attained in the French service.

It was here, too, that Napoleon organised the system which conduced so much to the subsequent success of the armies, of trusting to his subordinates the details of administration and of execution of strategical and tactical operations in his campaigns. Each marshal in command of a corps received general instructions as to the line of operations which he was to adopt and the end to which his efforts were to be directed. But he was left entirely master of the means by which these objects were to be attained. Napoleon was frequently extremely minute in his directions to his subordinates ; but he confined his directions more to making it clearly understood what his views and his objects were than endeavouring to interfere with the details, which should always be left to the discretion of lieutenants. The same system of confidence and of responsibility was established between the marshal of a corps and the general of his division. To all of these a certain discretionary power was granted in the execution of orders. Yet though Napoleon left to each officer discretion and responsibility, he maintained a most vigilant superintendence over all departments of the army. He did not interfere in the details of administration, and above all of organisation, but he was most particular and severe as to the result. Nothing escaped his vigilance, and if any defect was anywhere apparent, an immediate and stern reprimand from Berthier informed the officer to blame that the attention of the emperor had been directed to his shortcomings.

His attention was habitually turned to the subsistence of his troops. This branch of the service came under his particular care, and necessarily so. The forces which he led into battle were larger than those to which any system of supply had anywhere hitherto been accustomed. The rapidity with which he moved inaugurated a new system of warfare. There was no question now as to the foundation of magazines. Corps had to live on the country, and the whole system of regulation of supply had consequently to be established on a new basis.

The arrangements connected with the transport vessels were as perfect as those for the land forces. The fleet was divided into as many sub-divisions as there were sub-divisions in the army. All the stores, baggage, and artillery were embarked, so that nothing remained but for the men to step on board. So perfect were the arrangements that not only every division of the forces, but every regiment and every company had a sub-section of the fleet assigned to it. The point of embarkation and the vessel in which it was to take place was told off to every man and horse in the armament. Every soldier down to the smallest drummer knew at what point of the coast he was to step on board, what vessel was to contain him, and what station he himself was to occupy on the deck. From constant practice and unceasing exercise the troops had arrived at such precision in this branch of duty, which is one of the most difficult for soldiers to acquire, that it was found by experiment that a corps of 25,000 men drawn up on the beach opposite the vessels told off to them could be completely embarked in the short space of ten minutes. Had we not the authority of two such excellent military critics as Ney and Dumas for this assertion it would appear incredible. No one can doubt that the Prussian staff have brought the science of military organisation almost to perfection. Yet during the late wars it was proved in the German service that it was possible to place within a railway train, which would appear to be a more easy operation than embarkation on board ships, not more than 1,000 men per hour from a single railway station.

The gunboats and armed forces which lay at Boulogne were not intended to force a way across the Channel in the teeth of the British navy, but merely to provide transports for the conveyance of troops, with their fire to cover the landing of the soldiers, to drive away the few coastguard vessels which might possibly be found near the English beach, and especially to distract the attention of the enemy from the quarter whence the force really intended to cover the design was expected to arrive. To carry 100,000 men in safety from the shores of France to the coast of Kent would have been a most hazardous attempt so long as the British fleet swept backwards and forwards over the waters of the Channel. Napoleon accordingly determined not to embark his troops till, by a concentration of his naval forces in the Channel and by the command of the sea, he should acquire time at least for an uninterrupted passage. As the action of the British government in the rupture of the peace of Amiens did not allow him time to develop his infant navy to such a strength as to cope with the British fleet on superior terms, and to drive it by weight of ordnance into its harbours, he resorted to stratagem. It was determined to decoy our fleet to distant parts of the world, and the stratagem then conceived by the emperor would probably have been successfully carried out had its execution been entrusted to an admiral with stronger nerves than those which Villeneuve possessed. Not one person in the British dominions, except the far-seeing Admiral Collingwood, penetrated the real design, which was that the English fleet should be decoyed to the West Indies by way of covering our colonial possessions from an attack by the enemy's squadron, and that the latter should return immediately to Europe and cover the landing while the vessels of England were still far away on the Atlantic. Napoleon himself thus gives an account of his intention :—" What was my design in the creation of the flotilla at Boulogne? I wished to assemble forty or fifty ships of the line in the harbour of Martinique by operations combined in the harbours of Toulon, Cadiz, Ferrol, and Brest, to bring them suddenly back to Boulogne, to find myself in that way during fifteen days the master of the sea, to have 150,000 men encamped on the coast, 3,000 or 4,000 vessels in the flotilla, and to set sail the moment that the signal was given of the arrival of the combined fleet. That project has failed. If Admiral Villeneuve, instead of entering into the harbour of Ferrol, had contented himself with joining the Spanish squadron and instantly made sail for Brest and joined Admiral Ganteaume, my army would have embarked, and it was all over with England.

"To succeed in this object it was necessary to assemble 150,000 men at Boulogne, to have there 4,000 transports and immense material to embark all these, and nevertheless to prevent the enemy from divining my project. It appeared scarcely possible to do so. If I had succeeded it would have been by doing the converse of what might have been expected. If fifty ships of the line were to assemble to cover the design upon England, nothing but transport vessels were required in the harbours continually, and all that assembly of gunboats, floating batteries, and armed vessels was totally useless. Had I assembled together three or four thousand unarmed transports no doubt the enemy would have perceived that I awaited the arrival of my fleets to attempt the passage ; but by constructing praams and gunboats I appeared to oppose cannon to cannon, and the enemy was in that manner deceived. They conceived that I intended to attempt the passage by main force by means of my flotilla : they never penetrated my real design, and when, from the movement of my squadrons, my project was revealed, the utmost consternation prevailed in the councils of London, and all men of sense in England confessed that England had never been so near its ruin."

To accomplish this strategy Napoleon desired that Villeneuve at Toulon and Missiessy at Rochefort should put to sea at the first favourable opportunity. His idea was that they should sail straight to the West Indies. Thither he hoped that they might attract a large proportion of the English fleet, and thence they might suddenly return, forming one armada, and ride superior to the English squadron opposite Brest. The supreme command was vested in Villeneuve, an officer of courage, fidelity and energy, but who was rather inclined to shrink from great responsibility.

The English government, as soon as the Spanish war broke out, lost no time in taking measures to meet the new enemy that had been thrown into the hostile ranks. Five ships of the line under Sir John Orde commenced the blockade of Cadiz. Carthagena also was watched, and a fleet was stationed in front of Ferrol. These squadrons, however, were hardly equal to the enemy's strength in the harbours before which they were cruising, and were wholly unfit to prevent the juncture of these forces with any superior hostile fleet which might approach. Thus if one division of the combined fleets was able to get to sea, it might raise the blockade of all of the harbours and release the combined armament for the projected operations in the Channel.

Already in January orders had been sent for the Rochefort and Toulon squadrons to put to sea. Early in that month the former of these, under the command of Admiral Missiessy, favoured by a storm, managed to get out of Rochefort, and sailed straight for the West Indies. It arrived in western waters without falling in with any English vessels. The Rochefort fleet arrived at Martinique on the 5th of February, and having landed the troops and ammunition which were destined for that island, sailed for Dominica, St. Kitt's, and Nevis. In the latter island contributions were levied, and some valuable merchandise burnt.

The arrival of Admiral Cochrane in the West Indies forced Missiessy back to Europe, and he reached Rochefort in safety in the beginning of April, and there awaited another combination of the French and Spanish squadrons. This expedition to the West Indies created great alarm in England. It showed how exposed our colonial possessions were to sudden onslaughts from the enemy's fleets, and caused great anxiety among our naval commanders to pursue any hostile vessels which might break the blockade in order to prevent their inflicting damage on our outlying dependencies.

On the 30th March, Villeneuve seized the opportunity of sailing from Toulon with eleven ships of the line. Off Cadiz he effected his junction with the Spanish Admiral Guavina, and on the 14th May cast anchor at Martinique with eighteen ships of the line and ten frigates, which had on board 10,000 veteran troops. At the same time the Brest squadron under Admiral Ganteaume, consisting of twenty-one ships of the line, put to sea and remained three days off the Isle of Ushant; but retired to their harbours on the approach of Admiral Cornwallis with the Channel fleet, which only amounted to eighteen vessels.

When Villeneuve broke out of Toulon Nelson was commanding in the Mediterranean. He had been forced from his position in front of Toulon, but had left some outlying vessels to give him information as to the movements of the enemy, and on his return towards the coast of France, was met by the *Phœbe* with the intelligence that Villeneuve was putting to sea, and was steering for the coast of Africa. The British fleet immediately made sail for Palermo, under the idea that the French were about to descend on Egypt, but by the 11th, Nelson felt certain from the information brought him by his cruisers that the French admiral had not taken that direction. He turned about and bore up with the utmost difficulty against strong westerly winds to Gibraltar, in the utmost anxiety lest before he could overtake the enemy they might make an attack upon Ireland. Notwithstanding every exertion, Nelson, however, was unable to reach the Straits of Gibraltar before the 13th of February with ten ships, and even then the wind was so adverse that he could not pass through, and was compelled to anchor on the Barbary coast for five days. At length he received certain information that the combined fleet had made for the West Indies, and amounted to eighteen sail of the line and ten frigates. He had with him only ten sail of the line and three frigates, his ships had been for nearly two years at sea, and the crews were weary and fatigued; but he did not an instant hesitate what course to adopt, and immediately made signal to set every stitch of canvas and bear away to the West Indies.

The combined fleet had about thirty days the start of Nelson, but he calculated from his superior activity and seamanship upon gaining ten days upon them during the passage of the Atlantic. In fact Villeneuve reached Martinique on the 14th May, while Nelson arrived at Barbadoes on the 4th June, having in the meantime been joined by Admiral Cochrane with two more ships. The information of the English admiral being in those seas determined Villeneuve to return, and on the 9th of June he was already in full sail back to Europe.

Nelson on his part, with his twelve ships, was most eager to close with Villeneuve, but, misled by wrong intelligence, he sought the enemy at Tobago instead of Port Royal. Finding this information was false, on the 13th June, with his own ten and only one of Cochrane's ships, he set sail for Europe, and on the 19th July anchored at Gibraltar. Next day he says, "I went on shore for the first time since June 16, 1803." Thus he had been over two years on board the *Victory* without having touched land.

He, however, did not rest at Gibraltar; there he found his old friend Admiral Collingwood, with whom be consulted. The two naval commanders believed that the invasion of Ireland might be the ultimate object of the French and Spanish fleet. Accordingly Nelson set off again under full sail to protect the Irish coast. Finding that the French vessels had not been seen or heard of in that direction, without an hour's loss of time he steered into the British Channel, where he hoped to find them. On the 15th August he joined the fleet of Admiral Cornwallis off Ushant. In this pursuit of Villeneuve to and from the West Indies, Nelson showed skill in seamanship such as seldom has been equalled, and never surpassed. French writers, with honourable candour, have expressed this opinion in terms of even higher commendation of their gallant enemy than has even Mr. Southey, his own biographer.

The real purpose of Villeneuve was in the first place to set free the squadron at Ferrol. On his way to do so, off Cape Finisterre, he fell in with the fleet of Sir

Robert Calder, and on the 22nd July there ensued an action between them. Calder had with him but fifteen line-of-battle ships to face the twenty vessels which sailed with Villeneuve. Yet ere evening fell two of the Spaniards had struck their flags. Next morning, and for some time longer, the two fleets hovered near each other, and at last bore away in different directions, as though by mutual consent. For this both admirals were severely censured. The French officers complained that Villeneuve did not renew the battle when his superior force gave well-grounded hopes of victory. The English officers complained that Calder did not further pursue the advantage which he had already won. At the time public feeling was strongly aroused against Calder. He was tried by court-martial, and was found guilty, but only of an error in judgment.

It was due to the foresight of Nelson that this action of Calder's, which at least detained Admiral Villeneuve, was fought. When Villeneuve quitted the West Indies he returned to Europe as rapidly as adverse winds would permit. Napoleon was in the greatest anxiety for his return. He counted the days and hours till some intelligence should arrive of the approach of the great armament from the West Indies, which should be the signal for the completion of his profound and great combinations. Nelson, on hearing of the departure of the French, despatched from Antigua on the 13th of June some fast sailing vessels. One of these, making a more rapid passage than the line-of-battle ships, outstripped the combined fleet, and by the celerity of its sailing saved England. The *Courieux* brig arrived in the Channel on the 9th July, having made the passage from Antigua in twenty-five days. Within twelve hours the Admiralty despatched orders to the admiral who commanded the squadron before Rochefort to raise the blockade of that harbour, join Sir Robert Calder off Ferrol, and cruise with their united force off Cape Finisterre, with the view of intercepting the allied squadron on its passage towards Brest. The orders reached the vessels before Rochefort on the 13th July; on the 15th they joined Calder in front of Ferrol, and together they sailed out to sea with fifteen line-of-battle ships to take up their appointed stations, and intercept the enemy. Hardly had this squadron reached the place assigned for it, about sixty leagues west of Cape Finisterre, when the combined fleet of France and Spain hove in sight, with twenty line-of-battle ships, a fifty-gun ship, and seven frigates.

Though Calder had by his action checked Villeneuve, it had been necessary, in order to place the force off Cape Finisterre to intercept him, thus to raise the blockade of Rochefort and of Ferrol. Under these circumstances it can hardly be seen how Calder could have been expected to renew the hazard of an engagement on the following day with Villeneuve, as at any time the two squadrons realeased from these ports, might have come upon his rear while engaged in action with Villeneuve in front. It would appear he only acted with due discretion in falling back on the Channel fleet off Brest, concentrating there the whole force of the

English navy in those seas, maintaining the blockade of Brest, and preventing the junction of Admiral Ganteaume with Villeneuve and the squadron of Ferrol and Rochefort.

After the engagement with Calder Villeneuve, instead of pushing boldly forward, touched at Vigo, and then, after some days spent in refitting and making repairs, sailed for Corunna and Ferrol. The Spanish line of battle-ships ready to join him at the latter port increased his total number to twenty-nine. He found there renewed orders from Napoleon to sail straight to Brest to break the blockade of the port by an action with Cornwallis, and then to proceed into the Channel in conjunction with Ganteaume. The personal bravery of Villeneuve urged him to this attempt, but his fear of responsibility deterred him. He expected to find Nelson already in combination either with Cornwallis or with Calder, and he knew that such a combination would be sufficient to overpower his fleet. In this it happened that, nervous as to responsibility, he trusted too little to the favour of fortune. On the 22nd July the action with Calder was fought off Cape Finisterre. On the 19th of that month Nelson arrived at Gibraltar, ignorant of the movements of his adversary. Had Villeneuve pushed boldly forward to Brest he would have had time to have raised the blockade of Brest and penetrate up the Channel, so as to permit the passage of the army from Boulogne.

As it was, Villeneuve passed some days in great uncertainty and anguish of mind. When he had formed his resolution he did no more than hint it in private letters to Decrés, the Minister of Marine. He concealed it even from General Lauriston, and it was not until he had again put to sea from Ferrol that he announced the course which he meant to pursue. He had decided that his force was inadequate to the enterprise upon Brest, and therefore he held it to be his duty to steer in the very opposite direction and proceed to Cadiz, where he might expect to be reinforced by several ships of the line. It was on the 21st August, the day on which the emperor expected Villeneuve at Brest, that he arrived at Cadiz.

When Napoleon arrived at Boulogne at the beginning of August he was in a state of great suspense and most eager expectation as to the proceedings of his fleet. For hours and hours together he would stand on the sea-shore straining his eyes over the expanse of the water and watching for a sail to arrive in the distant horizon. Staff-officers stationed, telescope in hand, along the cliffs had orders to bring him the earliest information of anything they could discern.

His troops at the various small ports around Boulogne were prepared and ready to embark at a moment's notice. Not a moment was to be lost when the fleets of Villeneuve and Ganteaume should appear. His anxiety was the greater at this moment since the designs of Austria and Russia, which had been encouraged and fostered by Mr. Pitt, were no secret to him. Austria, indeed, had all but openly declared herself, and her army was already in movement to cross the frontier stream of the Inn. Still Napoleon trusted that he should have time to strike a quick, decisive, and deadly blow on England before he was called away from the shores of the Channel to wage a continental war in Germany. Under these circumstances every day and every hour became of the most pressing and paramount importance. It was under such circumstances that the tidings reached him that his fleet had left Ferrol, but instead of making for Brest was steering back to Cadiz. The scene which ensued has been described by Count Daru, his private secretary and the eminent historian of Venice :—"Daru found him transported with rage, walking up and down the room with hurried steps, and only breaking the stern silence by broken exclamations. 'What a navy!' 'What sacrifice for nothing!' 'What an admiral!' All hope is gone. Villeneuve, instead of entering the Channel, is taking refuge at Cadiz. It is all over; he will be blockaded there. Daru, sit down and write."

Thus the profound calculations of Napoleon for the invasion of this country were baffled and thwarted by the incompetency and moral timidity of an admiral. Fortunately for England, at the same time the offensive coalition which the skill and energy of Mr. Pitt had set in motion began to bear fruit. The Austrians were pressing forward towards the frontier of the Inn. The Russians were arming, and were ready to move up in support in their rear. It was necessary for Napoleon to relinquish the scheme of his descent on our country, and take some energetic measures against armies which threatened to invade his own territories.

Had it not been for this coalition and for the advance

of the Austrians at this time, England might have for years been threatened with invasion. The expedition of Villeneuve or some similar stratagem might have been repeated time after time, and it is probable that finally the mental capacity of the emperor would have arranged some combination by which for a sufficient time the Channel should have been in his power to allow the passage of his transports. It was this retreat of Villeneuve to Cadiz which suspended operations against England and ruined the project of invasion—the best conceived project, as Napoleon said, and the surest that he ever in his life had formed.

On the very day that news was received at Boulogne of the retreat of Villeneuve to Cadiz, Daru, by the orders of the emperor, wrote down, under his dictation, and for several hours transcribed a series of detailed instructions to carry out an entirely new plan of war on the Continent. Although the emperor could no longer deal his blow against England, he determined to strike at the Austrian armies before the Russians were prepared to join them in the field. With this view immediate orders were given, and the several divisions of the French army were withdrawn as silently as possible from the coast of the Channel, and moved by rapid marches to different points on the Rhine. The artillery and stores were sent forward to Strasburg and Mayence.

Possibly it was intended that after the campaign in Central Europe had been concluded another attempt should be made on the shores of our island; but all possibility of such an invasion was for many years destroyed by the energy and ability of Nelson. He arrived at Portsmouth from Gibraltar on the 17th of August, and there heard of Calder's action of the 22nd of July, and the retirement of Villeneuve. For one or two weeks he resided at his country house at Merton in Surrey, but he was earnestly intent to close with the French fleet now lying at Cadiz, which he had watched or chased without cessation for the last two years. Accordingly he wrote to Lord Barham, the head of the Admiralty, offering to undertake the command of the great fleet which was now being prepared to go out to meet and if possible engage the enemy off Cadiz. The offer so nobly made was most gladly accepted. At the interview which subsequently took place Lord Barham desired him to choose his own officers. Many an admiral might on such an occasion have thought kindly of his relatives or his hangers-on, but the answer of Lord Nelson was dictated by a nobler spirit, "Choose yourself, my lord," he said; "the same spirit actuates the whole profession: you cannot choose wrong."

On the 14th of September Nelson embarked at Portsmouth in his flag-ship, the world-renowned *Victory*, and on the 21st of the same month arrived off Cadiz with a great fleet, intent upon the destruction of the French and Spanish squadrons that were there assembled. The defensive measures of the English ministry for England were at this time in a favourable state. On the 26th of September Napoleon was at Strasburg, intent on resisting the advances of the Austrians. On the 29th of September Nelson was off Cadiz intent on destroying the fleet to which the French Emperor was forced to trust for the passage of the Channel. In Central Europe matters went badly. On the 2nd of November a rumour reached London that the great bulk of the Austrian army had capitulated at Ulm. It was not at first believed by the ministry, but on the following day, Sunday, the 3rd, a Dutch newspaper came to hand in which the account of the capitulation was inserted at full length.

Gloom settled down upon England. It was expected that the warlike genius of Napoleon would dash away the Austrian forces, fall upon the Russians single-handed, and smite them also to the earth. For four days men in London were anxious and gloomy; but on the 7th of November men were shaking each other by the hand and congratulating themselves on safety from invasion, although a deep feeling of sadness mingled with their joy. Great news had come that day from the fleet; but the joy that it roused was clouded with grief for the fate of the hero to whom the victory was due.

Nelson, who had been joyfully received by the fleet off Cadiz, had recourse to a stratagem to induce the French admiral to come out and test the hazard of battle. He caused his fleet to keep out of sight of the harbour, leaving only a few vessels to look out, to signal the moment the enemy appeared. Villeneuve, angry and excited by the reproaches of his chief and the sarcasms of his officers, seized the bait, and, eager to restore his fame, sailed out into the open sea and accepted battle. On the 21st of October was fought the great action of Trafalgar, which destroyed the combined fleets of France and Spain, and established so firmly the naval supremacy of England during the remainder of the war that it was hopeless for Napoleon longer to meditate an invasion. And thus, amidst the thunders off the coast of Spain, the last great danger to which our country has been exposed passed away, while the last faint glimmers of life of the great seaman, who achieved our country's safety, flickered out. Much does our country owe to the exertions of Nelson. The great naval actions in the French Revolutionary war may be regarded as six. The First of June, which for the time warded off the invasion that was then prepared by the mutilation of the French fleet; St. Vincent, in which the Spanish fleet, which would have combined with the remains of the French fleet to cover an invasion, was swept from the sea; Camperdown, in which the Dutch fleet, that also would have been combined against us, was placed out of the list of combatants; the Nile, by which the army of France in Egypt was cut off from its communication with home; Copenhagen, where, before the conclusion of the peace of Amiens, was destroyed the Danish fleet, which would have been ready, after its rupture, to join in covering the transports of the army from Boulogne; and Trafalgar, which finally established the naval supremacy of England on the sea, and disposed of the combined squadrons of France and Spain. Of these six four were achieved with Nelson's aid, and three with Nelson in chief command. It is certainly to these actions that the safety of our country from invasion during the wars of the Revolution and of the Empire may be ascribed. And they surely teach us with trumpet tones that the true safety of England lies in maintaining an invincible and insuperable navy as its first line of defence.

CHAPTER XX.

PROSPECTS OF INVASION.

THE true value of history is not to record merely facts that have passed, but to deduce from those facts lessons for our future guidance. In no branch of historical science is the adaptation of the light of experience of so much moment as in military history. The value of its study has been frequently proved, but there is no brighter instance of the great results which accrue from worship at the shrine of the deeds of past heroes than that of the First Napoleon. His words of counsel to those who would study under him were :—" Read and re-read the works of Alexander, of Hannibal, and of Cæsar, for from them you will learn the principles upon which you yourselves must act in the theatre of war."

We have seen from the records of the invasions of England that no invasion has been successful against this country since that which established William III. on the throne of England. It is hardly necessary for us to pay much attention at the present time to the invasions which preceded that which led to the Great Revolution of this country, as on account of altered circumstances, change of armament, and different modes of transport, few lessons of value are now to be derived from the feats of arms of the middle ages, or of the still older modern times. The first invasion to which we shall now devote our attention is that which tore the sceptre of this country from the line of the Stuarts, and placed our government on a liberal and enlightened footing. It has frequently been argued that the invasion of William III. owed its success to the fact that in this country there was a strong party ready to aid him as soon as he appeared upon our shores. It is undoubtedly true that a powerful political body was ready to give assistance to the Prince of Orange; but this party was totally unfit to take the field, and was neither equipped nor organised as an armed force. Its moral strength may have been great, but the real secret of the success of the invasion of William III. appears to have been that he was accompanied by an adequate military force. Had it not been that strong battalions marched under the Prince of Orange, the officers of the regular army who, moved by their political bias, deserted the cause of their liege sovereign, would not have dared to have done so. But what strikes us most in considering the descent of William is, that although it was well known that the invasion was in preparation, and although the fleet which bore the soldiers of the Prince actually saluted the Castle of Dover as they passed through the narrow straits of the Channel, and their passage was immediately reported to London, no attempt was made by a land force to oppose the descent at the moment of the disembarkation of the troops. It would surely be expected that at this moment the most favourable opportunity was given for a blow to be struck by the defenders of our shores, whether in the cause of a king or of a country.

After the troops of the Prince of Orange were once landed, the resistance to them by the regular army, much as it had been nurtured and fostered by James, was absurd and ludicrous. The skirmish at Reading is not worthy of being ranked amongst ordinary affairs of outposts. But we learn the lesson from this descent, of how easily a force invading our island can be disembarked, if, either by accident or stratagem, it is enabled to elude the vigilance of our Channel fleet.

From the time of the successful invasion of 1688 many attempts have been made upon our shores, universally without success; but the good fortune which has watched over our country in this respect appears to those who carefully study the matter to be much more due to good luck than to good management. In 1744 the invasion which was then prepared by France was only thwarted by gales and winds, which stirred up the stormy seas that rage around our island. The invasions prepared in the early wars of the French Revolution were baffled by the skill, the energy, and the enterprise of our naval commanders. That of 1804 promised every chance of success, and this was only apparently torn from it by the sudden death of Admiral Latouche. The great invasion planned by Napoleon in 1805 was apparently on the point of being crowned with, to us, most unhappy results, had Villeneuve only had the nerve to push forward; as by the dates which have been given in the main body of this work it will easily be seen that he had plenty of time to appear in front of Boulogne, and to hold for several days the mastery of the Channel, before Nelson could possibly arrive to disturb the passage of the French army by means of its flotilla.

It can hardly be doubted what would have been the result had a hundred thousand veteran soldiers of France, inured to battle, led by competent and able officers, appeared on the coasts of Kent or Sussex. We can well imagine that the bands of militia and volunteers, arrayed in our southern counties under the command of squires and country gentlemen unaccustomed to war, and ignorant of the life of camps, would have fared but badly before the clouds of skirmishers and the serried columns which had carried the standards of France beyond the Rhine and the Adige. Nor is it at all apparent that, although the volunteers and militia mustered in great numerical force, they were at all fit to enter upon a campaign even of a few days. They seem to have been totally unprovided with camp equipment, stores, reserves of ammunition, or, what is more vital than all these combined, commissariat arrangements. It is probable that after the first twenty-four hours this undisciplined and hastily-levied soldiery would have found themselves without provisions. Starvation would have rendered discipline amongst such a force impossible; self-preservation would have induced them to disband themselves to seek after sustenance; the country would have been pillaged by its own defenders; the army would have been disbanded; those that kept together would probably have been of little avail, except to fill the cottages and hamlets with wounded, and strew the downs and woodlands of our southern shires with corpses.

But, in looking towards the future, great changes have to be considered. In the time of the last invasion threatened by Napoleon the introduction of steam navigation was considered, even by the greatest minds of Europe, as a chimera, and the dream of a madman. Since then, steam navigation has been so much developed that steamers have almost, except in special trades, superseded the use of sailing vessels; and the number of voyages now performed by steamers are immensely superior to those performed by sailing vessels. Another advance of science has caused almost a revolution in the military art. When Napoleon was mustering his corps in the camps that stretched from the Texel to the Pyrenees, the orders sent from headquarters to the different commanders could only be carried by the comparatively slow means of mounted orderlies, or aides-de-camp; and, however hastily couriers pushed along the roads of France, it was an affair of days, and sometimes of weeks, to carry the simplest command from one flank of an army to another. The introduction of the electric telegraph has changed this. In one moment every division of the most enormous army can be set in motion by the simple will of a single man. Mistakes are much less likely to occur, as, if an order is not thoroughly understood, it is but the affair of a few minutes to refer it back to the source from which it emanated, and to receive further information and explanation. Had Villeneuve at Ferrol been able to communicate with Napoleon at Boulogne, how different, in all probability, would have been the fate of our country. An electric spark might have laid our island at the feet of a conquering invader, reduced the United Kingdom to an appanage of the Imperial diadem of France, and pressed the soldiery that conquered in the Pyrenees and on the slopes of Waterloo into a link of the heavy chain which would have quickly fettered the liberties of Europe.

It is a question that has been considered, whether the introduction of more rapid means of locomotion through the adoption of steam, and of more speedy methods of the communication of information through the adoption of electricity, will be more favourable in future wars to the attack or the defence. Both will no doubt to a certain extent be benefited, but as the essence of the success of an attack in most cases depends upon surprise, and in all cases on rapidity of action, it appears certain that the assailant will derive more advantage from these improvements than those who have to resist his assault. In case of an invasion being at a future time directed against our shores, it will not now be necessary that the transports or the armed vessels that are to convoy them should be assembled in any particular port, or collected beneath some well-marked feature of the shore, where their concentration must be known to the cruisers of the enemy. It will be only necessary that a certain point should be fixed upon the chart as the rendezvous for the flotilla, out of sight of land, and only known to the commanders who have to direct the operations. These, too, would not necessarily be acquainted with the spot, until they had already left their ports, and were out of sight of land. The power of steam would allow these vessels to be collected at a certain point, without danger of delay, or of being blown back to friendly harbours by unfavourable breezes. The introduction of the electric telegraph would allow various descents to be made on different parts of the coast simultaneously, and would thus prevent the great advantage which hitherto has accrued to the defence, of acting on interior lines in such a manner as to allow different parts of an assailant force, attacking at intervals, to be overwhelmed by the superior force of the defendant thrown judiciously on particular points, while other points of assault were watched and defended by weak detachments.

Science has made another alteration in war. The introduction of rifled small arms and rifled cannon has, it may be assumed, necessitated almost as great a change in tactics as did originally the invention of gunpowder. The invention of gunpower tended to reduce the large numbers of levies who formerly were able in a few days or a few weeks to learn the use of the arms which were needed in hand-to-hand combat. It made the military profession a peculiar and special calling for which a certain training was required, and reduced the large levies of ancient times to small bodies of regular soldiers. The introduction of rifled arms would probably have tended in the same direction, and the skill required to wield the new weapons would have reduced the numbers of standing armies to smaller and smaller proportions. But the course of this natural revolution has been arrested. The stringent rules insisted upon by Napoleon after his conquest of Prussia, that the Prussian government should not maintain an army of more than 30,000 men, led the genius of Scharnhorst to devise means by which, without more than that number of soldiers under the colours, a large force should be trained for the great effort for the liberation of the Fatherland from foreign oppression. He devised the means by which a large number of men should be rapidly passed through the ranks of the regular army, taught the use of their weapons, and then, relegated to civil life, should be available, in case of the outbreak of war, again to take their places in the ranks.

The advantages of this system were little regarded by European powers, till the wonderful successes of the German army in 1866 and 1870 showed that this mode of arming a nation was the only one which allowed a country to enter into a war with a great numerical superiority of fighting strength. All nations have more or less within the last few years adopted the rudiments of the plan first devised by Scharnhorst; and although opponents may argue against it, it appears only according to common sense that some such method must be adopted in future by all countries that wish to maintain a military position. No doubt everybody would desire that soldiers should be perfectly drilled, admirably disciplined, and accustomed by constant repetition of the manœuvres of the parade-ground to perform their evolutions with the most mechanical accuracy. But to have such soldiers so highly perfect they must be retained for many years in the ranks. As long as Continental nations place armies, not of thousands, or hundreds of thousands, but of millions of fighting men in a theatre of war, it is impossible that any country, however rich, can maintain an army able not indeed to cope with such armaments, but even to act in such force as to be worth consideration as an ally. Lord Cardwell perceived this in our country, and with a wisdom which will be more and more appreciated, endeavoured to graft upon the British military system a means by which soldiers should be taught their duty by a short service in the ranks of the regular army, passed into the reserve, and be liable to recall into their regiments in case of war. Should time elapse before the necessity arises for the employment of our army on an active campaign, we shall in a few years be able to place in the field a force which, although not so large as that of many Continental powers, will be at least respectable, and which could oppose, if properly handled, with every chance of success, an army that had once landed on our shores.

It would appear tolerably certain that in future greater facilities will be afforded to a government that designs the invasion of England for eluding the British fleet intended to cover our coasts than in the days of our ancestors, through the result of the introduction of steam navigation and of the electric telegraph. There is also more probability that in future the British fleet is more likely to be equalled, or even overpowered, than in times past. England is no longer so superior in relative wealth as she was in the early days of this century. The amalgamation of Germany under the House of Hohenzollern, has concentrated and knit together the energies, the determination, and the great mental capacity of the German people. The iron works of Essen, the development of manufacture throughout the Fatherland, shows that in Germany, which numbers a larger population than England, there is an industrial activity which may place Germany ere long close to England in the race for wealth. The great development of manufacture in Belgium has not indeed raised Belgium to the rank of a formidable enemy to the liberties of our country, but has placed within easy reach of our shores a field for the industry which the lamentable squabbles between capital and labour have done their best to divert from our own land. Trade and commerce are fickle mistresses, once insulted and turned away, they are most difficult to win back. In France the increase of wealth has been enormous; and in that country wealth is not only developed, but it is stored up. The economy of the peasantry is proverbial, and has long been acknowledged; but few men even among the greatest financiers, were aware of the latent power of pecuniary resource in France, until the Stock Exchanges of Paris and Frankfort were startled by the rapidity with which the indemnity after the last German war was paid off. So little was the recuperative power of France appreciated, that it is said, and probably with truth, that a Board of Bankers was assembled at the headquarters of the German army, to settle the highest indemnity which France could possibly pay without being entirely crushed; and that on their report the conditions of peace were based. In Russia there is at the present time a strong development of industry; several cotton mills have been erected in various provinces, and it is openly avowed by Russian statesmen that they desire to make their country independent of the English market. At the same time a dangerous canker is gnawing at our own vitals. The maintenance of our pauper class, which sits lightly upon us in time of peace and of prosperity, is assuming proportions which would weigh upon us heavily in the hour of adversity and of a close and dangerous war. The maintenance of modern navies depends more and more upon the power of the purse; and as the relative superiority of England with regard to wealth fades away, so does the danger proportionately increase, that foreign navies will be found equal, if not superior, to our own. For these reasons, it appears that hourly, though insensibly, the command of the Channel, is slipping from our hands, and that before many years are over the naval superiority of the world will be so evenly balanced, that we must be prepared to view without apprehension, the possibility of the disembarkation of a hostile force upon our shores.

Nor is it unlikely that this will be soon attempted. At the present time the great wealth of this country and its defenceless position expose it as a ready prey. The indemnity which a Board of foreign Bankers might arrange for the City of London would probably be quite in a proportionate degree to the exaggerated estimate which is entertained on the Continent of our wealth. Such a stake would be well worth a hazard, especially when the hazard of a counter stroke is infinitesimally small. Here is the weakness of England. Our navy is at the present time very powerful, but our navy is totally incapable of acting offensively against the capital of a hostile power. If at the present time an enemy were to threaten us with invasion, we must remain on the defensive, as long as it pleases the enemy to threaten us. We have no means of carrying an offensive war into hostile territories; but as has been proved repeatedly, over and over again in history, and as was laid down energetically by the genius of Pitt, the true defence of any country must be in its power of offence against its assailants. A country which is only able to stand on the defensive is in the same position as a prize-fighter who enters the ring, bound by some spell that would prevent him striking his adversary, and forced to stand only upon his guard; it follows that the guard must sooner or later be broken down, and that the pugilist who has no fear of a counter-stroke can drive his blows home with an effect which must in the end lead to the total defeat, if not annihilation, of his opponent.

At the present time the regular army assembled in

England is a larger force than it has been since the close of the campaign of Waterloo. It is roughly estimated at 100,000 fighting men; but within this number are included all recruits, sick, and soldiers who from age or infirmity would not be able to take the field. It can hardly be doubted that at the present time our country could not send into the theatre of foreign war a larger effective force than 50,000 men; such a force, in comparison with the armaments of France, Germany, Austria, or Russia, is so small as to be contemptible. For defensive purposes, to guard the shores of our island, we have in addition a force of militia and a force of volunteers; but if the true principle of defence, that of power of assuming the offensive, is to be observed, the militia and the volunteers are utterly worthless. Nor even are they competent to take part in a campaign in Surrey, Sussex, or Kent. They are totally unprovided with transport, hospital equipment, reserve of clothing, ammunition, or commissariat arrangements; while the regular army is encumbered with enormous masses of camp equipment, which are utterly unnecessary in a country such as England, where towns and villages for the cantonment of troops are abundant. If the enemy is so near that corps cannot be cantoned, he must be so near that tents could not be pitched, or the roads encumbered with the transport waggons which are necessary to carry the camp equipage. If, on the other hand, the enemy is so distant that camps can be formed, there can be no danger in separating troops, so that they may take advantage of the house accommodation of the theatre of war. It would certainly appear that for defensive purposes it is absolutely unnecessary that the militia and volunteers should have in the time of peace a certain organisation prepared which would enable them within a few days, or a few hours even, to take the field and take part in a campaign; but that if the true principle of defence is carried out, by some radical change, the militia certainly, and a proportion of the volunteers, should be enrolled and enlisted on such a footing that they would be liable in case of European war for service on the Continent.

If an invasion were to take place, and our fleet had either been eluded or overpowered, in what position are we? The troops which could be collected to oppose a landing or bar the progress of an enemy from the coast towards the capital are unprovided with the material which would allow them to take the field. There is in England hardly sufficient military transport or administrative service to permit of even the small division at Aldershot being mobilised and placed in line of battle. It is improbable that an enemy would land upon our shores in the case of a serious invasion with a less force than 100,000 men. Against such an attack even the most stalwart Englishman can hardly argue that the Aldershot division would suffice. It would probably be swept away in the battle of a few hours, and crushed beneath an enormous superiority of numbers. Nor can we believe that after having cleared its passage of the Aldershot division the army of the enemy would be kind enough to remain inactive while the militia could be collected from Ireland and Scotland, and could be provided with an impromptu transport service made up from the cab cripples and omnibus horses of London. Nor even if they would, would these valued animals be immediately available. The inhabitants of London would probably be unwilling to remain to share their houses and homes with, and to part with their plate and valuables to, the soldiery of the invaders. They would probably be inclined to make at this period of our history an exodus more universal than that which occurs annually from the metropolis at the commencement of August. Our government, which depends so much upon popular opinion, would hardly venture to sequestrate the cab-horses upon which would depend the means of numerous families getting to the railway stations in order to seek safety beyond the actual area of operations.

If a battle were once fought between the coast and London, it appears that there would be no means for checking the further advance of the enemy. The total want of fortifications round our metropolis places London in the same position as Paris occupied when the allies entered it in 1814. It would be able to make no resistance, and the enemy must march in as if into an open town. Simultaneously with the fall of London would occur the fall of Woolwich Arsenal, and with that great seat of military manufacture in the hands of the enemy, not only could no ammunition be obtained for our troops in the field, but no guns, shot, or shell could be provided for either our artillery or our navy.

Yet the fall of Woolwich would be of slight importance compared with the capture of the metropolis. The threat to fire the city and light up in flames the forests of masts below London Bridge would probably be sufficient to force our government to make peace on any terms that could be obtained. Among these terms probably would be included the cession of India, and with that cession the total repudiation of the Indian loans, which have been raised under the guarantee of the Secretary of State for India. Thousands of families would be thrown into misery and destitution. Such is, however, but one of the results that might accrue from an invasion. Another result which may tolerably certainly be anticipated would be the payment of an immense war indemnity, which would increase to a crushing extent the weight of taxation of our impoverished country for many many years to come.

Nor is it probable that an enemy who directed a large force against London would be content with inflicting injury on the metropolis alone. If our navy were overpowered the sea would be open to hostile cruisers; even if our fleet were concentrated so as to attempt to bar the passage of the Channel, vessels could not be spared to perform the duty of watching our outlying ports. It may be certainly anticipated that powerful cruisers from the enemy's harbours would, impelled by steam, appear suddenly and unexpectedly at Glasgow, Liverpool, Leith, Hull, Newcastle, Bristol, and every other port where there were dockyards to set in flames or municipalities to terrify. In every port an indemnity would be raised, under the threat of an immediate bombardment. These ports are undefended, except at Liverpool, where a few earthworks, which are almost contemptible, have been erected. Against a bombardment directed against warehouses, stores, and vessels in docks, or alongside quays, the energies of the local volunteers would be useless. In time of peace it would certainly appear only prudent that some fortifications should be thrown up to bar such passages and to hinder vessels on buccaneering expeditions from entering our important harbours.

For a similar reason it would appear only prudent that the metropolis should be fortified by a circle of forts, such as proved of immense value to Paris when the Prussians advanced against that city in the late war. The introduction of rifled arms has not succeeded in making the military profession a smaller and more select body, as might have been anticipated from a comparison with the results of the invention of gunpowder. This has been due to the necessity of Continental powers bringing a great numerical strength of soldiers into the field; and their reason has been just, because a small force of marksmen, however skilful, and however intelligent, must be surrounded by a very large force of opponents, and then the line of communication, on which their supplies of ammunition depend, would be cut off. When they were surrounded at a distance, beyond the range of their bullets, so that their ammunition, when once expended, could not be replenished, the most skilled body of marksmen, under these circumstances, would be left as defenceless as if they were armed with claymores or broadswords. In order to allow soldiers to shoot well with rifles, time for drill is necessary. The system adopted in European armies, by which soldiers are passed through the ranks, and serve there a certain number of years, gives them time sufficient to become tolerable marksmen. In our country, where the main auxiliary force, the militia, does not serve in the regular ranks, and is only called out for a few days comparatively in the year, the men are unable to be taught rifle-shooting, which in future wars must be the key to the efficiency of an army. Consequently our militia are at present totally unable, as effective soldiers, to take the field, even in the case of an invasion. Time would be required after the militia was embodied to drill its constituent members into marksmen. This drill could not be carried on in the open field in time of a campaign; but if London were surrounded with forts of sufficient strength to prevent the enemy closing in between them upon the city, within the shelter of those forts, the militia might be drilled and brought to such a degree of perfection that they would within a certain number of months be able to take the field with hopes of success, and to march out from under shelter of those forts to engage the enemy.

The second great auxiliary force of our country is the volunteers. The great body of our volunteers are good marksmen; and probably in the volunteer ranks are to be found a larger proportion of better riflemen than in the regular service. But while the militia have a certain amount of discipline without power of shooting, the volunteers have a certain power of shooting without discipline. In order to bring the volunteers into that compact and homogeneous state of crystalised discipline which is necessary for the execution of field movements, time would be required, and such time could only be gained if an enemy which had once landed on our shores could be delayed. It would appear that the only way in which this delay could be ensured would be by a series of fortifications which would force an invader either to open trenches, or to rely upon the slow and tedious measure of a blockade.

The fortifications alone would be of small avail, unless measures were adopted that the troops which held those fortifications should be well supplied with provisions and with ammunition. No system of fortification of the metropolis would be complete which did not include Woolwich Arsenal; and if Woolwich Arsenal were successfully held, it could turn out sufficient supplies of ammunition to provide for all the defensive purposes that would be required. Food is another and very serious consideration. The vast population of our metropolis is not self-supporting in the smallest degree. Every article of consumption of its numerous inhabitants, which now muster nearly four millions of mouths, has to be brought in from the outer country; and but a small portion of this country could be included within the area covered by fortifications. Power could be taken by the government to compel all useless mouths to leave London in case of an invasion; but this power should be taken in peace. Nor would it be possible to confine the inhabitants of our metropolis to merely the number of fighting men who would be required to hold the works. Business could not be suspended, the public offices could not be closed, and it would be necessary that a certain number of men should be retained to carry on the necessary work of every-day life. Great misery would also be inflicted upon the poorer classes, who might be driven forth by the edict of the government to allow of a longer defence being made of the works ; and to meet such a catastrophe measures ought certainly to be organised in time of peace, and arrangements made by which, either through camps of refuge or through agreements with municipalities of provincial towns, the wretched people who might be driven forth from their only habitations should not be left to misery or starvation, or thrown indiscriminately on the poor-rates of whatever parishes they might be enabled to reach. It would be necessary also in time of peace that provisions of food should be supplied for the garrison of London. Not only is our metropolis dependent for its food on districts of country beyond the space covered by its houses, but our whole island depends for its supplies upon distant lands. Were suddenly, as if by the stroke of a magician's wand, the British fleet swept from our seas, and a stern line of blockade established round our coasts, this country, within a certain time, though comparatively a long time, must be reduced to a state of starvation. Its teeming population of mouths is too large for its productions. If the metropolis of

England were to be put in the position to withstand a long blockade to give time for its militia to be made marksmen, its volunteers to be made disciplined soldiers, and for the great defensive energy of the country to be brought into play, measures should be taken during peace to store up and provide a certain amount of provisions within the area covered by the guns of the works which should protect the city.

It is unnecessary here to touch more fully upon the state of our regular troops. Within the last few years every exertion has been made by the War Office to place our military force in a more efficient condition. For the development of the ideas which now so wisely prevail time is necessary; and not only time, but an expenditure of money. The government of a country which depends upon popular opinion can hardly, however, be expected to come forward and make heavy demands upon the national purse, unless impelled by public feeling. In a country such as ours, where we all claim to have a voice in the government, through the organs of our opinion and through the press, we must be prepared to undertake individually, as well as collectively, some of the responsibilities of neglect, as well as some of the satisfactions of success. If money sufficient is not devoted to placing this country in a condition of safety, the fault cannot be laid to the charge of any particular minister. The crime lies at the door of every educated man who has not raised up his voice to impel the government to take the measures necessary for our national security. If we were willing boldly to sacrifice ourselves to the guidance of a despotic government, which would relieve us of all care and of all thought, we might also plead justly, we were thus relieved of all responsibility. Such is not the case in England. Every man can make himself heard, and it is the duty of every man to have a care for his national security, inasmuch as it is the duty of every father of a family who has not abundant means to insure his life, and as it is prudent of every man to insure his house and furniture against the possibility of fire. There can be no doubt that one of the main reasons that this rich country exposes its riches to the cupidity of an assailant is because of an unwise economy. No doubt it is distressing that taxation should be placed upon the people which presses heavily upon the middle classes, whose incomes are small, and on whom every increase of taxation weighs heavily; but the very wealth of England, which forms the bait to a probable assailant, should be our best bulwark against the possibility of that assailant being successful. Were the country at large to insist upon proper sums of money being spent for its defence, the financial talents of the ministry could with justice be called upon to devise a means by which those who were most interested in the defence of our wealth should be the most bound to subscribe for its security.

At the present time it is possible that war is not far distant. Let us be wise in time.

THE END.

LONDON:
R. CLAY, SONS, AND TAYLOR, PRINTERS,
BREAD STREET HILL,
QUEEN VICTORIA STREET.

www.ingramcontent.com/pod-product-compliance
Lightning Source LLC
Chambersburg PA
CBHW030429300426
44112CB00009B/916